NOTHING REMAINS BUT TO FIGHT

Above: Lieutenant J. R. M. Chard,
5th (Field) Company, Royal Engineers,
Officer Commanding Rorke's Drift.

Right: Lieutenant G. Bromhead,
2nd Battalion, 24th Regiment,
Second in Command, Rorke's Drift.

NOTHING REMAINS BUT TO FIGHT

THE DEFENCE OF RORKE'S DRIFT, 1879

Ian Knight

Greenhill Books

To my parents, John and June Knight, who have always supported and encouraged my curious fascination with events of long ago in far-away places.

This edition of *Nothing Remains but to Fight* first published 1993 by

Greenhill Books,
Lionel Leventhal Limited, Park House, 1 Russell Gardens, London NW11 9NN

British Library Cataloguing in Publication Data
Knight, Ian
Nothing remains but to fight: the defence of Rorke's Drift, 1879
I. Title
968.4045
ISBN 1-85367-137-1

Library of Congress Cataloging in Publication Data
Knight, Ian, 1956–
Nothing remains but to fight: the defence of Rorke's Drift, 1879
by Ian Knight
168 p. 28 cm.
ISBN 1-85367-137-1
1. Rorke's Drift (South Africa), Battle of, 1879.
I. Title.
DT1879.R68K57   1993
968.04'5—dc20

Designed and edited by DAG Publications Ltd, London in QuarkXPress via Typesetters (Birmingham) Ltd, Warley.
Designed by David Gibbons. Edited by Michael Boxall. Layout by Anthony A. Evans. Indexed by Kate Ryle. Quality printing and binding by The Bath Press, Avon.

CONTENTS

FROM ISANDLWANA TO RORKE'S DRIFT

The British invasion of Zululand in January 1879 (left) and the advance of
the Zulu main army to Isandlwana and Rorke's Drift

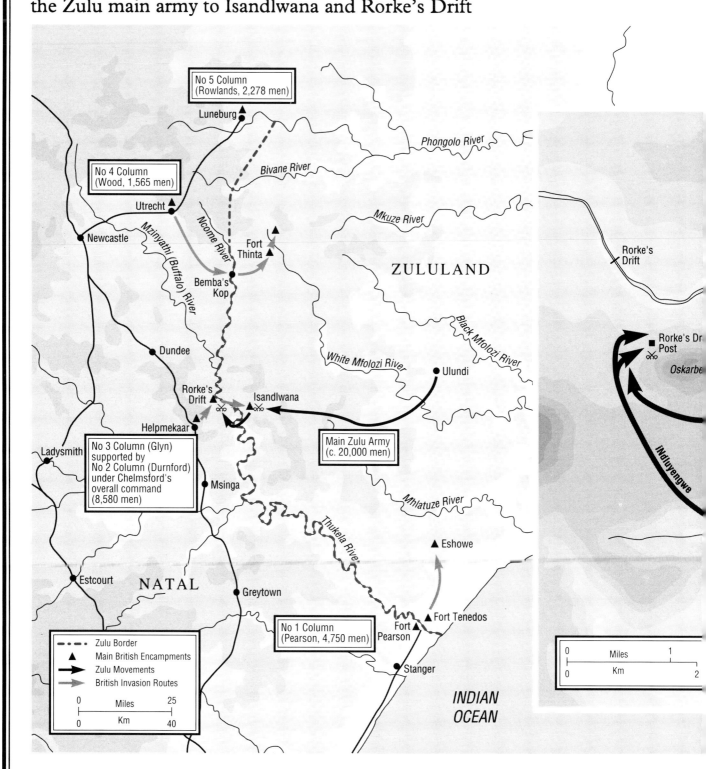

No 5 Column
(Rowlands, 2,278 men)

No 4 Column
(Wood, 1,565 men)

No 3 Column (Glyn)
supported by
No 2 Column (Durnford)
under Chelmsford's
overall command
(8,580 men)

Main Zulu Army
(c. 20,000 men)

No 1 Column
(Pearson, 4,750 men)

ZULULAND

NATAL

INDIAN
OCEAN

Luneburg

Utrecht

Newcastle

Dundee

Rorke's
Drift

Helpmekaar

Ladysmith

Msinga

Estcourt

Greytown

Fort
Thinta

Bemba's
Kop

Isandlwana

Ulundi

Eshowe

Fort Tenedos

Fort
Pearson

Stanger

Phongolo River

Bivane River

Mkuze River

Mzinyathi (Buffalo) River

Ncome River

White Mfolozi River

Black Mfolozi River

Mhlatuze River

Thukela River

Rorke's
Drift

Rorke's Dr
Post

Oskarbe

iNdluyengwe

Legend:
- — · — Zulu Border
- ▲ Main British Encampments
- ➤ Zulu Movements
- ➤ British Invasion Routes

Miles 0 — 25
Km 0 — 40

Miles 0 — 1
Km 0 — 2

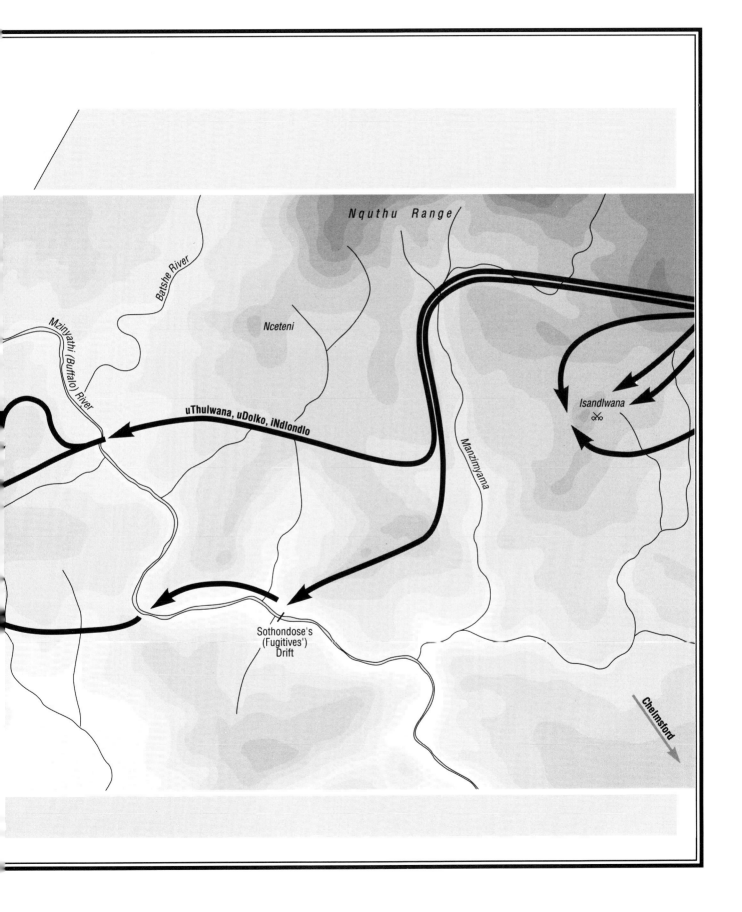

CHRONOLOGY

Afternoon of 22 January 1879	**3.15**	First reports of Isandlwana disaster reach Rorke's Drift. Chard returns from posts to Mission. Garrison begin building barricades.
	3.30	
	3.45	Party of Natal Native Horse arrives at post and is deployed behind Shiyane Hill to harass Zulu advance.
	4.20	First shots of battle are fired by Natal Native Horse, who then break and flee towards Helpmekaar. NNC infantry also then bolt.
	4.30	First appearance by Zulus. Attack by '500 or 600' warriors on back of post. This attack is checked and the Zulus veer around to attack the front of the hospital.
	4.40	Remainder of Zulu force appears. Some riflemen occupy the Shiyane terraces. The rest attack the front of the hospital. Zulus launch a series of attacks on the front of the hospital, finally overrunning the barricade there and forcing a way into the building. They also extend their attacks right across the front of the post. No attacks are made on the back of the post, where the garrison attempt to suppress the fire from the hillside. This fire is at its most severe at this period, and several of the garrison are injured by it.

6.00	Chard withdraws to the area in front of the storehouse, abandoning the yard. Zulus advance to occupy abandoned barricades.		**6.00**	The fight for, and evacuation of, the hospital.
6.15				
6.30	Zulus surround the post on all sides, but attempts to attack from western face are repulsed because they are too conspicuous in the light of the burning hospital.			
			7.00	

8.00	Zulus repeatedly assault the eastern end of the post and drive the defenders out of the cattle pen.	
9.00		
	Last Zulu attacks on the barricades. Assault losing momentum.	
10.00	Sporadic firing on post. Last shots fired 2 a.m. on 23rd. Zulus begin withdrawal at this time, under cover of darkness.	
Midnight		

HOURS OF DARKNESS

Morning of 23 January 1879	**4.30**	Dawn. Zulus have withdrawn.
	7.00	Reappearance and withdrawal of Zulus.
	8.00	Arrival of Lord Chelmsford's force.

The times in this diagram are largely based upon Chard's letter and report and are intended as a very general guide to the sequence of events. All times are approximate only. This applies especially to the period about 8.00 to 9.00 p.m.

INTRODUCTION AND ACKNOWLEDGEMENTS

The Battle of Rorke's Drift is arguably one of the best known incidents in the military history of the British Empire. In many ways it has achieved a level of interest far out of proportion to its political and strategic significance. The defence of the Reverend Otto Witt's Mission station on the Natal/Zulu border by the men of 'B' Company, 2/24th, and a handful of others, on that hot afternoon of Wednesday, 22 January 1879, was, in truth, little more than the aftermath of the far greater disaster that had taken place on the grassy slopes below Mount Isandlwana, across the river in Zululand, a few hours before.

That successful defence of Rorke's Drift by its stubborn garrison may have done something to restore the British Army's tattered honour, but in reality Isandlwana had smashed the whole of Lord Chelmsford's invasion plan. The repercussions of this, both for the British policies which had provoked the War, and for the Zulu kingdom itself, would be colossal. Indeed, it is probably true to say that the Anglo-Zulu War itself was little more than an Imperial side-show; it had no great bearing on the broader issues of British influence around the world; even Disraeli's government considered it an irritating distraction from a far more important crisis looming in Afghanistan.

While it is true that the Anglo-Zulu War played its part in shaping the subsequent development of South African society, by rights both the War itself and the Battle of Rorke's Drift should, so far as the rest of the world was concerned, have sunk into that murk of history wherein reside all the half-forgotten feats of arms whose purpose now seems hard to discern. It was, after all, not very different from the numerous other heroic stands, sieges and slaughters which inevitably marked the expansion and contraction of the British Empire across the globe. Yet the very opposite seems to have happened. From the beginning Rorke's Drift struck a chord in the public consciousness and, despite changing attitudes towards concepts of heroism and glory, it continues to exert a remarkable fascination among a broad cross-section of people who know little about the Zulus, and have no idea why the British wanted to defeat them. Celebrated at the time in popular verse and song, it has since been recalled in at least two feature-films, in popular novels, and in a stream of histories that have crossed the great divide between the scholarly and the popular.

What, then, is the point of telling the story again? None, perhaps, except that it seems to the present author that the layers of myth that have grown up about the battle have become increasingly a barrier to the understanding of what really happened there. Not that this work is intended in any way to be iconoclastic, or to detract from the desperate courage of the men who fought on both sides; nevertheless, exaggerated notions of glory and heroism seldom help to make facts clear, and they often obscure the reality of the human experience. Rorke's Drift was a particularly brutal battle, a struggle for survival in which the participants fought each other to a standstill; the men who took part had no illusions on that score, and it was not they who romanticized the fight. The associations of glory and gallantry were added by a British public keen to celebrate the achievements of 'the thin red line' at a time when most of the news from Zululand was grim. Some members of the garrison came to accept their role as 'Heroes of Rorke's Drift' happily enough, but there is sufficient evidence to suggest that many were haunted by the horrors of that night for the rest of their lives.

I have based this account largely on the words of the participants themselves, both as a means of presenting the battle as factually as possible, and of evoking the scene as experienced by those who endured it. There are short-comings in this approach, because in battle a man's perception is notoriously limited, and the common soldier often has no idea of the part he is playing in the broader scheme of things; at Rorke's Drift, however, the limited area of the field, and the fact that many of the British participants knew one another, tends to alleviate this problem a little. Sadly, however, it places an inevitable emphasis on the British participants, simply because most surviving accounts were written by them; Zulu society was not literate at that time and, although a considerable body of evidence relating to the Anglo-Zulu War was subsequently collected from the Zulus by travellers and scholars, remarkably little of it is concerned with Rorke's Drift. Naturally enough the Zulus had no wish to celebrate a defeat, but it also seems to be the case that they recognized the marginal importance of the battle. To them, the great battles of Isandlwana, Khambula and Ulundi, which steadily broke their military strength and paved the way for the dismemberment of their kingdom, were of far greater importance. Nevertheless, I have tried to stress the Zulu perspective wherever possible.

I have not attempted a general history of the

Anglo-Zulu War in this volume, nor have I described Isandlwana, and the strategic context of Rorke's Drift, in any detail. For my views on these aspects of the campaign readers are referred to *Brave Men's Blood* and *Zulu: The Battles of Isandlwana and Rorke's Drift* respectively. I have, rather, chosen to concentrate on the narrow confines of Rorke's Drift, and the men whom fate and circumstance had drawn to that spot on that particular dramatic occasion. Many people have, over the years, shared with me their knowledge and enthusiasm, and without them a book such as this could not have been written. My longest-standing and greatest debt is to that great Natal expert on Zulu history and culture, Sighart 'SB' Bourquin. SB has been unfailingly generous, both with his own superb collection of records and photographs, a knowledge accumulated over fifty years of association with the Zulu people, and with his hospitality. I am eternally grateful to him for the adventures which we have shared on our expeditions to the battlefields together, which have brought the mystery and magic of Zululand and its past alive for me. Zululand is changing rapidly. Five years ago SB and I were able to camp close by the battlefield of Rorke's Drift itself; with the increased — and very positive — moves to protect the battlefields, this is a privilege which few will have the chance to experience in the future. My thanks are due, too, to my friends David and Nicky Rattray of Fugitives' Drift Lodge, who not only provided hospitality on my visits to the region, but also a good deal of stimulating conversation, and their own quota of adventures. David is a fund of local stories concerning the action, and his passion for exploring the sites exceeds my own. Graham Dominy, the historian at the Natal Museum, helped me to find my way through the various collections of records in Natal and, together with his wife Anne and son James, also proved a most entertaining host.

Dr John Vincent of the Natal Museums' Service, and his colleagues Gilbert Torlage and Mark Coghlan, could not have been more generous in allowing me access to the site and its records. I am particularly grateful for their permission to consult the report of the archaeological surveys of 1988-9 and to use some of the photographs from it. Graham Smythe, curator of the new museum on the site, allowed me the fullest access to the museum facilities, and Mrs Sheila Henderson filled me in on the background to the settler community. My thanks are due, also, to Professor John Laband, and to Dr Barry Marshall of the kwaZulu Monuments' Council.

Many people have helped with my research, both in Britain and South Africa. Gillian Berning and her colleagues at the Local History Museum at Durban, Jenni Duggan and her staff at the Killie Campbell Africana Library, and Mrs E.B. Nagelgast of the Africana Museum, Johannesburg, all tackled my persistent inquiries, both in person and by correspondence, with rare patience. Major Bob Smith, curator of the Royal Regiment of Wales Museum at Brecon, and his archivist Diana Roberts, allowed me the fullest access to their collection of records and relics. The staff of the National Army Museum in London, and various regimental museums around the country, were also unfailingly kind and helpful. Colonel Ian Bennett, whose own book, *Eyewitness in Zululand*, shed much-needed light on the problems of transport and supply, gave me much invaluable advice on the role of the commissaries, as well as valuable advice and support. Ian Castle, a regular travelling companion who has footslogged across the battlefields with me on many occasions and in all weathers, read the manuscript, and allowed me access to his own researches on the Natal Volunteer units. Keith Reeves, another fellow traveller, also allowed me to plunder shamelessly his collection of photographs and artefacts. Rai England gave me access to his superb collection of contemporary newspaper engravings, while Tim Day and Ian Woodason shared with me their researches into the subsequent careers and fate of many of the participants. Indeed, I have greatly benefitted from my association with the enthusiasts of the Zulu Study Group of the Victorian Military Society over the years.

Several debts are of a purely personal nature: my parents, John and June Knight, have always supported my curious fascination for Zulu history, even when it would have been far more sensible to re-assess my priorities and settle instead for a 'proper job', while my fiancee Carolyn has seen me through all those times when the midnight oil burned low to no avail. My thanks to them all. Needless to say, the responsibility for any conclusions drawn in this work are all my own.

1.BACKGROUND AND SETTING

In 1849 a trader named James Rorke bought a farm of a thousand acres on the banks of the River Mzinyathi (Buffalo river) in the province of Natal in South Africa. His property included one of the best crossings on the river, and in giving his name to it Rorke set in motion a train of events that would lead to the enactment of one of the almost legendary epics of the British Empire — one which still holds a popular currency when others, more important in their time, have long been forgotten. The grim drama of the Well of Cawnpore has slipped from the public consciousness, and the Relief of Mafeking has come to represent nothing more than the quaintness of a by-gone age, but the story of the Battle of Rorke's Drift continues to exert a particular fascination. It has been told over and over again, losing nothing in the process, and usually couched in terms which not only stress such timeless and appealing themes as valour and self-sacrifice, but which also project a certain, rather more ambiguous, image of the British Empire in Africa. And the origins of that particular image, of why Rorke's Drift took on such a

Right: The man who started it all. The frontier trader, James Rorke. (Killie Campbell Africana Library)

mythical quality, is part of the story itself.

When Rorke first arrived to claim his land, Natal was still a wild and rugged country, its only outlet to the wider world, in those days of sailing ships, being the treacherous, reef-studded south-eastern coast of Africa, beaten eternally by the crashing surf of the Indian Ocean. From the coast the land rises in a series of steep terraces towards the barriers of the Qahlamba and Drakensberg mountains, and the rain-bearing winds from the sea have given birth to a series of major river systems which have cut deep, winding gorges on their way through the rolling green hills. The variation in altitude has given rise to several distinct climatic zones, from the humid, sub-tropical reaches along the coast to the cool inland heights. The summer months, December, January and February, are blisteringly hot and very wet, and the grass grows tall and green; in the dry winters the temperature can drop below freezing overnight, and the landscape takes on an entirely different aspect, turning a golden yellow-brown. Before the introduction of Western farming methods, the coastal strip was covered with lush, semi-tropical bush, while in the hotter, drier midlands, age-old forests of trees with such exotic names as stink-wood, yellow-wood and sneeze-wood crested the ridge-tops. The baking valley floors, which trap the heat like an oven and stifle the slightest breeze, were carpeted with dense thorn bush. Up-country, the undulating mountain foothills provided an endless vista of unbroken grassland.

Natal earned its unusual name on Christmas Day 1497, when the Portuguese explorer Vasco da Gama, sailing north up the coast, logged its discovery for the European world, and christened it Terra Natalis, in honour of the birth of Our Lord. For more than three hundred years, however, Natal remained cut off from the grand rivalries and petty squabbles that characterized the emergence of the European empires. The Portuguese established a trading enclave in Mozambique to the north, but the malarial lowlands of Maputaland which lay between them and Natal discouraged them from moving south. In 1647 the Dutch established a way-station at the southernmost tip of the continent, the Cape of Good Hope, to service their ships on the long haul to the Indies. The indigenous Khoi-San peoples, whose simple culture proved unable to withstand the more robust technology of Europe, gave way before the onslaught, and the Dutch settlement gradually expanded, despite the opposition of the bureaucrats who thought that colonial settlement was more trouble and expense than it was worth. By the middle of the eighteenth century Dutch farmers, moving on the fringes of the Cape's fluid boundary, encountered the first black groups moving in the opposite direction. Since both parties were essentially pastoralists, this led to an endemic confrontation which for nearly a century effectively prevented European penetration of Natal.

The competition for good grazing land would, indeed, characterize much of the interaction between black and white in southern Africa. It gave rise, in the end, to a series of brutal and bloody conflicts which fail to compare in terms of genocide with the experience of the native Americans only because the blacks in southern Africa were too numerous to be annihilated. It would not be true to suggest that this conflict over natural resources was purely racial, but it may well have been responsible for the self-inflicted devastation wrought among the African population of Natal at the beginning of the eighteenth century. Natal was extremely good cattle country; it had a mix of sweet and sour grasses, which matured at different times throughout the year, and a relative absence of the tsetse fly and other debilitating livestock diseases. And it is no coincidence that the black people who inhabited Natal on the eve of the colonial encounter valued cattle above almost everything else.

Scholars have preoccupied themselves with the origins of black groups in Southern Africa, partly because, with no written records to illuminate them, they are lost in the mists of time, and partly because the historical record has been blatantly distorted in recent times for a variety of political ends, which has made the issue one of some sensitivity. Suffice it to say that archaeological deposits dating back to the African Iron-Age have been found across much of Natal, while the accounts of ship-wrecked sailors have confirmed that an African group, classified loosely by language and culture as the Nguni, were present in the region by the fourteenth century. The Nguni are a polygamous people whose basic political unit is the clan, a kinship group which traces descent to a supposedly common ancestor. The Nguni used cattle as a means of governing all aspects of social relationships, and of assessing wealth and status. Life for the Nguni, both male and female, was a succession of rites of passage, in which they passed from childhood and youth, when they were considered an extension of their parents' household, through adulthood to venerable old age. The most important step in the journey was marriage, since this was the point at which men, in particular, were thought to have passed from boyhood to the independent rights and

Below: *The Mzinyathi valley at Rorke's Drift; Shiyane hill in the centre, with the river beyond. The cluster of buildings where Rorke once had his store can be seen at the foot of the hill, centre left. (Author's collection)*

Sirayo's Krantz, ou
Pest a été livré le premier combat de la
guerre. Le "Krantz" ou village du chef Sirayo
est situé sur cette montagne, d'un abord extrêmement difficile.

pour un peintre délicieusement beau. Espèce de palais

Krantz pour   Krantz où a été   S'montel qui a été
but de ni   bien que   pour ce combat
                    le Krantz ou bastions

pour Berg, &c. des
de la maison. Pendant le
s'attaque des Zulus ne trouver
aux susceptible qui servent
en plein dans l'individuelle

Specimen du retranchement
barricade que a été form
hi's Drift

CAPTIONS TO COLOUR ILLUSTRATIONS

A and B

Two sketches by Lt. Col. Henry J. Degacher, 2/24th, of the defence of Rorke's Drift. Degacher commanded the 2nd Battalion in Zululand, and was present with Chelmsford's force which returned to the post on the morning of 23 January. His sketches show the two buildings and their surroundings, and one of the wagons built into the barricade on the south wall. These sketches were used by the artist Alphonse de Neuville as a reference for his famous painting of the battle.
Top: Rorke's Drift Post 1879. (pencil, watercolour wash 25.6 x 35.9cm, Art Gallery of New South Wales).
Bottom: barricade at Rorke's Drift 1879. (pencil, watercolour wash 25.6 x 35.8cm. Art Gallery of New South Wales).

C

Alphonse de Neuville's painting of the battle. Arguably the most spirited rendition of the scene, it telescopes several famous incidents from the fight: Corporal Scammell, here incorrectly shown in the uniform of the 24th, hands his cartridges to Lt. Chard, right. In the centre Surgeon Reynolds tends the wounded Dalton; behind him Chaplain Smith hands out ammunition, while in the background Cpl. Schiess fights at the barricade. Lt. Bromhead points, centre. The viewpoint is from the front of the storehouse looking west and the overall scene is extremely accurate, although the evacuation of the hospital did not occur until after the yard had been abandoned. (Alphonse de Neuville, 1835–1885, oil on canvas 180.9 x 301.4cm, Art Gallery of New South Wales).

D

'The Defence of Rorke's Drift' by Lady Butler. Like de Neuville, the artist has included several incidents which took place at different times during the battle. Chard points to Bromhead, centre;

behind them Schiess leaps on to the rampart, and Chaplain Smith distributes ammunition. In the foreground, Louis Byrne is shot handing a drink to Cpl. Scammell while Surgeon Reynolds looks on. Fred Hitch, right, his wounded arm thrust into his waist belt, carries packets of ammunition to the line. The viewpoint is from the front of the hospital, looking towards the storehouse, and while the painting accurately reflects the gloom of the gathering dusk, it, too, errs in its depiction of the evacuation of the hospital at this stage of the fight. (Royal Collection, St. James's Palace © HM the Queen).

E

A modern rendition of the battle by American artist Keith Rocco. The viewpoint is similar to Lady Butler's, and represents the battle at about 6pm, when the Zulu assault on the front barricade was at its fiercest. Chard is shown firing at a warrior, centre, while nearby Bromhead leads a group of men to reinforce a weak-spot. Private Cole lies dead, left, with Private Bushe – struck on the nose by the bullet that killed him – kneels next to him. Chaplain Smith is depicted right, whilst Dalton carries ammunition boxes to the line. In the background, Walter Dunne struggles to build the redoubt at the front of the storehouse. (Rorke's Drift © Keith A. Rocco, 1990).

F

The struggle for the hospital quickly became part of the mythology of the battle; in this contemporary print, one of the defenders – presumably the bearded William Jones – holds the Zulus at bay, while another helps a frail and sickly patient to safety. The ferocity of the fighting is suggested by the image of the wounded Zulu, still clutching at the blanket of the sick-bed. (Rai England)

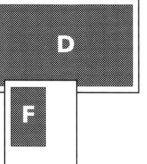

responsibilities which characterized manhood. Before a man could marry, he had to transfer cattle to the family of his betrothed; this custom, known as *ilobolo*, was both an indication of his own status and a guarantee of the future standing of his wife. As a man accumulated more cattle, so he could afford to support more wives, raise children, and attract adherents. Thus there was a very real connection between the levels of cattle in Nguni society and the rate at which that society expanded.

This system worked very well until it reached an ecological limit. Despite its geographical riches, there is a harshness which lurks not far below the surface of the African environment. Every few years nature withheld its bounty through a period of prolonged drought. The grasses shrivelled and withered, and the competition for good grazing land among people dependent upon cattle became intense. Since the Nguni practised no comprehensive form of stock control, the very ideal cherished by their society — the possession of endless herds of sleek, well-fed cattle —contributed to a breakdown of the natural resources. Over-grazing destroyed the grass cover which held the soil together, and when rain did come it flushed away the top-soil, and left the countryside scoured by deep erosion gulleys, called dongas. At the end of the eighteenth century, Natal was struck by such a drought, which is still remembered as the *Madlathule* — 'Let him eat what he can and say naught'. It coincided with a violent social upheaval, and, though the connection between the two is still hotly debated by scholars, the inference is difficult to ignore. There may well have been other contributing factors. The spread of Portuguese trading patterns out from Mozambique in the north may well have had an unsettling effect — the first violence occurred across such routes — by introducing a new element of competition. The slave-trade, which various European powers occasionally indulged in through the same ports, may also have been an element. But the importance of cattle and the land on which to graze them should not be under-estimated.

At the beginning of the eighteenth century, some of the larger clans in Natal began to attack one another. At that time the most sophisticated political unit appears to have been the chiefdom, but as a result of these pressures, clans began to draw together to extend their power and influence. Bigger and stronger units began to emerge, both through conquest and through alliances of convenience. Warfare at this stage was not particularly destructive: each clan chief was able to command an army composed of young men who, being unmarried, were considered tied to him by obligations of service. Although cattle raids and night attacks were not unknown, the usual method of settling disputes was for the aggrieved parties to muster at an appointed place and indulge in ritual

combat. The warriors were armed with light throwing spears and oval shields of cow-hide, and, after a prolonged session of ritual challenge, a few heroes would indulge in individual combat. Then the armies of both sides would throw spears at each other until one side gave way. Casualties were usually light, and a gift of cattle served as a formal declaration of submission, and was usually enough to restore peace.

As the process of conflict accelerated, however, so the military methods employed became harsher. The dubious credit for this is usually given to one man, King Shaka kaSenzangakhona of the Zulu. Although King Shaka's meteoric rise has undoubtedly attracted a fair share of bogus legend, he was none the less an extraordinary individual. He was born in about 1787, the illegitimate son of Chief Senzangakhona of the amaZulu people. The amaZulu — Zulu's people, from the name of their legendary progenitor, which itself means 'the heavens' — were a small clan living south of the White Mfolozi river in the northern part of Natal, which subsequently became known as Zululand. Shaka endured something of an unhappy childhood, wandering among his mother's relatives to escape the rigours of the drought; unwelcome, apparently, among the Zulu because of his father's disapproval. He gave service to another chiefdom, the Mthethwa, and it was during this period that he is supposed to have conceived his innovative military techniques. Instead of lamely throwing his spears at the enemy, Shaka would rush down on them with a heavy-bladed stabbing spear of his own invention, and fight them hand to hand. When he rose to command part of the Mthethwa forces, he trained them in a new tactic, the *impondo zankomo*, or beast's horns, in which one group of warriors (the *isifuba* or 'chest') assaulted the enemy head-on, while two flanking groups (the *izimpondo* or 'horns') rushed out on each side to pin him in place. This tactic was apparently so successful that Shaka was established by the Mthethwa on the Zulu throne, a position which he exploited so successfully that the Zulus emerged from the power struggle as the dominant force in the region. At its height, Zulu influence extended from the Black Mfolozi in the north, south across the mighty Thukela River and into Natal proper.

Shaka astutely refined existing structures to produce a political system which concentrated power in the king's hands. The Zulu kingdom was made up of all the clans who submitted to Shaka's authority, and there was an inherent tension between the chiefs, who wished to retain their traditional prerogatives, and the central authority of the king. Many clans gave their allegiance to the Zulu as equals, and their hereditary chiefs had the right to sit in the powerful *ibandla*, or national council, which could overrule the king's decisions. In the case of subjugated clans, however, Shaka often interfered in the royal line, killing off the legitimate ruler, and raising up some junior member of the family who was loyal to him. This effectively stacked the balance of power within the *ibandla* —and the country — in his favour. So, too, did the way he appropriated the system whereby young men gave service to the chiefs. This became the prerogative of the king alone; young men were gathered from across the country and formed into guilds known as *amabutho* (sing. *ibutho*), which were created on the basis of the common age of the members. The *amabutho* were quartered in royal homesteads, known as *amakhanda* (sing. *ikhanda*), which were distributed strategically about the country as centres of royal authority. The *amabutho* gave service to the king in a number of ways: they took part in his hunts, tended his homesteads and crops, herded his cattle, acted as an internal police force, and, in times of war, formed the basic tactical units which made up the Zulu army. The young men were required to serve in the *amabutho* until the king gave them permission to marry and stand down, at which point their first allegiance reverted to their own families and their clan chiefs. It was not unknown for Zulu men to remain unmarried until they were forty, since this prolonged the period during which the king had them at his disposal; it did not, as the Victorians imagined with a thrill of prurient horror, channel frustrated sexual activity into aggression. In fact, Zulu moral codes allowed for limited sexual activity outside marriage. Indeed, service in the *amabutho* was often very attractive to its members, because their common age, and the awe with which the Zulu army was regarded by its neighbours, led to a high morale, and service offered the possibility of advancement and rewards of cattle.

Ironically, it was the very success of the kingdom created by Shaka that brought about its destruction. Rumours trickled down to the frontier of the Cape Colony, carried by the refugees fleeing from the upheaval, of a powerful kingdom whose herds were innumerable, and whose cattle-pens were ringed with ivory. By this time much had happened at the Cape, and Britain had assumed control from the Dutch as part of the fall-out from the revolutionary and Napoleonic wars in Europe. With the ending of these wars, the world was awash with ex-servicemen looking to make their fortunes and ready for any adventure. In 1824 a small party of British and Dutch traders, backed by the Cape merchants, sailed up to Natal in the hope of establishing a profitable contact with the Zulu kingdom. This was certainly a daring venture; for one thing, Natal boasted only one potential harbour, a bay which the Portuguese knew as the Rio da Natal, whose entrance was blocked by a dangerous sand-bar. The intrepid band crossed the bar into the still, quiet, beautiful lagoon, and camped that night on the shore, fending off hyenas

with flaming brands from their camp-fires. Eventually they duly made their way to King Shaka whom, with the typical arrogance of their time, they expected to be overawed by their white skin. They found instead that the Zulus already knew about white people from encounters with the sailors who were occasionally spat out by the surf on their shores. They called them *abelungu*, pallid sea-creatures, a term which was not entirely respectful. Unabashed, the traders made themselves firm favourites with the king, not merely because they were able to add new varieties of goods to those which, within the kingdom, he controlled as a monopoly, and distributed as a mark of his favour; but also because they introduced him to firearms. Shaka established them as a client chiefdom and gave them rights over much of Natal, and from this unconventional beginning date all British claims to the region.

These first traders were a thoroughly disreputable lot, but it is difficult not to be intrigued by their castaway life-style and their sheer cheek. They established themselves as Nguni chiefs, married African wives, established homesteads, collected adherents, hunted, traded, accumulated cattle, quarrelled, cheated and fought among themselves, and didn't hesitate to try to manipulate king Shaka to their own ends. Given the circumstances, successive Zulu kings treated them with a remarkable tolerance. They were not, however, so well received by their own government; they tried several times to persuade the Colonial Office to recognize their claims to Port Natal, but the British government would have none of them. Until, that is, there was the prospect of a rival European power intervening, at which point it acted with alacrity.

In the 1830s a significant part of the Dutch population of the Eastern Cape — who by now considered themselves to have a separate cultural identity, and called themselves Afrikaners, white Africans or simply Boers (farmers) — became disenchanted with British rule and expressed their dissatisfaction by emigrating *en masse* to the interior. They first arrived in Natal across the Drakensberg from the interior in 1838. They reached an accommodation with the traders at Port Natal, but their negotiations with the Zulu kingdom — and by now King Shaka had been replaced by his half-brother King Dingane kaSenzangakhona — went horribly awry and resulted in the massacre of the Boer envoys. A brutally destructive war then broke out — the first test of arms between Europeans and the Zulus — in which the Zulus were heavily defeated, first at the Battle of Blood River in 1838, then again two years later, when Dingane's brother, Mpande, defected to the Boers and was used by them as the instrument of Dingane's overthrow. The Boers hoped that Mpande would prove a compliant

Above: *The Drift itself; a recent view showing the shelf of rock (right) which created the ford on the River Mzinyathi at Rorke's Drift. Mount Isandlwana is on the sky-line, right. (Author's photograph)*

client-ruler, and in Natal they set about establishing their own ideal state. With the Zulu threat reduced, however, those parts of Natal that had been depopulated in Shaka's time, for fear of his raids, began to fill up as their original inhabitants came out of hiding to reclaim them. The Boers, attempting to control black settlement and ensure that they retained the best farm-land, tried to dump the 'surplus' black population on Natal's southern frontier. This had an unsettling effect at the Cape, an area about which the British were particularly sensitive. They became even more alarmed when the Boers tried to open diplomatic contacts with Holland via Port Natal. At this juncture it was conveniently remembered that Shaka had granted land around the port to British subjects, and in 1842 troops were promptly dispatched to secure it for the Empire.

A force of two hundred British redcoats, supported by artillery and locally raised cavalry, marched up from the Cape. It must have been an extraordinary journey; several of the soldiers had their wives with them, and one gave birth along the way. At one point they marched along the beach, marvelling at the traces of old ship-wrecks and the skeletons of beached whales. When they arrived at the Port the Boers gave them a frosty reception and the tension erupted into open warfare. The British planned a night attack on the Boer camp, but were discovered, intercepted and badly shot-up. They

retreated to an improvised earthwork fort where they withstood several weeks of siege. One of the British traders managed to slip away and, accompanied by his African servant, covered the gruelling journey to the Frontier outposts in ten days — it usually took three weeks.. A warship was promptly dispatched to land reinforcements, and the Boers were driven off. When the echoes of the gunfire had ceased to reverberate about the lagoon, the British had arrived to stay, but it was not until 1845 that Natal was fully accepted into the colonial administration.

Thus Jim Rorke had come early to British Natal. The story is that his father was a soldier with an Irish regiment that had fought in the Eastern Cape, and that Rorke himself had served with the commissariat in the seventh Cape Frontier War, the War of the Axe (1846). Apparently he had gone north to Natal a year later to try his luck, one of no more than a trickle of settlers, at that stage, to do so. In 1849 the upper reaches of the Mzinyathi were among the most remote and undeveloped areas of the colony. The British had taken over Pietermaritzburg, the town fifty miles inland from Durban, which the Boers had built as their capital, but the process of extending imperial administration took its time. Like the Boers, the British divided the land up between the black and white populations, and the whites got the best of it. The blacks were settled in reserves known as locations and, since they lacked the power to do anything else, the British allowed them to rule themselves by their existing political institutions — the chiefdoms — which had survived the passing of Shaka and the coming of the whites with varying degrees of power and cohesion. White settlers took over the remainder of the country, and both were overseen by a scattering of magistrates, who represented the best that law and order had to offer. Hunting and trading was still the most important economic activity among the settler community, although over the next two decades it gave way to an increase in cattle-ranching and, on the coastal strip, the introduction of the sugar-cane industry. The colony's roads consisted of no more than wagon-tracks, and along these sprang up little hamlets which, with a way-side inn, a trading store and a church, were to constitute most of Natal's urban development for nearly thirty years.

Politically, the British had come to an agreement with King Mpande kaSenzangakhona, who was relieved to be free of his obligation to the Boers. The disastrous Boer–Zulu war of 1838-40 had cost the lives of several thousand Zulus, and seriously weakened the king's grip over the state apparatus. The various clan chiefs who made up the nation had gained a good deal of independence, the price of their support for Mpande in his struggle against Dingane, and, for the first time since King Shaka's day, the young men in the *amabutho* had an alternative means of establishing their independence: throughout Mpande's reign many preferred to place themselves under Natal authority, where there were less rigorous means of obtaining cattle for *ilobolo*. King Mpande, a shrewd survivor who hid a calculating mind behind a façade of indolence, dedicated his reign to keeping the kingdom intact. He was happy to accept a definite boundary between the two countries, and the Anglo–Zulu accord had specified that the border between the two countries would follow the River Thukela, the most spectacular of the river systems which bisect Natal from west to east. Where the Thukela curled back on itself in the central midlands, the border branched off up the line of the Mzinyathi, which angled north-west towards the Drakensberg. Jim Rorke's farm was well sited on the banks of the Mzinyathi — the very frontier of the colony itself, and one of the best gateways into Zululand.

A drift is a ford, a place where South Africa's often treacherous rivers can most easily be crossed. At Rorke's Drift, the Mzinyathi flows over an exposed reef of hard bed-rock which has resisted erosion and is, therefore, when not in flood, shallow as a result. The country upstream is generally open, with flats on each side of the river giving way to rolling hills in the distance. One of these, a spur of the Drakensberg called the Biggarsberg, strikes down as a high, flat ridge,

parallel to the river. The first Boer settlers who came to the area combined to make a cutting across this ridge, and called it as a result Helpmekaar — 'help one another'. Some three or four miles below Rorke's Drift, the river enters a narrow, rugged gorge, and this difficult country continues down to its junction with the Thukela, and almost as far as the sea. An isolated hill, jutting out from this range, rises just above the drift; a hulking hog's back, it was known to the Zulus as Shiyane, 'the eyebrow', which the line of the summit resembles.

Jim Rorke was a trader, and the 1850s were the golden age of hunting and trading in Zululand. The track across Rorke's Drift led off into the heart of the Zulu kingdom, and must have seen the passage of a steady trickle of traders' wagons, heavily laden with cloth, beads and perhaps gin, as well as the self-contained expeditions mounted by professional traders bent on securing a concession from the king. Shaka had found the European trade a useful boost to his power, but by Mpande's time it was impossible to maintain a royal monopoly of exotic prestige goods. The king's subjects were keen to purchase on their own account, and the traders were keen to supply them; the process inevitably helped to erode royal influence still further. The best that Mpande could do was insist that every European working his territory should secure his permission first, at the expense of a fee. Where possible, Mpande liked to be paid in guns. Hunting, too, enjoyed a golden twilight in the 1850s; at that time the upper Mzinyathi — as its name 'the water of buffaloes' suggests — was still teeming with game. In the rolling country behind Helpmekaar there were still elephants in plenty, and the grassland was alive with giraffe, rhino and countless species of buck. Yet, with the slow but steady increase in the white population of Natal, the game that was not quickly shot out was driven into the inaccessible parts of the country by European farming methods. Professional hunters, whose capacity for slaughter was extraordinary, turned increasingly to Zululand, until by the 1870s the more profitable species were scarce even there.

Rorke established himself about a quarter of a mile from the crossing which bore his name, under the western foot of Shiyane. Here he built two large buildings in the typical style of the period, both thatched, with walls of brick and stone, and wide front verandas. One of these served as his house, the other was a general-purpose store and shed. He became well-known to the black population on both sides of the border, who knew his store as kwaJim — Jim's Place. If Rorke was a man who enjoyed the company of his fellow settlers, his life must have been a lonely one, for his nearest neighbours were the Vermaaks at Helpmekaar, ten miles away; even here, as late as the 1870s, there

was nothing but an isolated church and two stone houses. A small hamlet sprang up at Dundee, twenty miles away to the north-west, and this, with Newcastle farther to the west and the predominantly Afrikaner town of Utrecht to the north, formed the metropolitan centre for the farms and traders living lives of great self-sufficiency along the length of the border. Yet Rorke must have been a respected member of that scattered community; he married, and enlisted in the local defence unit, the Buffalo Border Guard.

It had been obvious from the beginning that the imperial government would not be in a position to provide military protection for the settlers. Natal was too large and backward, and its population too small and scattered, to justify the expense. A standing garrison was established at Fort Napier in Pietermaritzburg, with one or two outposts scattered about the country, but in the event of either an internal rebellion or a attack from outside, the colonists would have to look to themselves. By a fear of outside attack, of course, most settlers meant the Zulu kingdom, which was still the largest and most powerful group in the region, Boers included. During his war with the Boers, King Dingane had launched his armies against them in Natal, and the resulting civilian casualties had left a deep impression on the settlers' collective consciousness. Although, in retrospect, there was never any serious danger of a war erupting between

the British and Zulus prior to 1879, there were times of tension, and each crisis produced a crop of rumours that a Zulu *impi* had crossed the border and was killing settlers and laying waste to their property. The settlers reacted by forming a number of small Volunteer units. These were loosely based on the Rifle Volunteer movement in Britain, adapted to local conditions, which is to say they were mounted units, not infantry. The men met once or twice a year to train, and provided their own horses and uniforms, while the government supplied them with weapons and equipment.

The Buffalo Border Guard had been formed when the undercurrent of uneasiness had intensified in 1873, during the 'rebellion' of a chief named Langalibalele kaMthimkulu, whose Hlubi people lived in the Drakensberg foothills. In 1868 diamonds were discovered at Kimberley, north of the Cape, an event which was to transform the history of the continent. For one thing it created an insatiable demand for black labour, which employers tried to satisfy by promising to pay wages with guns instead of cash. Although the effects of the diamond-rush were limited in Natal, whose communication infrastructure was not best suited to exploit the chances it offered, none the less a large number of Hlubi men had crossed the Drakensberg to work at the mines, and returned home duly rewarded. The Natal authorities regarded this influx of arms into the black population with some alarm, and ordered Langalibalele to surrender them. Caught between two fires — his young men refused to give them up — he prevaricated, and, when the Natal authorities called out their militia prematurely, Langalibalele panicked and fled across the mountains. A force sent to intercept him was badly cut up at Bushman's Pass. Although the rebellion soon fizzled out — Langalibalele was arrested, and his people suffered a retribution out of all proportion

to their crimes — the shock waves reverberated through the rural settler communities, reinforcing their sense of isolation and vulnerability. Along the Mzinyathi border the result was the formation of the Buffalo Border Guard in which James Rorke enlisted as a First Lieutenant.

For perhaps thirty years Britain and Zululand remained good neighbours, quarrelling occasionally it is true, but never quite coming to blows, and generally respecting each other's laws, customs and territorial integrity. By the end of the 1860s, however, tensions were becoming more pronounced and the implications were felt first on the Mzinyathi border. Following their defeat at Port Natal in 1842, many of the most independent-minded Boers left Natal, trekking back inland over the Drakensberg mountains to the Afrikaner Republic of the Transvaal. Some, however, lingered in the north-western section of the country, which was as far as they could get from British rule without actually emigrating. Here, the Zulu border runs north from the Mzinyathi, roughly along the lines of the Ncome (Blood) River, towards the Phongolo River, which the Zulu kings claimed as the north-western corner of their territory. This area is a long way from the centre of authority of any group, however, and, since strictly speaking it abutted the territory of the Boer Republic of the Transvaal, the Anglo-Zulu accord had not specified an exact boundary line. The Boers had asked King Mpande's permission to graze their cattle on these high grassy uplands, and the king had agreed. Mpande was astute enough to see the advantage of maintaining a vestige of friendly contact with the Boers and, in due course, he was able to exploit this in his internal power-struggle against his son, Prince Cetshwayo. By the 1870s, however, the Boers had encroached more and more on territory claimed by the Zulu, and a bitter wrangle had developed as a result.

Left: *Rorke's store, which the Reverend Otto Witt used as a church, and the Army turned back into a store, photographed at the end of the Anglo-Zulu War, c.June 1879. The strong loop-holed wall was part of the defences built after the battle, but the picture gives a good impression of the basic design of both buildings; large bungalows with verandah and thatched roof. ('SB' Bourquin collection)*

Right: The Reverend Otto Witt, the Swedish missionary whose society had purchased the buildings at Rorke's Drift in 1878. (Natal Museums Service)

In 1873 King Mpande died and his son Cetshwayo succeeded him. Mpande had successfully and deliberately ducked the issue of the succession throughout his life, however, with the result that Cetshwayo was sufficiently unsure of his position to ask for a gesture of support from the Natal authorities. This was given, but would rebound to spectacular effect when the disputed border question landed squarely in Britain's lap. Although Cetshwayo was keen to avoid conflict with the British, he repudiated any agreements his father had made with the Boers, and was keen to restore his control over the full extent of his territory.

Below: The grave of James Rorke, who died in October 1875, and is buried at the foot of Shiyane, overlooking the River Mzinyathi. (Author's photograph)

Rorke's house was at the extreme southern tip of the inverted triangle of the disputed territory. Rorke would have been all too aware of the tensions, and perhaps this is why, towards the end of his life, he considered selling the property. In July 1875 the Norwegian missionary, Karl Titlestad, urged his Society to purchase Rorke's land. It must, indeed, have seemed attractive to the Church, not just because Rorke's buildings were in good repair, but because of its proximity to Zululand. There was considerable rivalry among the various mission groups to establish successful stations in Zululand, but so far they had not had much luck. The first Missions, established in Dingane's time, had to be abandoned when war broke out with the Boers. King Mpande had encouraged the missionaries, but for political rather than spiritual ends; he gave one of his sons into their keeping as a hostage against the ambitions of Cetshwayo. So Cetshwayo turned instead to traders for support within the white community, and his attitude towards missionaries was decidedly luke-warm. Nor did they succeed in prying many Zulus from their traditional beliefs, but merely attracted converts from among those who were alienated from their own communities so that Mission settlements earned something of a bad reputation. A Mission close to the border would offer the best of both worlds.

Jim Rorke did not have time to enjoy the proceeds from the sale of his property. He died in October 1875 after a two-day illness.

'I was sorry not to have seen him before he died,' wrote Titlestad. 'I went to see Mrs Rorke as soon as I heard the news. Together with another man I helped to make the coffin and Mr Rorke was buried two days later. A Scottish missionary conducted the funeral service. There was a large gathering of white people at the graveside. My wife and I later visited Mrs Rorke and subsequently I have seen her several times. Mrs Rorke has not been left too well off which increases her plight.'

Rorke was buried behind his old store, at the foot of Shiyane, at a spot which overlooks the Drift. His colleagues in the Buffalo Border Guard paid for the erection of a tombstone. And so Jim Rorke passes out of our story, almost unnoticed, leaving nothing behind but his name, not to remember him by, but to recall events with which he had no connection.

Because the political sympathies of the border Boers led them to lend their support to the Transvaal Republic rather than Natal, Britain was not, initially, over-concerned about this wrangle and, if anything, tended towards support for the Zulu claim. Following the discovery of diamonds, however, the home government suddenly became interested in South Africa. Hitherto it had seemed no more than a costly backwater on the fringes of the empire, and policing the endless bickering between the locals was a price Britain was prepared to pay for the convenience of owning the Cape. Diamonds, however, meant that Britain could at last get a return on all those years of trouble and expense, and it moved quickly to secure its claim to the Kimberley district. If this important resource were to be properly exploited, however, a new economic infrastructure would have to be established, since there was, at present, no way of moving the necessary equipment and labour across the region. Not only was the transport system hopeless, but the area was a patchwork of mutually antagonistic Boer republics, British colonies and black kingdoms. For South Africa to be properly developed, it was argued, it would be necessary for all of these groups to be placed under one umbrella authority — British. This scheme was the brain-child of the Secretary of State for the Colonies, Lord Carnarvon, and was called Confederation. It would not, of course be a popular scheme in South Africa, not only because the Boer republics had been born out of an anathema for British rule, but because the most prosperous British possession, the Cape, resented the idea of being shackled to under-developed Natal. Carnarvon went ahead, however, and the Transvaal was the first plum to fall into his lap. Because its citizens were of such independent mind that they resented paying their taxes, the Transvaal had hovered on the brink of bankruptcy since its foundation; it was pushed over the edge by an unsuccessful campaign waged against one of its African neighbours, King Sekhukhune's Pedi. British agents discreetly canvassed a highly selective cross-section of Boer opinion — mostly among British immigrants — pronounced it favourable to British intervention, and in 1877 raised the Union Flag at the capital Pretoria. With the Transvaal, of course, came the border dispute, and King Cetshwayo found that his hitherto friendly relationship with Britain went decidedly sour when they switched their support to the Boer claim.

Britain had, in any case, adopted a more aggressive forward policy as a result of the Confederation scheme. A new imperial pro-consul, Sir Henry Edward Bartle Frere, had been sent out to South Africa with the expressed intention of pushing the scheme through. Frere was an extremely able man who had had a long and distinguished career in the Indian Civil Service, and was, if anything, considered over-qualified for the job. He arrived on the eve of the Transvaal annexation, and turned his considerable energies to manipulating colonial politicians and the representatives of independent states alike. Frere clearly felt that the Zulu kingdom was an anachronism — he referred to King Cetshwayo and his warriors as 'magnificent animals' — which was dangerously out of place in the new order of stable

economic progress. A war with the Zulus, furthermore, could be extremely useful. Frere needed an excuse to unleash a little of Britain's military might in aid of the hard-pressed settlers, both to remind them of the benefits of imperial rule, and to demonstrate the fate that might befall those who opposed Confederation too vigorously. At the end of the 1870s a wave of unrest was sweeping through southern Africa's black population. A war — the ninth — had broken out on the Cape frontier, the Pedi were still unrepentant, and there were stirrings of discontent among the BaSotho. In fact, there is nothing to suggest that these outbreaks were anything other than an unco-ordinated reaction to the common experience of dispossession and economic impoverishment which was becoming the black man's lot across the region as the century wore on. Frere, however, was convinced that a hidden hand lay behind it, and he found it in the form of King Cetshwayo of the Zulus.

Frere felt that the Zulu kingdom posed an

Above: Lieutenant-General Sir Frederick Thesiger, 2nd Baron Chelmsford, the British Commander-in-Chief in South Africa, 1878-9. This is the uniform Chelmsford wore in the field during the Anglo-Zulu War ('SB' Bourquin collection)

intolerable threat to Natal's security. He characterized its military institutions as a celibate man-destroying machine, bent on 'washing their spears' in the blood of its innocent white neighbours. King Cetshwayo, who was a more vigorous personality than his father, was represented as a blood-thirsty tyrant who wallowed in the blood of his own subjects, and whose aggressive intentions were manifest in his stubborn policy regarding the Transvaal border. Frere felt that even if Cetshwayo were not actively encouraging the upsurge of black resistance, the strength and unity of the Zulu kingdom at least served as a beacon which encouraged other groups by its very existence. By the same token, it was clearly an obstacle to progress, since the kingdom had not, by and large, been drawn into the mainstream of white economic development in the region; there were no Zulus working in the diamond fields. A war with the Zulus, therefore, could fulfil several very useful purposes: it would serve to break the spirit of black opposition to colonial exploitation and, by removing the supposed threat to the kingdom's white neighbour-states, it would provide a tangible proof of the beneficence of imperial rule.

There were those in Natal, however, who were not so sure. In particular, the head of the civil administration, Lieutenant-Governor Sir Henry Bulwer, feared that a Zulu War would cost Natal dear. Apart from the handful of Volunteer units, very little had been done to put the colony into a defensible condition, and there was an obvious danger that its civilian population – both black and white – would suffer heavily should the Zulus be provoked into an offensive. Furthermore, such a war could poison race relations for years to come and, far from benefiting the colonial economy, might ruin it. In an attempt to head off the increasingly war-like attitude of the High Commissioner, Bulwer proposed that a Commission be set up to take evidence from both the Zulus and the Boers and come to some impartial judgement on the question of the border dispute. Frere accepted, presumably in the expectation that the Commission would support the Transvaal's claim.

The Commission convened at Rorke's Drift in March 1878. The parties in dispute were each requested to send three representatives, and the Commission also consisted of three members. These were Lieutenant-Colonel Anthony Durnford, Royal Engineers, who had played a significant part in the Langalibalele rebellion, John Wesley Shepstone, Natal's Secretary for Native Affairs, and M.H. Gallway, Natal's Attorney-General. The Three Transvaal representatives were Henrique Shepstone — brother of John — who was Secretary for Native Affairs in the Transvaal, Gert Rudolph, the Landdrost of Utrecht, and Petrus

Lefras Uys, a prominent farmer in the disputed area. The Zulu representatives were Chief Sihayo kaXongo, who lived on the Zulu side of the Mzinyathi near Rorke's Drift, and Gebula and Mundula, two of the king's officials. The king also sent one of his *izinceku*, or personal servants, a man named Sintwangu, to bring him a confidential report on the proceedings.

The Commission made a polite but firm show of impartiality. The Commissioners were accompanied by an escort of twenty men of the Natal Mounted Police, which gave an air of importance to the proceedings. When the Transvaal representatives tried to sit with the Commissioners, they were discreetly moved to a place equally distant as that of the Zulu representatives. The Commission began its work in the second week of March, and sat for more than a month. It sifted through a great deal of evidence, both written and oral, and finally came to the conclusion that the balance of right lay with the Zulus. Many documents produced by the Transvaal were highly suspect, and often the tangled web of claims and counter-claims simply could not be unravelled. Durnford thought it clear that

'...the white man wanted the black man's land — that he got leave from the black to graze cattle in the first instance, then came over and put up a shanty, then a house. Then more Boers came, and so on, until, as the Zulus told us, the Boers were like a toad that comes hopping and hopping until it hops right into the middle of the house.'

When the Commission broke up and reported its findings to Frere, it suggested that, while there was no evidence that the Zulus had ever ceded land to the Transvaal, the Boers should be allowed to keep the areas they had settled most heavily, and the remainder should be restored to the Zulus. It was not the decision Frere had hoped for. Had the Commission backed the Transvaal claim, he would have had a legitimate reason to confront the Zulus. Taken against the background of his over-all aggressive posture, the Commission's decision looked remarkably like a climb-down. Rather than publish the report immediately, Frere sat on it while he took advice from a variety of local sources, pondering his next move.

At this point the Zulus played into his hands. In July, two wives of Chief Sihayo fled across the border from Zululand, seeking sanctuary in Natal. Both were apparently pregnant, neither of them by Sihayo, and one of them was implicated in acts of witchcraft. Both adultery and witchcraft were terrible crimes in the Zulu community, punishable by death; Chief Sihayo, moreover, was an important man. His brother, Mfokazana kaXongo of the Ngobese family, had been a favourite of King Mpande, and had been appointed by him *induna* of the Qungebe people. This was a responsible position, precisely because the Qungebe lived on the border, opposite the crossing at Rorke's Drift. Sihayo had personally supported Cetshwayo during the succession crises of the 1850s and 1860s, and he was rewarded when Cetshwayo came to the throne with the position previously enjoyed by his brother. Sihayo was a progressive man, at ease in European society; he often wore European clothes, and dined at table with missionaries. He had extensive trading contacts both in Natal and through Swaziland to Mozambique, and possessed horses, wagons and guns. His affluence was apparent in his Sokhexe homestead, which was built on a knoll at the foot of the Ngedla mountain overlooking the Batshe valley, which boasted an impressively large stone cattle-kraal. In many ways Sihayo was perhaps the epitome of the frontier chieftain; he looked to both sides of the border and had a foot in each camp. Nevertheless, he was close to the king and his first loyalty remained to Cetshwayo.

Sihayo was, indeed, visiting Ulundi at the end of July when his sons discovered that his runaway wives had taken the foolish step of moving close to the border. One was living in the homestead of one of Natal's black Border Policemen, Mswagele. Sihayo's sons were outraged at this apparent flouting of their father's honour, and his eldest son, Mehlokazulu, an active and decisive young man who was an attendant of the king's and a junior commander of the iNgobamakhosi *ibutho*, reacted quickly. On 28 July Mehlokazulu, accompanied by his brothers Tshekwana and Bhekuzulu, and their uncle Zuluhlenga kaXongo, crossed the Mzinyathi below Rorke's Drift in broad daylight, at the head of thirty mounted men armed with rifles and spears, and a large force of men on foot. They went to Mswagele's homestead and arrested one of the women. Mswagele, supported by a group of Natal blacks, tried to intervene, but the Zulus were too strong for them. The woman was taken back across the river and put to death. It is variously suggested that she was clubbed to death, or strangled, and that her teeth were knocked out first. The next day Mehlokazulu crossed the border again and carried off the second woman.

White opinion in Natal was appalled, both by the violation of its territory and by the apparent brutality of the deed. In fact, of course, the two women were citizens of the Zulu king, and had been dealt with according to Zulu law, so the legal position was not as clear-cut as it seemed; nevertheless, it confirmed all the latent fears within the settler community regarding their savage and barbarous neighbours. On this issue, at least, it brought Bulwer and Frere together, since Bulwer was adamant that Mehlokazulu be surrendered for trial in Natal. King Cetshwayo prevaricated. He admitted that the young men were in the wrong, but put their behaviour down to an excess of zeal,

and offered £50 in compensation. In fact, since there was probably little British cash available within the kingdom, this was quite a significant sum, but Frere and Bulwer chose to regard it as derisory. Frere's stance became increasingly belligerent.

If war were to come there was an obvious need to make military preparations. The senior British commander in South Africa was Lieutenant-General Sir Frederick Thesiger. Tall, bearded, rather aloof but with perfect manners, he had arrived in South Africa in February, and had brought to a close a messy little war against the Xhosa on the Cape Frontier. In September he and his Staff arrived in Natal, and Frere asked him to prepare a plan for the invasion of Zululand. Since Frere was pursuing his policy with little support from the home government, Thesiger could expect little enough in the way of reinforcements, and would have to make do with the troops already in South Africa. Although these were hardly sufficient for a major war, Thesiger decided that they would advance into Zululand in five separate columns, starting from widely spaced points along the border. His experience on the Cape Frontier had suggested that black armies were reluctant to face massed firepower in the open, but he was also anxious to limit the Zulus' chances of a counter-strike in Natal, which remained largely unprotected. In the event, the problems of supplying five columns in the field forced him to reconsider. Each imperial infantry battalion required a minimum of seventeen wagons to carry its ammunition, equipment and supplies, and Thesiger had no fully integrated support services to call on for back-up. There were no more than a handful of trained commissariat officers in South Africa, and the short-fall would have to be made up of special-service officers with no experience in the field. Furthermore, the supply of transport vehicles was limited, and would have to be augmented by the hire or purchase of civilian vehicles. Each wagon needed a minimum of sixteen oxen to drag it at a rate of two miles an hour for no more than ten or twelve miles a day; unless properly treated and well fed, the oxen could be expected to drop like flies from a variety of fatal diseases. In the end, Thesiger opted for three offensive columns, with two in reserve on the borders. One of the offensive columns would cross the river at Rorke's Drift.

Frere, meanwhile, had brought events to a crisis. He decided to add a significant caveat to the Boundary Commission's award, and Cetshwayo's representatives were invited to hear its findings at a meeting on the Lower Thukela on 11 December 1878. They sat patiently while the award was read out, and expressed themselves pleased at the impartial result. Then, to their astonishment, they were informed that, because of the raid by Sihayo's sons and other minor incidents, King Cetshwayo

was expected to comply with certain terms within thirty days. These included the surrender of Sihayo's sons, and — most incredibly — the disbandment of the *amabutho* system. As one incredulous Zulu commented, these terms, if obeyed, would reduce the Zulu nation to the level of the *amakhafula* — the blacks living under British authority in Natal. This, of course, was Frere's intention; if Cetshwayo accepted the demands, the Zulu menace would be effectively removed. If he didn't, he could be broken. With heavy hearts the Zulu envoys retired across the river to take the news to the king.

Once the ultimatum had been delivered, Thesiger — who had just succeeded to the title Lord Chelmsford — was able to prepare for his campaign. Troops began to march up to their starting-points, and a levy, the Natal Native Contingent, was hastily raised from among Natal's black population. Because Bulwer did not altogether approve, the NNC had not been authorized until November 1878, and did not begin to muster until the middle of December. Warriors were drawn from clans across northern and central Natal, the NCOs being recruited from white veterans of the Cape Frontier War, who had little knowledge of Natal. In the end, the officers, most of whom were either imperial regulars or ex-imperial regulars, had something like two weeks to drill the men into shape before they were pitched into combat. The NNC were poorly armed. Because of Natal's anxiety about arming its black population, only one in ten was given a firearm, the remainder carrying their own shields and spears. They wore no uniform other than a red rag tied around the head. Under sympathetic officers, and employing their customary fighting techniques, the

NNC had the potential to become excellent light infantry, but in fact most of their officers and NCOs despised and bullied them, and it is hardly surprising that in the event their showing was poor.

Chelmsford's No. 3, or Centre Column, was technically under the command of Colonel Richard Glyn of the 24th, although Chelmsford decided to accompany it in person, which effectively reduced Glyn to a cipher. The Column assembled at Helpmekaar on the Biggarsberg plateau. This was chosen simply because it was a fine, airy, healthy spot on the so-called Border Road which ran up from the capital Pietermaritzburg, through Greytown before turning off from Helpmekaar to Rorke's Drift. It was therefore usefully situated along a tolerably efficient supply route. The two solitary stone houses soon disappeared in a sea of tents and wagons as the troops appointed to the column gradually came up. The backbone of the Column were the two battalions of the 24th Regiment. It was unusual for two battalions of the same regiment to serve together — one was always supposed to remain on garrison duties at home — but in practice the Empire required a lot of policing, and both battalions had been dispatched separately to the Cape frontier. They were re-united at Helpmekaar, much to their delight. The 3rd Regiment of the NNC mustered at Sandspruit, on the Natal side of the Biggarsberg and, as the time allotted for compliance with the ultimatum ticked away, moved up to join the regulars at Helpmekaar. Also attached to the Column was N/5 Battery of the Royal Artillery. With no regular cavalry at his disposal, Chelmsford had to fall back on the services of a squadron of Mounted Infantry, and the small Natal Volunteer units. Among those camped at Helpmekaar was

Below: The windswept heights of the ridge at Helpmekaar. Helpmekaar was chosen as a supply depot on the route to Rorke's Drift; the earthwork fort visible in this photograph was erected after the battle of Isandlwana, when Zulu raids were expected along the border. (RRW Museum, Brecon)

Rorke's old unit, the Buffalo Border Guard.

Rorke's widow had finally sold her husband's store to the missionaries, and in 1878 had moved up to a farm at Knostrope on the Helpmekaar escarpment. Here she lived with her sister who was married to Quartermaster-Sergeant Adams of the Buffalo Border Guard. As the Column began to shuffle towards the border, the Volunteers moved forward and pitched their camp at Knostrope. The new owner of Rorke's Drift was a Swedish missionary, the Reverend Otto Witt. He had not been in residence long, and had not yet had time to impose his personality on Rorke's buildings; he had simply taken over Rorke's house and was using the store as a make-shift church. He had, however, christened Shiyane 'Oskarberg', after the King of Sweden. Chelmsford had another purpose in mind for Witt's buildings; they were ideally suited as an advanced supply depot. In the first week of January No. 3 Column began to move down from Helpmekaar and camped at Rorke's Drift. The army took over Witt's church and used it to store supplies. A few sick and injured men were placed in Witt's house. Witt himself stayed on to keep an eye on his property, but sent his wife and daughter to a safer house a few miles from the river.

The final military preparations had been accomplished despite appalling weather. For three or four years South Africa had been suffering from one of its periodic droughts. Major rivers had shrunk to a trickle, and crops and grass had withered. The colony's civilian transport infrastructure ground to a halt, since the oxen had soon stripped the roadside bare of pasture, and none was growing afresh. Then, with the onset of the summer, the rains had returned with a vengeance. Each evening the skies would fill with leaden-grey clouds, and down would come long spears of rain. The parched earth, too hard to absorb it, simply sluiced it off into dongas, and the rivers rose at an alarming rate. The troops encamped at Helpmekaar found themselves living in a sea of mud, and each downpour brought the chance of some new unexpected stream taking a wayward course through their tents. With heavily laden wagons working the roads in convoys, the surfaces soon disintegrated into a quagmire. At Rorke's Drift, the Mzinyathi rose to become a sheet of brown water, chest deep and higher, surging in a torrent over the rocky shelf, making it impassable for wagons and men on foot. A portable pontoon was therefore brought up and assembled at the Drift, together with an improvised barrel raft. Each was capable of carrying either a company of infantry or a wagon at a time.

The British ultimatum expired on 11 January 1879. Frere had received no response to his demands, beyond a request to allow more time for them to be considered, which was refused. In fact, King Cetshwayo had been boxed into a corner. Some of his important chiefs wanted him to surrender Sihayo's sons —thinking them not worth

Below: The invasion of Zululand; a sketch of Lord Chelmsford's Military Secretary, Lieutenant-Colonel J.N. Crealock, of the 3rd Regiment, Natal Native Contingent, crossing at Rorke's Drift on the morning of 11 January 1879. (Sherwood Foresters Museum)

ruining the country for — but it was quite impossible to disband the *amabutho* system. This was not only the basis of Zulu military might, it was also the fundamental prop of royal authority, and without it the kingdom would fall apart. Reluctantly the king called up his regiments and waited apprehensively for the inevitable.

The Centre Column crossed into Zululand at Rorke's Drift a little after dawn on the 11th. It was a cold, misty morning, and it was widely rumoured that the Zulus would oppose the crossing. The 2/24th were drawn up on a rise commanding the river, while the guns were unlimbered downstream. The infantry crossed on the ponts, while the mounted men and NNC crossed through shallows on either side, the NNC linking arms and plunging into the water through which they pulled themselves across in a body. It was a tense time for those left on the Natal bank; the mist blotted out the view of the far side, and all that could be seen were the shapes of men moving about in the gloom. Suddenly, however, the sun broke through and the mist lifted. The column moved out, shook itself down, and formed up on the Zulu bank. There was not a Zulu in sight; the crossing had been unopposed.

Chelmsford established his first camp on Zulu soil just back from the river. On the morning of the 12th he made a sortie against Sihayo's important homestead, Sokhexe, a few miles farther along the road in the Batshe valley. Neither Sihayo nor

Mehlokazulu was at home, but Sihayo had left another son, Mkhumbikazulu, with forty or fifty retainers to guard his property. The Zulus had taken up a position among the rocks at the foot of the cliffs which line the Ngedla mountain, on the eastern side of the valley. The 1/24th and NNC made a frontal assault against the boulders, while the Volunteers were sent round to the right flank to get on to the hills above them. The 2/24th moved farther up the valley to destroy Sokhexe itself, which was found to be deserted. The Zulus stuck to their position as long as possible, but after a sharp skirmish, broke and fled. Chelmsford then marched the entire force back to the camp, well pleased with their performance.

Progress over the next few days was slow, however. The road beyond Rorke's Drift was far from perfect at the best of times, and the continuing bad weather made it almost impassable. Chelmsford intended to push forward in a series of leaps and bounds, co-ordinating his advance with the Left Flank Column, No. 4, which was moving down from the direction of Utrecht. Work parties were out improving the road every day, but it was not until the 20th that he was able to move forward to his next temporary camp. This was established a few miles beyond the Batshe at a distinctive hill called Isandlwana.

Below: The ponts at Rorke's Drift, with Shiyane in the background. This photograph dates from later in the war, probably from the end of June 1879. The 'floating bridge' pont is on the right, with the improvised 'barrel raft' moored to it. The small rowing boat is visible in the foreground. (Local History Museum)

2. DRAMATIS PERSONAE

When Lord Chelmsford's Column moved forward towards Isandlwana from their camp on the Zulu side of Rorke's Drift on 20 January, those who remained at the Mission had a distinct feeling of being left behind. They were, after all, guarding a post on the Natal side of the border, scarcely a position of any danger, and their duties would be both arduous and boring. If there were any hope of seeing active service, it would obviously fall to the General's Column.

It is interesting to see who had been left behind at Rorke's Drift, and why. The post was under the overall command of Brevet Major Henry Spalding, 104th Regiment, who was the Deputy Assistant Adjutant and Quarter-Master General attached to the Headquarters Staff in South Africa, and had been for two years. Spalding was temporarily in charge of the line of communications forward from Helpmekaar, and it was his responsibility to see that the line was kept open, posts properly garrisoned, and supplies kept moving. Indeed, the importance of Rorke's Drift to the Column lay in the fact that it was its advanced supply depot. Provisions were shuffled forward down the line to be accumulated at Rorke's Drift, before they were ferried across the river and on to the Column. Upwards of thirty-five wagons, loaded with supplies, had gone up with the Column on the 20th; they were unloaded at the new camp at Isandlwana on the 21st, and were due to return to be reloaded on the morning of the 22nd. Consequently there was a huge stock-pile of stores at Rorke's Drift.

There was a large pile of mealie-bags covered by a tarpaulin in front of Rorke's store, and the inside was crammed to the ceiling with sacks of tea, coffee, sugar and flour, and heavy wooden crates containing biscuits and tinned meat. Mealies, which have achieved a certain international fame through their providential presence at Rorke's Drift, were simply the local variety of maize. They were a useful general-purpose food which served both humans and animals. According to Chelmsford's Field Force Regulations, members of the NNC were entitled to a daily ration of a pound of mealies, or flour or biscuit, and mealies could also be fed to draught oxen when grass was in short supply. White troops, incidentally, were supposed to receive fresh vegetables instead, if they were available. The biscuits were small oblong blocks of hard-tack, not unlike the notorious ships' biscuits beloved by the Royal Navy; indeed, there is a suggestion that some might have been ships'

biscuits. The mealies were packed in large sacks weighing 200 pounds; the biscuit boxes weighed about 112 pounds. Sizes and construction of the boxes differed, apparently, but it is difficult now to be precise about their specifications. The biscuits were purchased under contract from Nabisco, who presumably made the boxes to War Office specifications, but no records survive. The boxes that held the tinned meat were apparently the smaller of the two, and contemporary sketches suggest that one or the other of them resembled tea-chests, simple wooden boxes bound with metal at the edges. One surviving crate, however, is more solidly built, having a stout wooden frame with rounded edges and thick wooden slats at the sides. Access to the contents was via a panel at the top, with a metal ring attached as a handle. This may have been the type used for the tinned meat.

The stores were under the watchful eye of a handful of commissariat officers under the command of Assistant Commissary Walter Alphonsus Dunne. A tall, pleasant-looking man, not yet 26, Dunne had joined the then Control Department in 1873, and had come to South

Left: Acting Assistant Commissary Walter Alphonsus Dunne, the senior commissariat officer at the depot at Rorke's Drift. (Author's collection)

Above: This heavy crate formed part of the barricades at Rorke's Drift during the battle. Although described as a biscuit box, it might equally be one of the tinned meat ration boxes. (Local History Museum, Durban)

and other ranks, and the Control Department, which still had a decidedly civilian outlook, was created to provide the officers. In 1875 the Control Department had been streamlined into the Commissariat and Transport Department, but as Colonel Ian Bennett has pointed out in his perceptive study of the transport débâcle in the Anglo-Zulu and Transvaal Wars: 'A pitifully inadequate establishment of dedicated and usually overworked Commissariat Officers was expected to improvise a transport system for each and every campaign as and when it occurred anywhere in the world at the minimum cost to the exchequer.'

Indeed, Dunne's command at Rorke's Drift suggests just how improvisatory this system could be. Dunne expected to move forward and join the main column shortly, leaving Acting Assistant Commissary James Dalton in charge of the depot. The Commissariat Department had its own system of ranks: Assistant Commissary was the equivalent of a lieutenant. Dalton's varied career had seen him enlist in the 85th (Shropshire) Regiment in 1849 — he was probably under-age at the time — where he rose to the rank of sergeant. He transferred to the Commissariat Staff Corps in 1862, and when he left the Army in 1872 he did so as a senior warrant officer with twenty-two years' service behind him. He retired to South Africa, and when the Ninth Cape Frontier War broke out he volunteered for service. Because of the desperate shortage of trained staff, he was accepted with alacrity, and was appointed Acting Assistant Commissary in December 1877. He was placed in charge of the supply depot at Ibeka during the first phase of the war, when the post was in a dangerous and exposed position. Supplies from Ibeka kept a number of British columns in the field during the gruelling sweeps through the bush which characterized the campaign, and Dalton was mentioned in dispatches for his efficiency and energy. He had followed the Army to Natal, and had ridden up to the front from Pietermaritzburg in pouring rain on New Year's Day 1879, in the company of Acting Storekeeper Louis Byrne. A civilian volunteer as, technically, was Dalton, Byrne had given up a job in the Natal Civil Service in response to a request for commissariat personnel. Acting Storekeeper was a rank, however, and he was classed as an officer. One wonders if Lord Chelmsford had selected Dalton for what promised to be, after all, a post of no less importance than Ibeka. There was only one other commissariat man at Rorke's Drift, Corporal Francis Attwood of the Army Service Corps. Attwood had volunteered for service in South Africa, but had been unhappy in the clerical duties in which he found himself at Pietermaritzburg, and had contrived a posting to Helpmekaar. There he had quarrelled with a sergeant-major and been sent forward to Rorke's Drift.

Africa two years earlier on his first overseas posting. He had already had an adventurous time of it, having served on the Cape Frontier, and then been sent to the north-eastern Transvaal to join an abortive British campaign against the Pedi. This war was in continuation of the Transvaal's long-standing quarrel with the Pedi, and its responsibility had passed to the British when they annexed the Transvaal. The war had fizzled out because the drought and horse-sickness made it impossible to sustain the army in the field, and Dunne had ridden the last hundred miles alone across country, through potentially hostile territory, to join the forces being assembled for the Zulu campaign. The Control Department of 1873 was a curious institution, the result of a fundamental inability on the part of the British Army to come to terms with its own supply requirements. The shambles of the Crimean War had exposed the inadequacy of a civilian supply and transport system, and the Army had created the Army Services Corps to undertake much of this work. The ASC, however, was composed only of NCOs

Far left: *Acting Storekeeper Louis Byrne, a civilian volunteer serving with the commissariat. (Colonel Ian Bennett)*
Left: *Second Corporal Francis Attwood of the Army Service Corps, wearing the DCM which he won for his part in the defence. (RCT Museum)*

Of secondary importance to its roll as a supply depot was Rorke's Drift's function as a field hospital. This was supervised by Surgeon James Reynolds, a 35-year-old Irishman from County Dublin. Reynolds had the joined Medical Staff Corps in 1868, and while attached to the 36th (Hereford) Regiment in India had received a commendation from Lord Sandhurst for his work during a cholera epidemic. He had come to South Africa with the 1st Battalion, 24th Regiment, and had seen action during the investment of Mpetu. With Reynolds were his groom, Mr Pearce, and Corporal McMahon and Private Luddington of the Army Hospital Corps.

There is some doubt as to the precise number of patients under Reynolds's care. Henry Hook, who was to become only too acquainted with the hospital, thought that there were about thirty, but Reynolds himself remembered only 'eight or ten'. Perhaps he was referring to the most serious cases, of whom Hook said 'there were about nine who could not move'. There were certainly seventeen or eighteen men on the site whose units were out with Chelmsford, and who had been left behind because they were sick, and several members of the garrison were also ailing. Only three men were actually suffering from wounds sustained in action: Lieutenant T. Purvis, Corporal Jesse Meyer and an unknown private, one of Prince Mkhungo kaMpande's people, a break-away section of the

Zulu Royal House which had settled in Natal. All three were in the 3rd NNC, and had been wounded in the action at Sihayo's stronghold. The details of Purvis's wound are not known, but it was evidently a severe one; Corporal Meyer had received a nasty stab wound '...in the lower end of the left ham, above the popliteal space'. The NNC had been interrogating a Zulu prisoner — and had no doubt removed any kid gloves for the occasion — when he had snatched a spear and tried to escape, stabbing Meyer in the leg. Although the wound was clean it kept breaking out in a severe haemorrhage. The African private had been wounded in the leg, which was heavily bound. The remaining patients were all suffering from the sort of accidents and illness sustained by any army on campaign, especially in wet weather. Gunner Arthur Howard, who was the servant to Brevet Lieutenant-Colonel Harness, the commander of N/5 Battery, RA, had been left behind suffering from diarrhoea. Nineteen-year-old Trooper Harry Lugg of the Natal Mounted Police had injured his knee when his horse had slipped crossing the Mzinyathi, and pinned his leg against a rock. His knee was swollen so badly that he couldn't walk. Corporal Christian Ferdinand Schiess of the 2/3rd NNC — who preferred to be called Friederich — had such bad blisters that he could no longer walk. Bombardier Lewis, RA, had a badly swollen thigh, following a wagon accident. Private John Connolly

Right: *Acting Assistant Commissary James Langley Dalton; a photograph taken just after the war, which suggests something of the iron will of the man whom many considered was the driving force behind the decision to defend Rorke's Drift. (Author's collection)*
Far right: *Surgeon James Henry Reynolds of the Army Medical Department, in charge of the hospital at Rorke's Drift. (Royal Archives, Windsor)*

of 'B' Company, 2/24th, had a partially dislocated left knee, again caused by an accident, while Sergeant Robert Maxfield of the same Company was suffering from an unspecified fever.

It should not be assumed that the Army had made any great alterations to Witt's house to turn it into a hospital; it was simply a convenient place for the sick to be tended. The house was a curious warren of rooms, many of which did not connect with one another, the only doors leading to the

outside. There were two large rooms at the front, facing the verandah, flanked by extensions on each side, and a row of small rooms at the back. A surviving plan for a house Witt later built on the same spot, and which greatly resembles Rorke's original, shows that the two front rooms were living-quarters, those at the back being servants' quarters or for storage. Witt was still living at Rorke's Drift and so presumably occupied his own bedroom; the Army, no doubt, had simply placed the patients in the most convenient of the remaining rooms. During the Anglo-Zulu War field hospitals could boast of little in the way of specialist facilities, and one witness suggests that the beds were nothing more than mattresses raised on boards a few inches above the ground. Raised on what is not specified; bricks, presumably. Whatever furniture Witt had remained in the house.

As the presence of Sergeant Maxfield and Private Connolly suggests, the garrison at the post was provided by 'B' Company of the 2/24th. In 1879 the British Army was undergoing a period of change and reform, and was deeply divided between an old, conservative, traditionalist school, led by the Commander-in-Chief, the Duke of Cambridge, and a progressive element, epitomized by General Sir Garnet Wolseley, that 'very model of a modern Major-General'. The origins of this schism date back to the much-publicized crises of

Right: *Dick, Surgeon Reynolds's fox terrier, which was with him throughout the battle. (Keith Reeves collection)*

the Crimean War, which threw the Army's short-comings into very public relief. The Secretary of State for War, Edward Cardwell, who had taken office in 1868, had tried to tackle the worst excesses of what amounted to a deeply entrenched inefficiency of attitude. He had, for example, abolished the system whereby officers purchased their commissions, and had tried to encourage a greater reliance on training and professionalism. Peace-time flogging, the worst aspect of the disciplinary regime that brutalized the men in the ranks, was abolished, although it was retained as a punishment on active service. Perhaps the reform which the conservative military establishment most resented, however, was the introduction of the short-service system. Previously, a man enlisting in the ranks had to do so for twelve years at a stretch; under the new system, a man could enlist for six years with the Colours, and six in the reserve. This was supposed to make army life more attractive to a better class of recruit, and to reduce under-manning by making a constant stream of new, young, recruits available. Its critics, however, argued that it filled the ranks with green youths who, deprived of the steadying influence of old sweats, were certain to be unreliable under fire. The Anglo-Zulu War was one of the first campaigns in which the system was put to the test and, whatever its merits, the many night-time scares and false alarms that bedevilled the later stages suggest that the critics had a point.

The introduction of the new system was very apparent in the ranks of the 2nd Battalion, 24th Regiment. The 1st Battalion, which had been on overseas postings since 1868, still had a high proportion of long-service men in the ranks, but the 2nd Battalion had ben based in Britain until February 1878. Its ranks were therefore filled with young men, many of whom had only a year or two's service under their belts. One such was Colour-Sergeant Frank Bourne, the senior NCO with the Company, a Sussex man, born in 1854, who attested in 1872. As Bourne himself wryly remembered, 'A' Company of any regiment in those days was always called the Grenadier Company and was supposed to have the biggest men. I think the Sergeant-Major must have been a wee bit humorous, for he posted me to our 'A' Company although I only stood five-feet six inches tall and was painfully thin.' He was promoted Colour Sergeant of 'B' Company in April 1878, when he was just 23 years old. Bourne was nervous of his new responsibilities, but soon settled in, only to find that he was known to his men as 'the kid'. He was not, in short, the imposing, mature man of popular myth.

Another corner-stone of the Cardwell system was the establishment of a regimental depot for each of the imperial line regiments, which served as its home base, where it concentrated most of its recruiting. Although the 24th's regimental title was 2nd Warwickshire Regiment, reflecting a long association with that county, the 24th's depot had been established at Brecon in South Wales in 1873. Many of the men recruited into the ranks after that time were drawn from southern Wales, or from the

Above: The 2nd Battalion, 24th Regiment photographed at Pinetown at the end of the Anglo-Zulu War. (RRW Museum, Brecon)

Above and above right:
Lieutenant-Colonel Frank Bourne, OBE. Bourne was the Colour-Sergeant of 'B' Company at the time of the battle; he rose through the ranks. He died in 1945, and is thought to have been the last survivor of the garrison. (RRW Museum, Brecon)

English towns and villages around Hereford and Gloucester, along the Welsh border. Because it had been overseas for so long, and because only the drafts sent out periodically from Wales to replace natural wastage exemplified the new policies, the 1/24th retained a high proportion of Englishmen — and men from Scotland, Ireland and Wales — in the ranks. The 2/24th did have a more pronounced Welsh character, however. 'B' Company alone had no less than five rankers named Jones, none of them related, and three men named Williams although at least one of these had enlisted under a false name. Nevertheless, there was a good cross-section of men from the British Isles in 'B' Company, hailing from London, Liverpool,

Birmingham, Dublin and counties as diverse as Devon, Leicestershire and Lancashire; not least of the mythical accretions about Rorke's Drift is that it was defended entirely by Welshmen.

At full peacetime strength each infantry company consisted of one hundred men, commanded by a captain and two lieutenants. There were eight companies in each battalion which — rather than the regiment — constituted the basic fighting unit of the British Army. When the 2nd Battalion had been sent to South Africa in February 1878, it consisted of 24 officers, eight staff-sergeants, 39 sergeants, 40 corporals, sixteen drummers and 746 privates. In other words it was pretty much up to strength. When the Battalion

docked at Cape Town the local press noted its youth with some concern, but concluded that they were a fine body of men who needed nothing more than experience in the field to mature them. And that they were to get, being dispatched immediately to the eastern frontier. The Ninth Cape Frontier War — the War of Ngcayecibi — was by now entering its final phase. It had been a scrappy affair, reflecting the erosion of the Xhosa tribe's power during eight previous wars with which they had been afflicted during the last 100 years. Many of the Xhosa lived in cramped reserves within colonial territory, where their political and economic independence had steadily declined. Those who lived outside the Cape's borders still clung to the authority of their paramount chief, but his power and prestige, too, had seen better days.

The Ninth Frontier War was the last, sad, desperate attempt of a declining people to halt the advance of colonial domination. In the early stages the Xhosa had taken the field in uncharacteristically large numbers, and the 2/24th's sister battalion, which had been at the Cape since 1875, bore the brunt of the fighting. By the time the 2/24th arrived, however, the Xhosa had retreated to their traditional stronghold, the

rugged, bush-covered Amathole mountains, and the 2/24th were employed in a series of sweeps through the bush. It was a particularly arduous type of warfare, since the Xhosa were an elusive enemy who had perfected hit-and run guerrilla tactics and ambushes, and who operated easily in an environment with which British troops found it hard to contend. The Amatholes are a maze of jutting spurs and vertiginous valleys, split here and there with spectacular gorges called kloofs, choked with jumbles of boulders, some as high as a house, all draped round with creepers and bush. In consequence operations were extremely arduous and frustrating, and much of the campaign consisted of a series of co-ordinated movements across unmapped terrain, in the endeavour — frequently unsuccessful — to pin down and destroy the Xhosa bands. In extremes of weather no less severe than in Zululand, the young men of the 2nd Battalion learned their trade, thrusting through dense undergrowth, snatched at by thorns and creepers, clambering up steep slopes, slithering down the other side, wading rivers, sleeping out at night with no tents in pouring rain — and all, as often as not, for no result. Such actions as did occur were usually short and sharp, the Xhosa

Above: A magnificent study of 'G' Company, 2/24th, taken at Pinetown at the end of the Anglo-Zulu War. Colour-Sergeant Ross is on the left, next to Captain F. Glennie. Lieutenant A.C. Wortlege, sitting centre. This picture gives a good impression of how the 2/24th would have looked in the field; the officers appear to be wearing the ORs' undress frock-coat, stripped of all decoration except possibly the green collar tabs. This seems to have been a fashionable item in the Battalion, and Bromhead may have been wearing it on the day of the battle. Note the crossed swords between the two officers. (RRW Museum, Brecon)

Godwin-Austen was one of three brothers who had been associated with the Battalion; his elder brother, H.H. Godwin-Austen, had retired in March 1878 with the rank of lieutenant-colonel, his younger brother Frederick was a lieutenant in 'G' Company. In an action on 9 May Captain Godwin-Austen was leading a file through the bush when the man behind him accidentally discharged his rifle. The bullet wounded Godwin-Austen in the back; his jacket — an OR's undress serge, stripped of all decoration except the green collar tabs — still exists, complete with a large rip up the back. One wonders how popular the Captain was with his men, and whether this was a nineteenth-century example of an attempted 'fragging'; but there is no evidence of anything untoward, and it was just the sort of accident that could easily occur under such difficult conditions. In any event, command now devolved upon Lieutenant Gonville Bromhead, who also had an elder brother, Brevet Major Charles J. Bromhead, with the Battalion. He seems to have been quite a popular figure within the battalion, despite the premature onset of deafness. It is difficult to assess, now, how severe this affliction was; it has been said that Bromhead's hearing was so bad that it led him to miss orders when on parade, and that his company was often given the most mundane duties as a result. However, none of the contemporary descriptions of his rather reserved personality, some of which are quite critical, mention his deafness, so it may be that its importance has been over-estimated. Nor is there any reason to suppose that 'B' Company was left at Rorke's Drift for this reason; although a dull and unglamorous duty for the men concerned, it was an extremely important one and would surely not have been entrusted to an officer whose efficiency was impaired.

In 1879 the British Army was still campaigning in uniforms more suited to the parade-ground than

Below: A company of the 2/24th at Pinetown, late 1879. As this picture suggests, most of the Battalion were young short-service men. (RRW Museum, Brecon)

fighting with a desperation born of despair.

'B' Company, commanded at that stage by Captain A.G. Godwin-Austen, took part in almost all the operations in which the Battalion was involved in the country around Ntaba-ka-Ndoda, from the end of March until May 1878.

Above: The band of the
2/24th, Pinetown, 1879.
(RRW Museum, Brecon)

the battlefield. Line infantry wore the scarlet jackets — either the seven-button dress tunic, or the loosely cut five-button frock-coat with cuff and collar patches in the regimental facing-colour which for the 24th, was grass-green. The cuff patches were framed by a piped white crow's foot design, and there was piping round the bottom of the collar and around the shoulder-straps. The regimental numeral was worn on the shoulder-straps; although it was brass for many regiments, the 24th were one of the few who had it in white metal. The regimental badge, a sphinx, recalling battle honours won against Napoleon in Egypt, was worn on the collar. Trousers were dark-blue with a red welt down the outside seam, and headgear was the white Foreign Service helmet. This was supposed to have a brass regimental device on the front — in 1879 it was the 1869-78-pattern shako plate, a design which had been officially superseded, but the new pattern had not yet been issued in Africa. However, the combination of a white helmet and a brass plate, both of which caught the glare of the African sun and made the wearer conspicuous for miles around, proved too much of a fatal attraction to enemy snipers, and veterans soon learned to remove the plate and dull

down the helmet with an improvised dye of tea, coffee, boiled tree-bark, mud or even cow-dung. It is possible that some men may have retained their helmet plate, even during the Zulu War, as a few have turned up since on the Isandlwana battlefield; but not in sufficient quantities to suggest that it was a common practice. In some photographs of the 2nd Battalion, men appear to be wearing a dull-coloured canvas cover over the helmet. This was not, at that time, an officially approved item, though it was not unknown in India. By the time both battalions of the 24th reached Natal, the harsh terrain and weather had taken a toll of clothing, and much of it had been repaired with an often bizarre variety of patches.

The men's equipment consisted of the 1871 Valise Pattern system. This incorporated two ammunition pouches worn on the waist-belt one on each side of the clasp, each carrying twenty rounds, and a black ball-bag, sometimes called an expense pouch, worn at the back when on the march, or on the right hip when in action. The wooden 'Oliver' pattern water-bottle was worn on a strap over the left shoulder, and a canvas haversack over the right. When on the march a rolled greatcoat and mess-tin were supported by braces

Right: The jacket worn by Captain Godwin-Austen when he was accidentally wounded on the Cape Frontier; it is an OR's undress frock-coat, stripped of all ornament except for the green collar tabs. It has a rip in the back where the Captain was wounded. Bromhead may have been wearing a similar frock-coat on the day of the battle. (RRW Museum, Brecon)

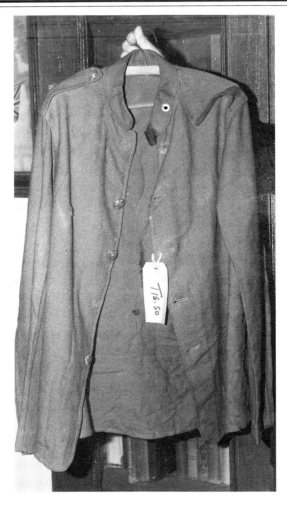

Below: 'B' Company, 2/24th, the men who defended Rorke's Drift. This photograph was probably taken at Pinetown after the War. Gonville Bromhead is on the extreme left, with Colour-Sergeant Bourne next to him. (Local History Museum)

worn around the shoulders. The heavy leather valise itself made marching difficult, and was usually carried on the regimental wagons. The Valise equipment was one of the first fully integrated systems and, although not without its faults, was generally effective. The design of the ball-bag was faulty, however, and it frequently came open, causing cartridges to be lost.

The main infantry weapon was the Martini-Henry rifle, introduced in 1874. This was a single-shot breech-loader with a falling-block system — a lever behind the trigger guard was pulled down to open the chamber, allowing a cartridge to be slipped in the top — which was sighted up to 1,700 yards, but was at its most effective at 400 yards and less. It fired a rolled-brass Boxer-pattern cartridge with a heavy .45in unjacketed solid-metal bullet which clipped through muscle and sinew to produce clean flesh-wounds, but which flattened out on striking bone, with shattering effect. Other ranks carried an 18-inch socket-bayonet whose wicked point had earned it the nick-name 'the lunger'; sergeants carried a heavy sword-bayonet. By the time 'B' Company arrived at Rorke's Drift, then, its members had learned something of both warfare and South Africa. They had seen action together, knew their Company officer and his ways, and knew how to use their weapons in combat. They had faced black Africans across the open sights of their rifles, they had heard the 'whizz and rip' of spears thrown in anger, and they had lived out in suffocating heat and torrential rain. They were, in

Left and opposite page: The other ranks' seven-buttoned tunic, c.1879. The undress frock-coat, a more comfortable jacket for every-day duties, was of the same basic pattern, but was looser cut, had five buttons, and was unpiped down the front and on the skirts. At the beginning of 1879 Long Service and Good Conduct chevrons were worn above the right cuff, not left, as here. (National Army Museum)

short, turning into a seasoned body of professional soldiers who must have thought they knew the worst South Africa could throw at them. In that, at least, they were to be proved very wrong. There was another element to the post's garrison, too, though it has received scant attention in the popular coverage of the events at Rorke's Drift. This was a company of the 2nd Battalion, 3rd Regiment, Natal Native Contingent, under Captain William Stevenson — or Stephenson, even the spelling of his name is in doubt. The 3rd NNC were part of Chelmsford's Column, and

Stevenson's company had been left as part of the garrison. So far so good. Yet no one seems quite sure how many men were in Stevenson's company; it should have included three white officers — the captain and two lieutenants — and six white NCOs, one black officer and ten NCOs, and 90 privates, a total of 110. Several eye-witnesses, however, gave their strength as between 100 and 300 men; Harry Lugg thought there were as many as 2,000 of them! Whatever the true figure, it seems that it was an unusually large company. The NNC wore no uniform, the men being

distinguished by a red rag tied around the head. Only one in ten had a firearm, the remainder making do with their own shields and spears. 'B' Company had pitched its tents behind the storehouse, on the flats at the foot of Shiyane, but there is no record of where Stevenson's men were encamped.

Down at the drift itself were pitched the two tents of a small party of Royal Engineers consisting of Lieutenant John Rouse Merriott Chard, Corporal Gamble, Sappers Cuthbert, MacLaren and Wheatley, and Driver Robson, Chard's batman. These were an advance party from 5th Company, Royal Engineers, one of the few units sent out from England in response to Chelmsford's request for reinforcements. It had arrived in Durban on 5 January and Chelmsford had ordered that '...an officer and a few good men' be sent up to join the Centre Column as soon as possible. Chard's party had arrived on the 19th, and found that one of the ponts had broken down, presumably as a result of the constant traffic across the river. At that time Chelmsford's Column was still encamped opposite the drift, and the Engineers set to work repairing the pont. Born at Boxhill near Plymouth, Chard was 32 years old. He had been commissioned into the Engineers in 1868, and had seen service in Bermuda and Malta, but had not yet been in action. By all accounts his was a relaxed, easy-going, affable personality; his commanding officer, Captain Walter Parke Jones, of the 5th Company, thought him 'a most amiable fellow', but '...as a company officer he is so hopelessly slow and slack'.

When Chelmsford at last began his advance from the drift, there was a bustle of activity at the post. Chelmsford was confident that he would soon make contact with a significant Zulu force, and he wanted to ensure that he was supported and that his line of communication was secure. There was a shuffling of troops along the line to ensure that all the important strategic points were duly protected. 'G' Company, 1/24th, was encamped at Helpmekaar, and was due to be replaced by Brevet Major Upcher's 'D' Company which was marching up from Greytown. Chelmsford ordered Rainforth's company down to guard the crossing at Rorke's Drift, while at the same time Lieutenant-Colonel Anthony Durnford, who had sat on the Border Commission, and who now commanded a column composed almost entirely of black troops, stationed fifty miles below Rorke's Drift on the Thukela, was ordered up to support Chelmsford's advance. Durnford was told to move

Left: An officer's belt clasp and OR's glengarry badge, 24th Regiment, 1879. (Keith Reeves collection)

Below: John Chard, RE, wearing his VC, photographed at the end of the Zulu War. He is wearing the Engineer Officers' undress frock-coat — scarlet with blue collar and cuffs and narrow gold piping — which he probably wore on the day of the battle. Beards were prohibited in peace-time soldiering, but allowed on active service. ('SB' Bourquin collection)

up to Rorke's Drift and await further orders. His column arrived late on the evening of the 20th, and crossed the river to camp on the site vacated by Chelmsford's force that morning. On the night of the 21st, however, Chelmsford's patrols, pushing out from Isandlwana, encountered a Zulu force in the hills above the Mangeni valley, about twelve miles from the camp. This was the first sign that the enemy might be mustering to oppose the Column's advance, and before dawn on the morning of the 22nd Chelmsford moved out with about half his men to attack them. As an afterthought, he sent a message ordering Durnford up to Isandlwana.

That same evening Chard also received an order from Headquarters ordering his men up to the advanced camp. Chelmsford's Staff was to prove less than efficient, and, typically, this order was ambiguous. It was not clear whether Chard himself was to go forward or stay at Rorke's Drift. Chard discussed the matter with Spalding, who said that he had been told that Chard was to select a suitable position to dig an entrenchment to defend the ponts, which would be occupied by Rainforth's company when it arrived. With Spalding's permission, Chard decided to ride up to Isandlwana the next morning and clarify the position.

Chelmsford's orders to Durnford also arrived early on the morning of the 22nd, and his column broke camp and moved off towards Rorke's Drift. Chard and his men loaded their equipment into their Engineers' wagon, and started off with them. Chard, who was on horseback, rode on ahead. When he arrived at Isandlwana, he found the camp buzzing with excitement. Large numbers of Zulus had appeared along the crest of a ridge to the north of the camp, and the troops had been formed up in expectation of a battle. The Zulus did not press their advance, however, and after a while retreated out of sight, and the men were stood down. Chard reported to the Column office, and received confirmation that his men were to stay with the Column, but that he was to return and build an entrenchment overlooking the Drift on the Natal bank. Reports from vedettes out on the hills suggested that some of the Zulus, at least, had moved away towards the left rear of Isandlwana, and Chard was concerned that they might have been trying to cut round behind the Column and strike at the crossing. Accordingly he set off back towards Rorke's Drift. He met Durnford's men along the way and told their leader the news. He ordered his own men to dismount from the wagon and march up to Isandlwana, as he would need the wagon and its equipment back at the Drift. Driver Robson was presumably needed to drive the wagon, so he returned with Chard together with an African mixed-race wagon-driver — which was, as it turned out, very fortunate for them.

Back at the Drift the morning was passing with the usual routine duties. Chard reported to Spalding, and found that Rainforth's company had not yet come down from Helpmekaar. In fact, Upcher's company, which was due to replace them, had been delayed on the road by bad weather, and Rainforth could hardly advance and leave Helpmekaar unprotected. In any case, it seems that Rainforth had not received most of the messages ordering him to move down to Rorke's Drift, and there was little sense of urgency among his command. In the absence of the redcoats, Spalding had issued the day's orders which made provision for a minimal guard on the crossing:

Camp, Rorke's Drift.
22nd January 1879.
Camp morning orders.
1. The force under Lt. Col. Durnford, R.E., having departed, a Guard of 6 Privates and 1 N.C.O. will be furnished by the detachment 2/24th Regiment on the ponts. A guard of 50 armed natives will likewise be furnished by Capt. Stevenson's detachment at the same spot — The ponts will invariably be drawn over to the Natal side at night. This duty will cease on the arrival of Capt. Rainforth's Company, 1/24th Regiment.
2. In accordance with para. 19 Regulations for Field Forces in South Africa, Capt. Rainforth's company, 1/24th Regiment, will entrench itself on the spot assigned to it by Column Orders para - dated -.
H. Spalding, Major,
Commanding.

The reference to Chelmsford's regulations is interesting. In the light of subsequent events, the issue of entrenching camps was to become a highly sensitive one, but paragraph 19 of Field Force Instructions merely stated baldly that 'The camp should be partially entrenched on all sides.' This seems unambiguous enough, but in practice Chelmsford clearly made a distinction between permanent depots and temporary camps along the line of march. In the Cape Frontier War, the former had certainly been entrenched, but the war had been too fluid to make it practical to entrench every over-night bivouac. So far, no attempts had been made to fortify any of the posts on the Zulu border, either by digging earthworks, or utilizing the locally preferred method, the wagon-circle or laager; neither Helpmekaar nor Rorke's Drift had been prepared for defence in any way. On the whole, this was because the prevailing opinion in the force, from Chelmsford down, was that the Zulus would not be capable of sustaining an attack on any post in the open. The orders to Chard to prepare an earthwork near the Drift clearly reflected the fact that a permanent garrison would be needed to protect this site, but Chelmsford had entrenched neither his first camp in Zululand, nor an advanced outpost established in the Batshe valley. Nor did he attempt to protect the camp at Isandlwana in any way. In each case he felt that these camps were too temporary to justify the effort, and that there was no serious danger. The officers of the 2/24th later maintained that this lack of preparation had worried Gonville Bromhead, and that he had made a mental note of what arrangements he would make if an emergency arose. Perhaps he did.

Certainly Chard wasn't happy about Spalding's arrangements. One NCO and six men of the 24th was clearly not a very strong guard in the event of a Zulu attack, and Chard was dismissive of the NNC. He explained to Spalding that the Zulus had been seen near Isandlwana, and Spalding decided to ride up to Helpmekaar to find out what had happened to Rainforth. Chard was just about to ride down to the Drift when Spalding called him back, and a deliciously ironic conversation took place:

' "Which of you is senior, you or Bromhead?" I said, "I don't know." He went back into his tent, looked at an Army List, and coming back, said, "I see you are senior, so you will be in charge, although, of course, nothing will happen, and I shall be back again early this evening." '

As a matter of interest, the Army List for 1878 lists Bromhead as having received his Lieutenancy on 28 October 1871, and Chard his on 15 July 1868. Chard went down to the Drift and whiled away the morning. The 24th detail was commanded by Lance-Sergeant Williams, while Stevenson's NNC came and, when their watch expired, went again, without being replaced. Having no sappers to supervise and no company to entrench, Chard does not seem to have allowed the Zulu threat to bother him any further and, by his own account, '...had some lunch comfortably'.

At about 12.30 p.m., the flat thud of gunfire in the distance attracted the attention of the camp, and the Reverend Otto Witt and Surgeon Reynolds decided to climb Shiyane hill to see if they could see any signs of fighting. With them went Chaplain George Smith. A Norfolk man, Smith was big and tall, with something of a stoop. He had come to South Africa in 1870 as a lay missionary under the auspices of the Society for the Propagation of the Gospel. In 1872 he had been ordained a priest by the Anglican Bishop of Natal, John William Colenso. Something of a free-thinker, passionately committed to the Christian ideals of justice and equality, Colenso was often out of step with the narrower, race-conscious outlook of the settler community. Smith, however, does not seem to have shared his patron's views, and was something of a muscular Christian who saw nothing wrong in forcibly prising stubborn Africans from their traditional beliefs. He had been Chaplain to the

Weenen Yeomanry, a short lived local volunteer unit, and had accompanied the expedition sent out to bury the colony's dead after the skirmish at Bushman's Pass. Colenso had argued that Langalibalele had been the victim of much injustice, but Smith, on the whole, felt that he had got what he deserved. It was entirely in keeping with his character, therefore, that he had volunteered to serve with the Centre Column as its Acting Chaplain. It has been suggested that Private John Wall of 'B' Company accompanied this party, but none of them mention him, and it seems unlikely that a private would be released from his duties to go for a walk; later historians seem to have confused him with a man named Robert Hall, of whom more later.

Witt, Reynolds and Smith toiled up to the top of Shiyane. As so often happens in the Natal summer, the torrential downpours of the night had given way on Wednesday, 22 January 1879 to an extremely hot day. This can mean shade temperatures of more than 100 degrees Fahrenheit, so it must have been quite a climb. A rocky terrace of broken strata, pitted with shallow caves and

Below: Lieutenant Gonville Bromhead, photographed in the early 1870s. ('SB' Bourquin collection)

Right: *Is this the face of the mysterious Lieutenant Adendorff? The original caption to this photograph was simply 'Adendorf'. (Talana Museum, Dundee)*

Below: *The regimental numeral and sphinx collar-badge from the tunic of Private William Jones, who won the VC at Rorke's Drift. The numerals are white metal and typical of the period; there were variations in size of the sphinx badge, the one illustrated here being slightly smaller than other surviving examples. (Xhawulisa collection)*

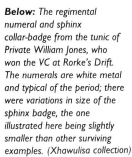

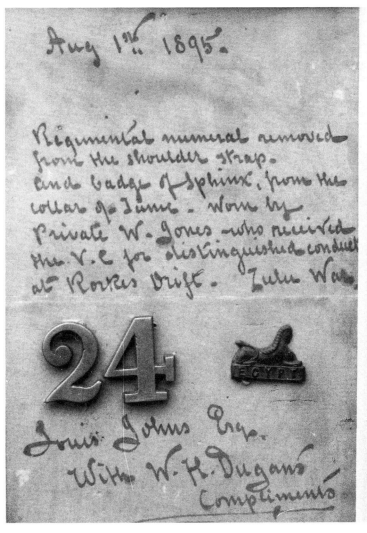

littered with huge slabs of fallen rock, runs round the base of Shiyane, and above it the slope rises steep and boulder-strewn. The top of this rise is a false crest, however, and the summit angles away steadily. Today, the summit is covered with thorn bush and aloes which tug at one's clothes and scratch face and arms. Photographs from 1879 suggest that the slopes then were largely bare, but it would have taken fit, active men a good half-hour to get to the peak, which is at the eastern end of the hill, at the farthest point away from the Mission. From there the ground drops away steeply, and there is a spectacular view of the Mzinyathi valley. The river stretches round from the left, across the drift, flowing past the junction with the Batshe, and the line of red cliffs on the Ngedla mountain which marked the site of Sihayo's stronghold. Just beyond them, to the right, Isandlwana lies like a lion in repose. Farther to the right the hills close in, and the Mzinyathi is squeezed through a narrow gorge and disappears from sight. By now it must have been after one o'clock, and the curious spectators could see a lot of movement in the hills around Isandlwana. A battle did indeed appear to be taking place. The Reverend Witt later claimed that he saw British troops advancing on the hills to the north of Isandlwana, and then being driven back towards the camp. The mountain itself shut out the view of the plain beyond, where most of the fighting was taking place, but in due course three long black lines of men were seen to be moving down the slopes behind Isandlwana, and a group of black troops appeared over a saddle to the right.

'These men', recalled Reynolds, 'we took for our own Native Contingent', and they continued to watch their movements for some time. While they were on top of the hill, incidentally, an eclipse of the sun took place, but no one at Rorke's Drift seems to have noticed it; which is odd, because many men, both black and white, on the Zulu side of the river were struck by it. Reynolds continued:

'Soon afterwards appeared four horsemen on the Natal side of the river galloping in the direction of our post. One of them was a regular soldier, and feeling that they might possibly be messengers for additional medical assistance I hurried down to the hospital and got there as they rode up.' Smith and Witt stayed on the hill-top for a while longer, watching the fascinating manoeuvres of the column of black troops moving leisurely across country towards the river downstream of the Drift. Both Bromhead and Chard had also seen riders approaching the post, and had sensed that something was wrong. Commissary Dunne and Bromhead were resting after lunch under an awning they had improvised by stretching a tarpaulin over some tent-poles when:

'Suddenly, we noticed at some distance across the river, a large number of mounted natives approaching, preceded by a lot of women and children driving oxen. We were going down to find out what they were, but had not gone many steps when we were called back by one of the men who said that a mounted orderly wished to see the officer in command. Turning back at once we met a mounted man in his shirt-sleeves riding hurriedly towards us. His first words were "The camp is taken by Zulus!" '

Dunne and Bromhead were stunned by this astonishing news, and Dunne was shocked into a sensation of *déjà vu*, of '...a strange feeling, which I cannot account for ... that I had heard this somewhere before'. The mounted man was probably Private Edward Evans of the 3rd Regiment (the Buffs), who was part of a squadron of Mounted Infantry attached to Chelmsford's Column, and with him was his colleague Private Daniel Whelan of the 1/13th. They must have given Bromhead the stark details of the catastrophe. While Chelmsford had been out of camp, searching for Zulus in the Mangeni valley, a Zulu army estimated at 20,000 strong had been lying undetected within five miles of Isandlwana. The Zulus Chard had seen in the morning were from one of the Zulu regiments, who had advanced to the edge of the hills under the mistaken impression that the battle was about to begin, but had then retired to their concealed valley. When Durnford had arrived in the camp, he had sent out patrols to reconnoitre Zulu movements, and they had stumbled on the Zulu bivouac, and precipitated the attack. The entire force defending the camp, about 1,700 men, had turned out to meet the Zulu advance, but their position was so over-extended that the Zulus had swept round them and burst through the line. No doubt Evans and Whelan would have been aware of few of the details, but six companies of the 24th — five from the 1st Battalion and one from the 2nd — had been annihilated, two guns had been lost, some 300 of the NNC had been killed, and both Durnford and the camp's commander, Lieutenant-Colonel Pulleine, were dead. The Zulus had cut off the road to Rorke's Drift early in the fight, and the survivors of the massacre had fled across country, chased all the way, and had struck the Mzinyathi at the gorge downstream of Rorke's Drift. Here, still harried by the Zulus, they had crossed the swollen river at a spot subsequently christened Fugitives' Drift. Having gained the comparative safety of the Natal bank, the senior surviving officers — Captain Edward Essex, a transport officer, and Captain Alan Gardner, 14th Hussars, attached to the Staff —had scribbled a pencil note of warning and sent it to Rorke's Drift. Then, together with most of the other survivors, they rode on to Helpmekaar. The catastrophe was all the more appalling because it had happened so quickly; the entire battle had lasted only about two and a half hours. The black troops Reynolds had seen from the top of Shiyane

were Zulus sweeping round to encircle the camp.

Bromhead immediately sent a message down to the Drift to warn Chard, but in fact Chard — who, curiously, doesn't seem to have noticed the black horsemen spotted by Dunne   had already heard the news:

'[I] was writing a letter home when my attention was called to two horsemen galloping towards us from the direction of Isandlwana. From their gesticulation and shouts, when they were near enough to be heard, we saw that something was the matter, and on taking them over the river, one of them, Lieutenant Adendorff of Lonsdale's Regiment, Natal Native Contingent, asking if I was an officer, jumped off his horse, took me on one side, and told me that the camp was in the hands of the Zulus and the army destroyed; that scarcely a man had got away to tell the tale, and that probably Lord Chelmsford and the rest of the column had shared the same fate. His companion, a Carbineer,

confirmed his story — He was naturally very excited, and I am afraid that I did not, at first, quite believe him, and intimated that he probably had not remained to see what did occur. I had the saddle put on my horse, and while I was talking to Lieut. Adendorff, a messenger arrived from Lieut. Bromhead, who was with his Company at his little camp near the Commissariat Stores, to ask me to come up at once.'

Lieutenant Adendorff has attracted a good deal of controversy and speculation, largely because his movements between Isandlwana and Rorke's Drift remain obscure, and because of a rumour that he was court-martialled for deserting his men. This rumour seems to be quite unfounded, and Adendorff's reputation has suffered unfairly as a consequence. Adendorff —whose name is sometimes spelt with one 'f', sometimes two, and whose initial is variously given as 'T' or 'J', though the latter is most likely since it was confirmed in

Standing Orders — was a lieutenant in Captain Krohn's No. 6 Company, of the 1st Battalion, 3rd NNC. Krohn's Company had been held in reserve at Isandlwana, and the battalion Adjutant, Lieutenant Higginson, who survived, had seen Adendorff on a number of occasions during the battle, so there's no reason to doubt that he was present. Years later, Adendorff's friend Walter Stafford, another NNC officer who survived Isandlwana, recalled that Adendorff had told him in 1883 that he and another man, as neither could swim, hugged the bed of the river up to the pont and were ferried across the river. This implies that they did not escape by the road, but across country like the other fugitives; they had, however, presumably managed to slip through the Zulu cordon at Fugitives' Drift. Adendorff, incidentally, seems to have been of European, rather than Afrikaner, descent; Stafford spelt his name 'Odendorff', and at least one other account refers to him as a 'foreigner': Higginson had noted at Isandlwana that he had difficulty in making himself understood when delivering a report. Chard makes the point quite specifically, however, that Adendorff stayed to assist with the defence, in which case he could claim to be the only man who was confirmed as having fought at both Isandlwana and Rorke's Drift.

Chard rode up to the Mission to confer with Bromhead, leaving the crossing in the charge of a handful of men under Sergeant Millne of the Buffs. When he arrived Chard found that Bromhead had already begun preparations to make the post defensible.

It is interesting to ponder the factors that made Chard and Bromhead stand and fight; not such personal elements as individual bravery, loyalty to one's comrades, discipline, or a sense of regimental honour, but the tactical pros and cons that led them to decide that the acceptance of battle was the best course. True, the crossing was strategically important and it was highly desirable that the supplies be prevented from falling into enemy hands. And yet, as the fugitives must have suggested, the Zulus were already over the river, so keeping the ponts safe must have seemed rather like shutting the stable door after the horse had bolted. Similarly, as the entire camp at Isandlwana had fallen into Zulu hands, a stockpile of stores,

even thirty-five wagon-loads, must have seemed of little consequence. Should the garrison have attempted to move out to check the Zulu advance? Could it have retired to the nearest supports at Helpmekaar? Even if the men had simply thrown down their weapons and run, would that have offered them a better chance of survival? There is no evidence that Chard ever thought about confronting the Zulus in the open. No doubt he would have heard how Pulleine's force, widely dispersed that morning, had been further scattered by the Zulus to the four winds.

There was no very clear indication of how many Zulus were approaching, except that they were in overwhelming numbers. To have taken them on in the open would have been suicidal. A retreat would have been a more practicable possibility, and in fact, unknown to the men at Rorke's Drift, there were now two companies of the 1/24th at Helpmekaar, Upcher's Company having arrived in from Greytown that very morning. Three companies of infantry must have stood a better chance than one. Yet Helpmekaar was several hours' march away, and the garrison had to contend with their sick. There were two open, colonial transport-wagons at the post, and the patients could have been loaded into these and evacuated. But such wagons moved at only two miles per hour, and the Zulus would undoubtedly

Below: A civilian ox-wagon. Chelmsford relied heavily on these vehicles as transport for his Columns; there were two at Rorke's Drift (without the tents). (National Army Museum)

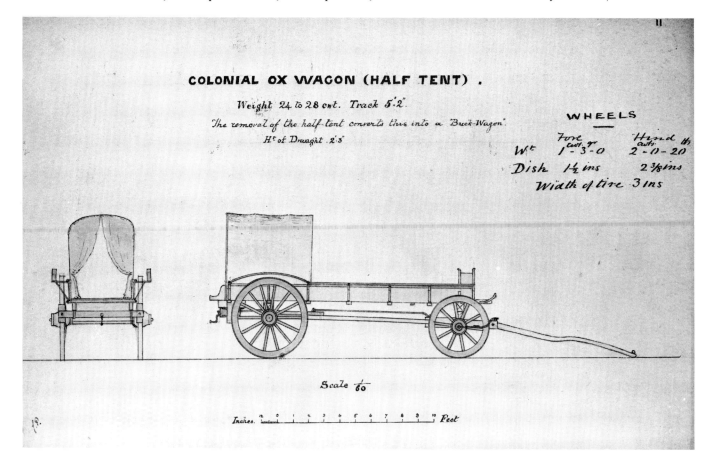

COLONIAL OX WAGON (HALF TENT).

Weight 24 to 28 cwt. Track 5'.2".

The removal of the half-tent converts this into a 'Buck-Wagon'.

Ht of Draught .2'.3"

WHEELS

	Fore cwt. qr.	Hind cwt. qr.
Wt	1 - 3 - 0	2 - 0 - 20
Dish	1½ ins	2⅜ ins
Width of tire	3 ins	

Scale 1/60

Inches. Feet

have overtaken them on the road and 'B' Company would have found itself fighting in the open and not on its own terms. Clearly the idea was discussed, because Chaplain Smith commented:

'A praiseworthy effort was made to remove the worst cases in the hospital to a place of safety. Two wagons were brought up after some delay, and the patients were being brought out when it was feared that the Zulus were so close upon us that any attempt to take them away would only result in their falling into enemy hands.'

As Surgeon Reynolds succinctly put it, '...in other words, removing the sick and wounded would have been embarrassing to our movement, and desertion of them was never contemplated.'

And open flight? Well, it must have crossed the minds of some men present; indeed, in the later stages of the Zulu War, panic among troops fresh out from England, especially when false alarms occurred at night, were not infrequent. There were, however, strong factors working against it. For one thing 'B' Company were not fresh troops; they had seen active service together on the Cape Frontier, and had gained some confidence in their ability to stand against African warriors. Nor should the ties of loyalty to friends and officers be underestimated. In any case, there is a natural tendency to draw together under such circumstances, and the prospect of 'every man for himself', fleeing alone in a hostile environment with fit and agile men in pursuit in large numbers, must have seemed decidedly unattractive. Under such circumstances, as Trooper Harry Lugg put it, '...nothing remains but to fight'. As Commissary Dunne commented, it was simply a choice of 'Do or Die!'

It may be that Bromhead had already mentally planned a line of defence, but Chard, Reynolds and Dunne were unanimous in the opinion that it was Acting Assistant Commissary James Dalton who first galvanized the garrison. According to Dunne:

'Dalton, as brave a soldier as ever lived, had joined us, and hearing the terrible news said "Now we must make a defence!" It was his suggestion which decided us to form a breastworks of bags of grain, boxes of biscuit, and everything that would help stop a bullet or keep out a man. An ox-waggon and even barrels of rum and lime juice were pressed into service.'

Chard agreed that Dalton's '...energy, intelligence, and gallantry were of the greatest service to us'. The barricades had, indeed, already been started by the time Chard rode up from the Drift, but he went round with Bromhead and Dalton, making suggestions for their improvements with the professional eye of the military engineer. Bromhead had already taken other precautions, according to Dunne:

'[he] at once ordered the men to fall in; outposts were thrown out, tents were struck, ammunition was served out, and the work of putting up the barricade was begun by all hands. Other preparations were also made: a water barrel was filled and brought inside, and several boxes of ammunition were opened and placed in convenient places. It was well for us that we had the help of 300 natives at this juncture, otherwise the work could not have been accomplished in time.'

The point about the outposts is interesting; Colour-Sergeant Frank Bourne is the only other man who mentions that they were sent out. He referred to them as 'skirmishers' – but they were more likely a picquet sent out to the slopes of Shiyane to give warning of the Zulu approach. Private Fred Hitch, a 22-year-old Londoner, who had been brewing tea for the company at a cook-house out the back when the news arrived, and who rushed in '...taking the tea and my rifle and ammunition and four kettles of tea', was sent up on to the roof of the store-house as a look-out. The water-barrel, incidentally, was actually a vehicle, a two-wheeled cart with a large barrel mounted on it.

How defensible was Rorke's Drift? Not very, according to the men of the garrison; Private Henry Hook thought that '...we were pinned like rats in a hole'. Yet in fact it was surprisingly secure, given the sort of attack it could expect. Rorke's two buildings backed on to and were overlooked by the Shiyane terrace some three or four hundred yards away. In front of the buildings the ground dropped away in another rocky step, three or four feet deep. In places, in front of the storehouse and between the buildings, this ledge consisted of exposed bedrock and collapsed boulders, as much as four feet high, but as it curled in front of the storehouse it gave way to a grassy slope which dropped away sharply in front of the verandah. A track branching off from the road from Helpmekaar to the Drift ran past the front of the building and off behind the shoulder of Shiyane; another leg ran up to the front of the storehouse. Immediately below the post was a jumble of bush and tall grass, which largely concealed an unfinished wall in front of the hospital. In places, this undergrowth extended to within five yards of the hospital verandah. A little beyond it, across the road, was a fine orchard which covered several acres and had been planted with '...standard grape vines, and many fine orange, apricot, apple, peach, quince, fig, pomegranate, and other fig trees'. Amidst the bush in front of the hospital was '...a grove of fine Cape poplars [and] some large gum trees'. There was no time to cut down any of this growth, and it would inevitably provide excellent cover for an attacking force. Nevertheless, the rocky ledge was quite advantageous; topped with a barricade three or four feet high, it presented an obstacle of more than head-height which a man on foot would have the greatest difficulty in surmounting.

A little in front of the corner angle of the storchousc was a neat, well-built stone cattle-kraal, or pen. This was about 4-feet high, and was divided by an interior partition. Below it, on the gently sloping ground in front of the ledge, was a larger, rectangular, roughly built cattle-kraal, the stones being piled up no more than two or three feet high. If the front of the post offered an interrupted field of fire, however, the back was wide open, apart from a brick cook-house and two ovens just to the right of the back of the storehouse, and a shallow drainage ditch. On the far end of the ledge, beyond the hospital, was a solitary privy — presumably of the locally traditional 'long drop' type, a hole in the ground with the seat mounted over it.

The buildings were about forty yards apart, both thatched, with a verandah at the front, but with comparatively secure back walls broken here and there by a door or window. The storehouse was set back slightly, so that its front edge was roughly level with the rear of the hospital. According to the Reverend Witt, the storehouse measured about 80 feet by 20 feet, the hospital slightly smaller at 60 feet by 18 feet. Apparently the storehouse was supported by several brick buttresses at the back, and had an attic reached by an outside staircase on the left. It was decided to leave the patients in the hospital, and Surgeon Reynolds, his hospital orderly and six men detailed by Lieutenant Bromhead — Privates Henry Hook, Robert Jones, William Jones, John Williams, Joseph Williams and Thomas Cole — barricaded the doors and windows and knocked loopholes through the walls. Most of the patients were well enough to bear arms, and Reynolds admitted that '...we did not consider either building would be taken unless with the fall of the whole place'.

The back of the post was sealed off by dragging the two wagons into the gap between the front left of the store and the right rear of the hospital. A line of biscuit boxes was drawn between them and under the wheels, and these were piled round with mealie-bags. The resulting barricade, nearly 4-feet high and very solid, stretched along the front of the post from the front left of the stone cattle-pen, across the front of the storehouse, along the line of the ledge, and finally across the front of the hospital verandah.

Having seen that the work was under way, Chard rode down to the Drift once more. He found that Mr Daniells, the civilian pontman, and Sergeant Millne of the Buffs, with Lance-Sergeant Williams of 'B' Company and his handful of men had already prepared the ponts for an attack by anchoring them mid-stream and sinking the cables. Mr Daniells was presumably a volunteer who had agreed to help with the running of the ponts, as there were several ferries of this type on the major rivers in Natal, but Sergeant Millne remains

something of a mystery. According to Chard, both he and Daniells had been part of the party originally working the ponts under Lieutenant MacDowell, RE, who had joined the Column at Isandlwana: this doesn't quite explain why Millne had been selected for the task. His regiment, the 3rd Foot, were part of the No. 1, Right Flank, Column, which was operating down at the Thukela mouth. It is tempting to think that he was a Mounted Infantryman, since the Buffs had supplied a large contingent to the squadron then operating with Chelmsford, but his name does not appear in any of the Mounted Infantry records. It may be that he had civilian experience of ferry work, or perhaps he was there purely fortuitously. In any event, Daniells and Millne offered to man the ponts and defend them mid-stream, and Sergeant Williams and his men were keen to join

Below: Sergeant F. Millne, the only man of the 3rd Regiment, the Buffs, present at the defence, photographed on his wedding day in the 1880s. (Family collection)

them, but Chard politely declined the offer. The party would have been completely exposed to Zulu rifle-fire, and the men could be better employed at the Mission. Chard ordered them to load the Engineers' wagon with the tents and equipment, and they returned to the post. The wagon was left by the rough stone kraal, and when the first shooting began Chard's wagon-driver freed the mules. In fact a number of animals was abandoned outside the post during the battle, Chard's and Dunne's horses among them, and probably the trek-oxen from the supply wagons. It was hardly practical to do otherwise, but most were subsequently killed, although the mules survived and were rounded up next morning.

According to Chard's reckoning, it was now about 3.30 p.m. The barricades were progressing well, although the front of the hospital was causing some problems. Not only was it the farthest point from the store to drag the mealie-bags — there must have been a natural tendency to dump them before they reached that far — but the slope made it difficult to form a stable barricade. In some of Chard's sketches he shows two lines of barricade in front of the hospital verandah: one almost at the foot of the slope and the other higher up. The lower one must have provided very inadequate protection, since the defenders would have had to stand on the rising ground behind it; in all probability, this line was abandoned early on, and another begun above it, but it was not completed. Dunne noted that '...this was the weakest point, for there was nothing but a plank to close the opening at one part'. Private Hitch also confirms that the front of the hospital was '...an open space which we had not time to complete'.

While the work was in progress a succession of fugitives had come past the post, most of them exhausted and utterly demoralized by their ordeal. According to Chard:

'...they tried to impress upon us the madness of an attempt to defend the place. Who they were I do not know, but it is scarcely necessary for me to say that there were no officers of H.M. Army among them. They stopped the work very much — it being impossible to prevent the men getting around them in little groups to hear their story. They proved the truth of their belief in what they said by leaving us to our fate, and in the state of mind they were in, I think our little garrison was well off without them. As far as I know, but one of the fugitives remained with us — Lt. Adendorff, whom I have before mentioned.'

Certainly the survivors had an unsettling effect on the garrison. One said to Surgeon Reynolds, '...no power on earth could stand against the enormous numbers of Zulus, and the only chance for us all was immediate flight'. Another whispered to Colour-Sergeant Bourne, 'Not a fighting chance for you, young feller.' The first man Lugg saw was a Trooper of the Natal Carbineers, who rode in without boots, tunic or weapons, and leading a spare horse. He muttered excitedly, 'Everyone killed in camp, and 4,000 [Zulus] on their way to take the mission station... You will all be murdered and cut to pieces.' Someone indignantly answered, 'We shall fight for it, and if we have to die we will die like Britishers.' Two of Lugg's fellow troopers in the Mounted Police, Doig and Shannon, came past, and Doig said, 'You will all be murdered.' This, thought Lugg, was 'consolatory'.

Shortly after his return to the Mission, a party of the Natal Native Horse rode up, and their officer reported to Chard. There were survivors from Durnford's Column which had included five troops of black horsemen, each of about fifty men. Three of these troops had been formed from the amaNgwane, a clan living in the Drakensberg foothills, who had a history of conflict with the Zulu Royal House. They were known to the British as Zikhali's Horse, after their chief, Zikhali kaMatiwane. One of the remaining troops was formed from the Natal BaSotho of Chief Hlubi, who had fought with Durnford at Bushman's Pass. The other was formed of Christian Africans from the Edendale Mission outside Pietermaritzburg. The men wore European clothes and were armed with Swinburne-Henry carbines. They had fought well at Isandlwana, but had lost heart in the final moments when the Zulus burst through into the camp, and made something of a fighting retreat on the trail towards Fugitives' Drift. It is not entirely clear as to which Troop these men belonged, and Chard doesn't mention their officer's name, but since the movements of most of their officers can be accounted for, the most likely candidate is Lieutenant Alfred Fairlie Henderson, who commanded the BaSotho troop. The men with him were probably predominantly Sotho, but no doubt some of the remainder of the NNH had rallied to them. With Henderson was a civilian meat contractor, a farmer named Bob Hall, who had been in the camp at Isandlwana. Chard was pleased to see them, and asked Henderson to extend his men in a screen beyond Shiyane, towards Fugitives' Drift, to try to delay the Zulu approach.

At about this time the Reverend Witt and Chaplain Smith came down from Shiyane. They had stayed up for quite some time, watching the movements of the Zulus between Isandlwana and the river, convinced that they were men of the NNC. Only when the Zulus had crossed into Natal and were close enough for Smith to see that they had no white officers with them, did the truth dawn. According to Lugg, Witt was very distressed; he was worried about his wife and daughters, and shocked by what the military had done to his house:

'...no one could help laughing at [his]

Left: *Alfred Fairlie Henderson who, as a lieutenant with the Natal Native Horse, is thought to have been the officer commanding the unit which arrived at Rorke's Drift before the Zulu attack. ('Henderson Heritage'/Natal Witness)*

Shortly after this, there was a smatter of shots from behind Shiyane, and Chard saw Henderson's men, 'about 100 in number', streaming off along the road to Helpmekaar. Henderson himself rode in and reported that his men would not obey him. Harry Lugg remembered that as Bob Hall galloped in he shouted that the Zulus were coming, '...as black as hell and as thick as grass'. According to Hall's own account, he and Henderson lingered near the orchard to watch the Zulu approach. They fired a few shots but, according to Hall, 'Mr Henderson and I had exhausted all our ammunition', so they, too, rode off to Helpmekaar. It is difficult to blame them; both officers and men had fought well at Isandlwana, but they must have been physically exhausted and in a state of shock. Having seen a much larger force cut up at Isandlwana, Chard's stand must have seemed to them hopeless. 'I have seen these same men behave so well since that I have spoken with several of their conduct — and they all said, as their excuse, that Durnford was killed, and that it was no use.'

More serious, however, was the defection that now occurred. The sight of the retreating horsemen proved too much for Stevenson's Company who suddenly leapt over the barricades and fled. 'I am sorry to say', said Chard, 'that their officer, who had been doing good service in getting his men to work, also deserted us. We seemed very few, now all these people had gone...' According to Private Hook, '...to see them deserting like that was too much for some of us, and we fired after them. The Sergeant was struck and killed.' The 'sergeant' appears, in fact, to have been a Corporal W. Anderson who fell among the trees in the orchard at the front of the post. Chaplain Smith thought that he was killed by the first shots fired by the Zulus; but perhaps he was just being charitable.

With the NNC gone Chard was left with fewer than 140 men to defend his perimeter. Clearly they were not enough, and he ordered them to make a new barricade of biscuit boxes, bisecting the yard from the left front corner of the store to the front barricade. Gaps were left for men to pass through, but this would serve as a reserve line of defence if necessary.

Up on the storehouse roof, Private Hitch could see the Zulus approaching just beyond the crest of the shoulder of Shiyane:

'I told Mr Bromhead that they were on the other side of the rise and was extending for attack. Mr Bromhead asked me how many there were? I told him that I thought [they] numbered up to four to six thousand. A voice from below — "Is that all?; we can manage that lot very well for a few seconds." There were different opinions.'

The infantry picquets now fell back towards the post, and the Zulus came into sight. The Battle of Rorke's Drift had begun.

gesticulations when [he] came back on seeing the best parlour paper being pulled down and loopholes being knocked out, while splendid furniture was scattered about the rooms. His first question was, in broken English, "Vot is dish?" Someone replied that the Zulus were almost on us, upon which he bolted, saying "Mein Gott, mein wife and mein children at Umsinga! Oh, mein Gott!" '

Witt remembered the conversation somewhat differently:

'Arrived at the house, we saw at once a new proof of the sad truth to which our eyes had just been opened. The tents which surrounded the house, and were used by a company left there under Major Spalding for the protection of the hospital and commissariat stores, had been pulled down, and a temporary barricade of meal-sacks was made between the house, which were a distance of twenty yards from one another. Here we were met by anxious questions from many lips, "Do the Zulus come here?" — and compelled to answer "In five minutes they will be here." '

Witt did not wait; he rode off towards Helpmekaar to find his family. He took with him Lieutenant Purvis of the NNC who, according to Chard, was '...very sick in hospital and only just able to ride'. Chaplain Smith looked about for his horse, but finding that his groom had fled decided to throw in his lot with the defenders.

3. ENTER THE ZULUS

When the troop of Durnford's Zikhali Horse, led by Lieutenant Charles Raw, discovered the Zulu army hidden in the Ngwebeni valley, some five miles to the north-east of Isandlwana, it precipitated a battle which the Zulus had planned for the following day. Traditional Zulu beliefs place great emphasis on the interaction between the every-day world and the spirit world, and the night of 22/23 January was the night of the new moon, an inauspicious time for launching battle — a time when the malicious and all-pervading evil influence, called *umnyama* ('blackness'), was unleashed, which could pollute not only individual warriors, but bring misfortune on an entire enterprise. Nevertheless, once the British had discovered the *impi*, any hopes of waiting until the following day were dashed, and the regiments streamed out of the valley in some confusion to attack the camp. The senior commanders lost all control of the battle within those first few minutes, and the regiments instinctively took up their traditional 'beasts' horns' attack formation without waiting for direction or instruction. The best the Zulu generals, Ntshingwayo kaMahole Khoza and Mavumengwana kaNdlela Ntuli, could do was to restrain those regiments that were on the far left of the Zulu camp, farthest from the British, and form them into a reserve.

Right: A prototype for the uThulwana. Most of the Zulus who attacked Rorke's Drift were, like this man, married men in their forties. He is wearing a typical charm necklace; for many, battle regalia consisted of nothing more than this and a loin covering. (Killie Campbell Africana Library)

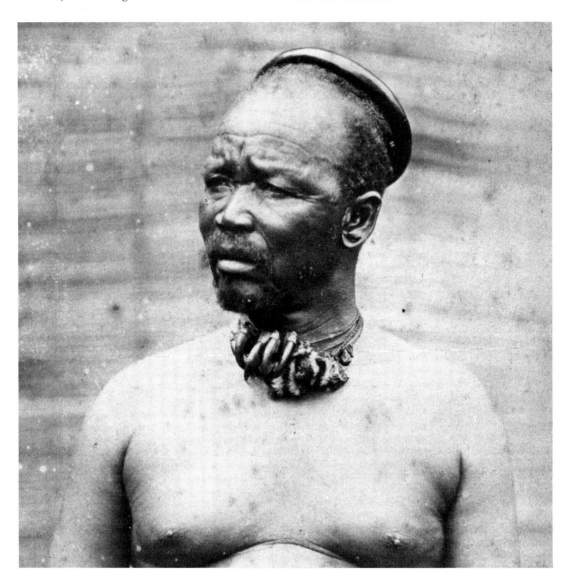

These regiments were known as the uNdi *amabutho*, as they were associated with King Cetshwayo's principal homestead, Ulundi, or Ondine — from the common root uNdi, meaning 'the heights'. Unlike the majority of the *impi* who were young, unmarried men, these were mostly senior married men, many of them middle-aged, and they comprised the uThulwana *ibutho*, and three regiments closely associated with it, the iNdlondlo, iNdluyengwe and uDloko regiments. Traditionally, at the start of a battle, the warriors were formed into a circle known as *mkhumbi*. This was to enable the commanders to address them and issue orders, and to allow any last pre-battle rituals to be observed. Even as the rest of the *impi* streamed across the heights towards Isandlwana, Ntshingwayo and Mavumengwana formed the

uNdi regiments into their circle. Speaking in the richly allegorical language characteristic of of the nineteenth-century Zulu, Ntshingwayo addressed them, recalling the glories of King Shaka's days, reminding them of their warrior tradition, using the shield as a potent image of glory, and telling them that there was no going back: 'Ntshingwayo kaMahole at [Isandlwana] declaimed the praises of Senzangakhona and Shaka, and holding up his shield said, "This is the love charm of our people." As he said this he shook his shield and said, "You are always asking why this person is loved so much. It is caused by the love-charm of our people. There is no going back home." '

The uNdi were then sent out on to the far right of the Zulu attack. They swung round behind the right horn, which was moving to confront the left

Left: *Prince Dabulamanzi kaMpande, the Zulu commander at Rorke's Drift, photographed in the early 1880s. (Natal Archives)*

Above: Prince Dabulamanzi, photographed at King Cetshwayo's 'coronation' in 1874. This picture suggests something of the Prince's confident personality; he and his retainers are carrying good-quality hunting rifles. (Killie Campbell Africana Library)

flank of the British line, and moved down into the valley behind Isandlwana. It is not entirely clear what their object was, but they effectively cut off the British force from its line of retreat, placing a large force between the camp and Rorke's Drift. As their younger colleagues surrounded the camp and closed in for the kill, however, the uNdi were deprived of a chance to join in the fighting. They moved south in the general direction of the Mzinyathi, keeping to the rising ground to the left of the Manzimyama stream. It was in this stream that much of the severest fighting took place, as the Zulus pushed the defenders through the camp, over the shoulder of Isandlwana, and brought them to bay in the valley beyond. The handful of British survivors scattered across country, slipping through the Zulu horns before they closed, and rode off towards the Mzinyathi. Yet the uNdi took no part in this, until it became clear that the fugitives might escape, at which point the iNdluyengwe were sent to head them off. They struck out straight for the river and, catching the survivors on a bluff above Fugitives' Drift, drove them down into the surging waters. The remaining regiments, the uThulwana, iNdlondlo and uDloko, moved at a more leisurely pace upstream, sweeping through the country towards the Batshe valley, and reaching the river a few miles above Fugitives' Drift. It was these movements that Witt, Reynolds and Smith, from the summit of Shiyane, had seen and mistaken for

the approach of the NNC.

The banks of the Mzinyathi gave the Zulus pause for thought. King Cetshwayo had given strict instructions that his army should not cross into Natal. The nation considered itself the victim of unprovoked British aggression, and the king was keen to play the role of the injured party. By limiting any military activity to his own soil, he hoped to win political advantage in any future negotiations. Indeed, with the odds in the war stacked so heavily against him, his one real hope of success was that he could swing the balance of British opinion against the war, by making the war itself too costly and the prospect of peace more attractive. He was only too aware that any attack on civilian targets in Natal — whatever the short-term advantages — would provoke a greater backlash in the end. So, when those elements of the *impi* in pursuit of the survivors reached the river they were presented with something of a dilemma; it was galling to watch the fugitives streaming away unchecked towards Helpmekaar, with the whole of the upper Natal border wide open. Yet the king's orders were not to be lightly ignored, and in any case many of the Zulus who had fought at Isandlwana were now exhausted.

The reactions of the various Zulu commanders in this sector reflect the mixed feelings within the *impi*. Prince Ndabuko kaMpande, one of the king's younger brothers, was keen to pursue the fight, and

he called out to members of his regiment, the uMbonambi, to follow him. They were not interested in doing so, however, pointing out that they had left too many wounded on the battlefield at Isandlwana who needed attention. They returned to take part in the looting of the camp, singing a great victory song which dated from the time of King Dingane. Some of the younger iNgobamakhosi *ibutho* were trying to find a way to get across the river but Vumandaba kaNtati, a senior commander and one of the king's most trusted councillors, called them back. Chief Zibhebhu kaMapitha, who commanded the uDloko, one of the uNdi regiments, apparently pleaded the excuse of a wounded hand to call off the chase at the river. Despite his youth, Zibhebhu was an extremely important man within the kingdom; his family line was descended from Shaka's grandfather, and was considered a section of the Royal House; he had also grown rich trading on his own account with whites, and he ruled his followers with an unusual degree of autonomy. He had commanded the Zulu scouts in the Isandlwana campaign, and was regarded as a daring and

resourceful leader. The fact that he urged restraint must have weighed considerably with his colleagues.

But the reserve regiments of the uNdi, the uDloko among them, were keen to carry on fighting. Why? Professional jealousy had a lot to do with it; the senior men were disappointed that the glory of the victory had gone to the younger men. Although their own role had been important tactically, they had not been among those engaged hand-to-hand, which was where the Zulus traditionally distributed their laurels. It was considered a great honour to be recognized as the first to 'stab' the enemy, the first to engage him hand-to-hand, and after each campaign the regiments argued hotly as to whom the honour belonged. Rivalry between the *amabutho* was, in any case, strong and the king traditionally exploited it to enhance his men's fighting spirit. When the *impi* was mustered on the eve of the war, the king called out regiments in pairs, and the warriors challenged one another to excel in the coming fight, laying wagers and boasting of their own martial prowess. Whoever had been the first to

Right: *Through a glass darkly. Sadly, this fascinating image is badly faded, but it suggests none the less something of the splendour of the full ceremonial costume worn by the amabutho. The men appear to be carrying a mix of the full-sized* isihlangu *and smaller* umbhumbhulozu *war-shields. (Natal Archives)*

'stab' that day, it had not been a senior man of the uThulwana.

Such challenges were traditionally reserved for the younger regiments who had yet to prove themselves, and were rather beyond the dignity of the uNdi. Nevertheless, at the end of the day, when the young men settled their bets and remembered who had lived up to his boasts and who had not, the uThulwana would have no tales of glory to tell, and no exotic loot to show off. This must have been quite a blow to their sense of honour. Certainly, their commander, Prince Dabulamanzi kaMpande thought so. Dabulamanzi was one of the king's younger brothers, and was about forty years old. He was an intelligent, aggressive man, whose photographs show him to have been good-looking, with a neatly trimmed, pointed beard, and a pleasant, open face which none the less has a suggestion of the mercurial about it. His principal homestead was at eZulwini ('the heavens), in the hot coastal country outside Eshowe, not far from the domain of the famous 'White Chief of the Zulus', the trader and hunter, John Dunn. Dabulamanzi's name meant 'part the

waters', an allusion to the time when King Mpande succeeded to the throne by the ploy of crossing into Natal and enlisting the help of the Boer Voortrekkers during his struggle with Dingane. In many ways it was an appropriate name, since Dabulamanzi also had a metaphorical foot in the white man's world across the river. Through his friendship with John Dunn, he had, unlike most Zulus, become both an excellent rider and a good shot. He liked to wear European clothes, and had a fondness for gin. He was not a man to be bamboozled by passing traders, and this gave him something of a bad reputation among the whites who felt that he drove too hard a bargain. The traveller Bertram Mitford gave one of his usual lively portraits of Dabulamanzi after the Anglo-Zulu War, which says as much about European attitudes towards him as it does about the Prince himself:

'Dabulamanzi is a fine-looking man of about thirty-five [sic], stoutly built and large-limbed like most of his royal brethren. He is light in colour even for a Zulu, and has a high, intellectual forehead, clear eyes, and handsome, regular features, with jet-black beard and moustache. But although a handsome face, it is not altogether a prepossessing one, for it wears a settled expression of insincerity and cunning which would cause you to have little doubt as to the deservedness of the public opinion about him if you had heard it, and if you had not, readiness of belief if you should come to do so. That opinion I have heard expressed by those who knew the man, in two wars, "a blackguard". With missionary and trader alike he is in dispute... '

In this case, 'cunning' might fairly be defined as a reluctance on the Prince's part to be taken in by white men, yet it does seem that Dabulamanzi had something of an impulsive and overbearing personality. He held no official command within the Zulu army in January 1879, but his status as a royal Prince and his haughty manner had given him a natural authority. After Zibhebhu retired from the field wounded, Dabulamanzi was the most senior man present with the uNdi, and he was all for crossing into Natal. Years later he told an interviewer that he had wanted to 'wash the spears of my boys' by allowing them a little mayhem along the border. Stafford, the NNC officer who had survived Isandlwana, visiting him after the war to talk over shared experiences asked him whether:

'...it had been your intention to invade Natal. He said "no", that [Cetshwayo] had told him that the flooded rivers were a bigger king than he was. I then said, "Then why did your men shout out, both at Isandlwana and at Rorke's Drift, *Nina manga* ... which means 'you are kidding yourselves, tomorrow night we will sleep with your wives and sisters in [Pietermaritzburg]'? He said that was only bravado – "But had Rorke's Drift fallen I should certainly have taken my army into Natal." '

That last statement is, to say the least, rather suspect. The Natal Colonists had a deep-seated fear of a Zulu invasion, and Isandlwana had come very close to realizing their worse nightmares. As Stafford explained, no doubt with a shudder, '...if that had happened all the Natal natives and Cape natives would have joined him as a matter of policy to save their own skins. It is too awful to contemplate what the result would have been (Hell on Earth).' In fact, many of the black groups in Natal had a history of hostility towards the Zulu kingdom, and might equally have turned out to defend their own territory, so Stafford's comments are more suggestive of the latent settler fear of the 'black menace' than of the balance of probability. The settlers lived isolated lives many miles from the nearest garrison, surrounded by and greatly outnumbered by a potentially hostile black population. They remembered the massacres inflicted on the Boers in Natal by King Dingane, and their insecurity, quite understandably, manifested itself in a fear of the Zulu king and his army. Such an attitude does not suggest, however, that the Zulus had any definite intention to undertake a military expedition in Natal in 1879.

Below: *Zulu headmen photographed in ceremonial regalia at the turn of the century. The basic elements of* amabutho *regalia are quite clear here: the cow-tail necklaces and arm and leg ornaments, and head-dresses with stuffed headbands and ear-flaps. The man in the centre has a bunch of* sakabuli *feathers at the front of his head-dress, with lourie feathers behind; the man on the right has a large bunch of lourie feathers. Most of this costume was impractical for wear on active service, however. (Natal Archives)*

Later, the British Army too, came to see the advantages of interpreting Rorke's Drift in terms of a determined and heroic stand against a black tide of savagery. In fact, the likelihood of such a raid was very limited, especially in the aftermath of Isandlwana, and not merely because the king's views were not to be lightly ignored.

Had Dabulamanzi tried to invade Natal, he would have had to do so with just twenty per cent of the forces engaged at Isandlwana. His men must have been tired before they reached the river, and they could not have hoped to overcome any major concentrations of British troops they met along the way. Exhausted, they would have been very vulnerable to a British counter-attack, and there would have been no warriors to support them or cover their retreat. If Dabulamanzi did make that boast to Stafford, it may have been out of bravado, but certainly if he intended to spread terror and panic over a limited area and at the same time pick up some easy plunder, KwaJim's trading post store would have been an obvious target.

Pride was undoubtedly an element in their decision. The uThulwana, the most senior of the uNdi *amabutho*, had a history of which they were extremely jealous. Formed by King Mpande, they had been something of a favourite of his; he had enrolled both his sons, the Princes Cetshwayo and Mbuyazi, in their ranks. Indeed, there were so many men of rank among them that they were also known as the iNhlabamasoka, 'the select ones'. Their arrogance was such that it was said that even the king stood in awe of the uThulwana, and only his most senior councillor, the nation's Prime Minister, Chief Mnyamana Buthelezi, could control them. In the 1850s, when the king's sons were coming of age and he refused to nominate an heir, a bloody civil war broke out between Cetshwayo and Mbuyazi. Prince Mbuyazi gathered his faction, the isiQoza, and tried to flee to Natal, to secure the support of the colonial authorities, but he was delayed by the flooded Thukela, and Cetshwayo's followers, the uSuthu, caught him on the banks of the river at 'Ndondakusuka. The resultant battle was one of the bloodiest in Zulu history, and ended with the virtual extermination of Mbuyazi and his followers. Most of the uThulwana had supported Cetshwayo, and the victory did little to diminish their sense of their own importance.

As the uThulwana approached middle age, they continued to reflect the divisions that characterized the Zulu kingdom in the 1860s and 1870s. The defeat of Mbuyazi meant that Prince Cetshwayo had effectively established himself as heir apparent, but King Mpande was determined not to acknowledge him officially until absolutely necessary; to do so would have severely weakened his own hold on the throne. So he withheld permission for the uThulwana to marry for as long as he could. The significance of marriage within the *amabutho* system was that it marked the point at which the men were officially recognized as adults. As such, their first allegiance reverted to their families and their clan chiefs, and the king could no longer count on their service. They dispersed to establish personal homesteads, and only reported to the *amakhanda* when specifically summoned. This change in status was signified by the *isicoco*, a ring of fibre woven into the hair, plastered with black gum and polished with beeswax to a glossy shine. Married men often shaved the head around the ring to make their status the more apparent. When in 1867 Mpande finally gave the uThulwana permission to marry he was in effect acknowledging his son's right to succeed him. From that moment his own power and authority began to slip into the hands of Cetshwayo.

In fact, the uThulwana seem to have been unusual in that they spent more time serving the king after marriage than was customary. In the 1840s and 1850s Zululand was afflicted by a man-power crisis. The civil war between Dingane and Mpande had weakened the bonds that held the nation together and many important men and their followers defected to Natal. Here they could look forward to a degree of autonomy not found under the Zulu system, and to means of accumulating cattle for *ilobolo* which were less demanding than military service. The *amabutho* system had worked very well in the political vacuum of Shaka's day, but the presence of a rival political system gave young Zulu men an alternative to serving the king. If, however, there were viable alternative systems nearby, the king's subjects could afford to look elsewhere. To counter this, Mpande followed a long and careful policy of reconstituting royal authority which gradually pulled the nation back from the brink of collapse. One means of achieving this was the creation of *amabandla amhlope* ('white assemblies'). These consisted of *amabutho* who were married, but who spent long periods living in the *amakhanda*, taking their wives and families with them. Under such circumstances service conditions were fairly relaxed, and the men could come and go pretty much at will. Following King Cetshwayo's coronation in 1874, the uThulwana themselves filled this role. They were quartered at the king's homestead of Ulundi, on the Mahlabatini plain.

A certain tension between the generations was inherent in the *amabutho* system, as senior regiments married and new regiments, eager for glory, were formed. In due course Cetshwayo began to raise his own regiments and, in the same way that King Mpande had favoured the uThulwana, so he favoured the iNgobamakhosi, the 'benders of kings'. The iNgobamakhosi were one of the largest of the *amabutho* on the eve of the 1879 War, and the king regarded them as the

bravest and the best. Initially, the iNgobamakhosi were also quartered at Ulundi, and were considered part of the uNdi grouping. However, such was the tension between themselves and the men of the uThulwana that they later had to be given their own *ikhanda* as a barracks. Even so, in 1878 a clash between them developed into open violence.

This outbreak was a consequence of both the king's policy of revitalizing royal authority, and the wider tensions within the kingdom. In the old Zulu kingdom, women were also organized into age-based guilds, although their functions were social rather than military. When the king allowed an *ibutho* to marry, he directed them to seek their brides from a specific female guild. In 1877 he allowed some members of the iNdlondlo and iNdluyengwe *amabutho* to marry. Both of these regiments were younger than the uThulwana, but had been incorporated with it to make up its strength. These men were directed to seek their wives from a guild known as the *iNgcugce*. The *iNgcugce* girls were much younger than their prospective husbands, however, and many had already chosen partners from among the iNgobamakhosi. They refused to obey the king's order, and the issue became a challenge to the

king's authority. When the girls continued to flout the law, several were killed and the remainder promptly found it expedient to transfer their affections.

When the next First Fruits ceremony took place, however, the lingering resentment between the uThulwana and iNgobamakhosi exploded. This ceremony, held in December or January each year, was a gathering of the nation to usher in the new harvest, and was one of the few occasions when the Zulu *impi* was mustered in its entirety. In 1878 the newly married men could not resist taunting the iNgobamakhosi about their lost lovers, and the iNgobamakhosi responded by grabbing their fighting sticks and setting about them. When word of this reached Prince Hamu kaMpande, the uThulwana's commander, he was so angry that he told his men to take up their spears. Hamu's reaction was no doubt influenced by the fact that he was a powerful figure in his own right, who was not entirely reconciled to Cetshwayo's rule; he regarded the arrogance of his brother's boys as a personal slight. Anyway, the uThulwana laid into the iNgobamakhosi, and as many as sixty men were killed before the king's messengers could separate the antagonists. This incident had happened just a year before the outbreak of the Zulu War, and

Above: *Chief Ngoza kaLudaba, the head of a breakaway section of the Zulu kingdom, photographed in Natal c.1868. This picture gives a good impression of the sort of regalia worn by senior men: headrings, otter-skin headbands and single crane feathers. Note, too, the two types of war-shield. The uThulwana would have been of roughly this age-group. (Author's collection)*

Above: *Where the iNdluyengwe crossed? The rock fissure in the bed of the Mzinyathi upstream from Fugitives' Drift. (Author's photograph)*

must have been fresh in the minds of the participants. The fact that the iNgobamakhosi had played such a prominent role at Isandlwana can have only spurred the uThulwana on.

The Zulu reserve crossed the Mzinyathi in two groups. The iNdluyengwe, who had been pursuing the fugitives, crossed a mile or two upstream of Fugitives' Drift. Chaplain Smith could see them emerge from the steep valley on the Natal bank, just below a bend in the river. Interestingly enough, a tradition has lingered locally that they crossed at a particular point where the river flows through a deep fissure in the rock. This fissure is eight or ten feet wide, and when the water is low the surface is about ten feet below the top of the fissure. When it is high, however, the narrow cleft fills to the brim with a surging torrent. It would take a brave man to attempt to cross it on his own, but a large group of men could help one another over without much difficulty. Certainly, the river was in flood, and was impassable along most of the stretch around Fugitives' Drift, as the fugitives themselves had found to their cost. The hills closing in on each side forces the Mzinyathi through a narrow gorge at a terrific pace, and it is difficult to see where else they might have crossed. Having got across the river, the iNdluyengwe thoroughly searched the

valley for any sign of British survivors, beating through the bush, and firing into caves on the rocky slopes. 'Being satisfied with the result, so far', they climbed the hills on the Natal side, and sat down to rest and take snuff. The Zulus placed a great importance on the taking of snuff, which they carried in gourds, horns, or carved bone containers around their necks or in their pierced ear-lobes. Beautifully carved wooden or bone containers were used to convey it to the nostril. The snuff was often mixed with crushed aloes, which gave it a bitter tang; it may well have also been mixed with narcotics, such as cannabis sativa, in which case its application on the eve of battle takes on a particular significance.

The uThulwana, iNdlondlo and uDloko approached the river farther upstream, above the hills, near its junction with the Batshe. Smith, Witt, and Reynolds, if he were still there, could see them, 'going through various exercises, dividing off (apparently) into hundreds, then into tens, wheeling and quickly reforming'. The Mzinyathi was wider and shallower here, and the current less strong. They formed a long line across the river in the traditional Zulu manner, making a chain and helping one another across. They did this at a leisurely pace, apparently spending time washing themselves and cooling off. When they reached the Natal bank, they too sat down to take snuff.

Unfortunately, we cannot say as much about the individual Zulus in the ranks as we can about their British counterparts at Rorke's Drift. Few accounts by participants in the battle have survived, nor do we know more than a handful of their names. The Battle of Isandlwana made far more impact on the Zulu nation than the fight at Rorke's Drift, and participation at the latter was to bring no great glory. Also, the men who fought at Isandlwana were younger and there were more of them; there were still plenty alive to tell their story fifty years later, when the last of the uThulwana must have been long gone. As a result, there are virtually no detailed Zulu accounts of Rorke's Drift, and we know little about the men who were facing Assistant Commissary Dunne, Sergeant Millne of the Buffs, and Privates Fred Hitch and Henry Hook. We have a rough idea of their ages: the uThulwana were in their mid-forties, the iNdlondlo a couple of years younger, and the uDloko two years younger than that. All these men were married, and at a time of life when active campaigning must no longer have offered the thrill that once it had. They had already spent a week living out on campaign, surviving on spartan rations of meat from slaughtered cattle and handfuls of roasted mealies. The iNdluyengwe, who were brigaded with the uThulwana to revitalize it, were younger, not quite thirty, and unmarried. It is even difficult to compute the total strength of these regiments. According to a list compiled at Chelmsford's request before the war began, the uThulwana were about 1,500 strong, the iNdlondlo 900, the uDloko 4,000, and the iNdluyengwe about 1,000. These figures are imprecise, for a number of reasons. The Zulus did not generally reckon a regiment's strength according to its total number of warriors, but rather according to the number of companies it contained. Each regiment was organized internally into two wings, made up of a number of companies called *amaviyo*. These often consisted of men who had first reported for service together in a particular locality, and their size varied accordingly. In favoured regiments, they might have been 200 strong; for the remainder they averaged fifty men apiece. The figure for the uDloko seems particularly large, and probably includes the amaKwenkwe, an *ibutho* incorporated into it; it is impossible to say whether all of these men were present on the day. The king's strategy had been to direct men living in parts of the country threatened by other British columns to stay and defend their homes, and as a result many of the *amabutho* who mustered at Ulundi were under strength. In any case, some warriors had slipped away from the reserve early in the fight at Isandlwana to join in the attack on the camp. Thus, although according

to imperfect British sources the regiments that crossed into Natal had a total and theoretical strength of 7,400 men, the actual numbers were probably between five and six thousand.

On ceremonial occasions, such as the First Fruits ceremony, the *amabutho* wore the most lavish costumes. It is not always easy to be precise about the composition of these costumes, because the surviving evidence is incomplete and contradictory, but curiously enough there are several descriptions of the uThulwana's regalia. All the regiments wore dense bunches of the fluffy part of cows' tails attached to thongs around the knees and elbows, and worked into a necklace so as to

Above: A warrior in the full ceremonial costume of the younger regiments: his head-dress consists of sakabuli feathers and a white cow-hide crest called amaphovela. *The tall plume is a bunch of sakabuli feathers. The ceremonial dress of the iNgobamakhosi ibutho was similar to this. (Royal Archives, Windsor)*

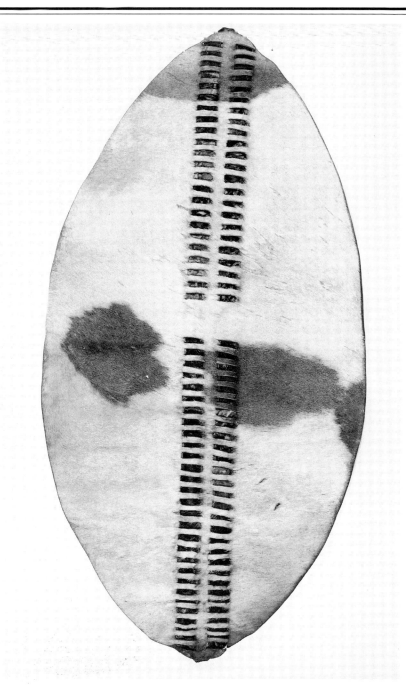

Above: A full-sized war-shield of the uThulwana ibutho, taken at Ulundi. The uThulwana shields were white with red patches. (Africana Museum, Johannesburg)

seen in the head dress. Around the forehead the uThulwana wore a headband of otter-skin, stuffed with a dried bull-rush or cow-dung and sewn into a roll that was tied at the back of the head. Flaps of samango monkey-skin hung down over the side of the face, and a single long blue-grey crane feather was worn at the front. White ostrich feathers were worn at the sides of the head, pointing to the rear, but the great men wore bunches of split and twisted scarlet and green lourie feathers — worn only by chiefs —instead. They may also have worn bunches of glossy black sakabuli feathers on either side of the head. The iNdlondlo's ceremonial costume was similar, but seems to have substituted a bunch of sakabuli feathers for the crane feather. There are varied, but not necessarily conflicting, descriptions of the uDloko's head-dress; according to one account, they wore long white ostrich feathers attached to a skull-cap of straw hidden by their otter-skin headbands, interspersed with black ostrich feathers, and with a crane feather at the front. Another account makes no mention of the ostrich feathers but confirms the crane feather. In each case, however, these head-dresses feature the typical ingredients of the senior warrior: otter-skin, crane feathers, white ostrich feathers. The younger iNdluyengwe's costume was indicative of their more junior status; it consisted of a leopard-skin headband, and bunches of sakabuli feathers arranged over the ears. At the front was a bunch of black ostrich feathers surmounted by one or two longer white ostrich feathers.

Very little of this finery was worn into action in January 1879. Much of it was both fragile and expensive, and not at all suited to the rigours of life in the field, and the king had specifically ordered his army to muster ready for combat, without its ceremonial uniforms. Instead, the men had turned up in war-dress, which was a much abbreviated form of the uniform. It is impossible to say exactly what this consisted of, as each warrior apparently retained whatever items he thought appropriate, and left the rest at home. On the whole, the regional armies harassing the British flanking columns — who were, by definition, operating closer to home — retained more costume than the main *impi* assembled for each campaign at Ulundi. Similarly, the more senior, conservative *amabutho* tended to retain more than the younger warriors, who often fought with no regalia at all. Nevertheless, even the uThulwana probably went into action wearing nothing more than a headband, with perhaps a crane feather here and there. A few might have worn the heavy cow-tail necklaces, and the leg and arm ornaments of the same material may well have been retained, but the valuable kilts and lavish displays of ostrich feathers were clearly quite impracticable. Indeed, most of the men who crossed the Mzinyathi into Natal on the afternoon of 22 January 1879 probably wore nothing more

hang to the waist at the front and the knees at the back. The every-day loin-covering was the *umutsha*, a thin strip of hide tied around the waist, with strips of fur, sometimes twisted together to resemble tails, dangling at the front, and a square of hide known as *ibeshu* covering the buttocks. Over this, the senior regiments, including the uThulwana and iNdlondlo, wore a lavish kilt. This was made by twisting together the pelts of civet cats and samango monkeys to form 'tails' which were tied in bunches so as to encircle the waist. Such pelts were extremely expensive, and reflected the status of many of the men in the ranks. The main regimental distinctions, however, were to be

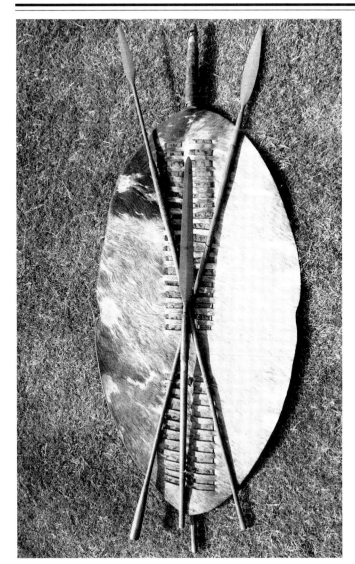

Above left and above: A trophy of Zulu arms picked up at Rorke's Drift on the morning after the battle by Major Dunbar, 2/24th. The shield is a very typical example of the umbhumbhulozu type, and is the colour of the uThulwana ibutho. Note the stabbing spear at the front of the display. (Xhawulisa collection)

than the ordinary *umutsha* loin covering.

It had been traditional since the days of King Shaka for the *amabutho* to carry war-shields of a distinctive uniform colour. When the regiments were serving the king they were supposed to be maintained at his expense, and he would grant them a herd of cattle from the national pool. These cattle were carefully matched according to the colour of their hides, and when the cattle were slaughtered for any purpose, the hides were used to make war-shields. These shields were not the property of the individual warrior, but of the state, and were kept in special stores in the *amakhanda*, raised off the ground on stilts to protect them from damp and rats. In Shaka's time the full-sized war-shield, the *isihlangu*, was nearly five feet long and almost three feet wide; each warrior would select a shield from the store which suited his own build. In the 1850s, however, Cetshwayo introduced a smaller war-shield, the *umbhumbhulozu*, for his followers. This was about three feet long by two feet wide and was lighter and easier to wield than the full-sized version. Both types were apparently in use in the 1879 War, although the *umbhumbhulozu* was the most popular, particularly among the younger regiments. Many of the shields that have survived are uThulwana shields taken by the British from Ulundi after the last battle of the war; most of them are of the full-sized *isihlangu* type. This no doubt reflects the preference of the looters rather than the prevalence of that type of shield; it may even be that such shields had been left at Ulundi precisely because the smaller type was taken into battle. But shields of both types were picked up at Rorke's Drift after the battle.

In Shaka's time, the uniformity of *amabutho* war-shields was very carefully maintained. Each regiment had its own colour, and there were often quite precise and subtle differences between them. On the whole, senior regiments carried shields that were predominantly white; junior regiments carried black shields. As a regiment progressed in age and experience, so it would be granted a new shield-colour with more white on it, reflecting its increased seniority. Grey, speckled, dun-coloured and red shields were also carried. By the 1870s, however, this practice was beginning to die out. Many of the younger regiments in particular seem to have carried shields of no particular colour, although they remained predominantly black. One can only speculate as to the reasons for this. King Cetshwayo's attempts to revitalize the military system may have outstripped the nation's cattle resources, which had suffered severely following an epidemic of lung-sickness which swept the country from 1874. It may simply have been impossible to amass sufficient matched cattle to provide shields for a thousand men at a time, and it is possible that some companies or sections of an *ibutho* had different shield colours, creating a mixed effect overall; the evidence is inconclusive either way. Most sources agree, however, that the uThulwana carried white shields with small brown or black patches, and surviving examples tend to confirm

this. The iNdlondlo apparently carried the same shields as the uThulwana, while the uDloko carried either white shields or red shields with white spots. The iNdluyengwe, as a younger, unmarried regiment, carried black shields with white patches on the bottom half.

Another significant difference in the warriors' armoury since Shaka's day was a high proportion of firearms. There is a suggestion that the first white hunters and traders who visited Shaka supplied him with a handful of old Brown Bess muskets, and during the reign of his successor, King Dingane, this was established as a regular feature of trade between the fledgling settlements in Natal and the Zulu kingdom. When, during Mpande's time, white traders and hunters operated in Zululand, which they did frequently, the king demanded that they pay a facility fee in firearms. In the aftermath of the civil war in the 1850s, Prince Cetshwayo relied heavily on his friend John Dunn to obtain guns for him to bolster his position within the kingdom. By the 1860s and 1870s large numbers of guns were flowing into the country, both clandestinely across the border from Natal — the trade was prohibited by the Natal authorities — and openly through Portuguese Mozambique in the north. As many as 20,000 guns a year may have entered Zululand through this source in the three or four years preceding the Anglo-Zulu War. Most of these guns were obsolete patterns of poor quality, since it was a common practice for the European powers to dump condemned firearms on the unsophisticated world market when new models became generally available at home. The majority of those in Zululand were probably Brown Bess flintlocks bearing Tower marks from the 1840s and 1850s. There were, however, quite a few European models from France, Germany and Austria in the country, together with a number of American makes. Even the British Enfield, the standard British military percussion firearm of the 1850s and 1860s, had found its way on to the market in large numbers. For the most part, however, these weapons were in a poor state of repair, and the traders seldom supplied the training and spare parts to keep them operable. Most Zulus failed to understand the true significance of sights, and aimed high, believing that the higher a gun was aimed, the further it would shoot. As the crisis with Britain loomed, King Cetshwayo stockpiled a store of nearly a thousand pounds of powder near one of his *amakhanda*, and hired the services of a BaSotho specialist to make him more. It was not of the best quality, however, and his warriors were usually only able to carry one powder-horn full into action, which allowed them very few shots. Moreover, there was a permanent shortage of musket balls, and the Zulus were forced to improvise with pebbles or irregular pieces of scrap metal which the British nick-named 'pot-legs'. Nevertheless, when

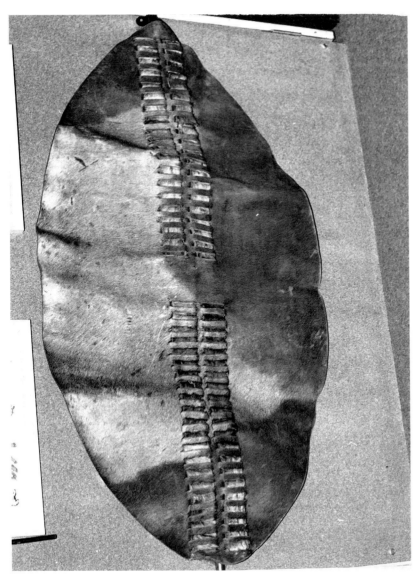

Below: An isihlangu *shield, believed to have been picked up at Rorke's Drift by Major Dunbar, 2/24th. It is red and white, the colour some sources attribute to the uDloko* ibutho. *(RRW Museum, Brecon).*

the *impi* mustered at the start of the campaign, the king was keen to ensure that as many of his men as possible had access to some sort of firearm, and by the time they were launched against Lord Chelmsford's Column, it seemed that most of them had.

It should be noted, however, that the men on their way to attack Rorke's Drift were not armed with British Martini-Henrys. It is true that the Zulus did take hundreds of British rifles from the dead at Isandlwana, but the uNdi regiments had not been involved in the fight. Even if they had been it is unlikely that they would have been able to learn how to use them at only a few hours' notice. Whatever firearms they had with them were their own.

When the two groups that had crossed the river had finished their snuff-taking, they rose and began to move at an easy pace upstream towards Rorke's Drift. Smith and Witt could see them quite clearly; one group, evidently the iNdluyengwe, had drawn ahead of the other and begun to advance along the undulating ground above the river, screened by a line of scouts. The other group split into two sections and advanced closer to the foot of Shiyane. Half moved out as if to swing round the foot of Shiyane, following the course of the river. This would have allowed them to approach KwaJim's from both sides, but they had much farther to go, across difficult country at the foot of the hill, and apparently changed their mind and moved back to rejoin the other party. There were two stout chiefs leading this unit on horseback, whom Smith and Witt at first mistook for British officers; it was only when they drew close enough for their black faces to be discerned that the spectators realized their mistake, and scuttled back down the hill as fast as their legs could carry them. At this stage, the Zulu advance seems to have been, if not undecided, at least relaxed. After the war, the Zulu summed up their attitude in an apparently light-hearted phrase, 'O! Let us go and have a fight at Jim's!' No doubt the commanders were casting about for the best prospect for loot. KwaJim was well-known to them, and any scouts observing the British movements over the previous week must have known that there was a small garrison there. Rorke's Drift was a very easy and tempting target, but it was not the only possibility; at least one deserted European farm-house lay close to the river downstream of Rorke's Drift, and there were numerous abandoned African homesteads along the valley. Furthermore, some of the Zulus may have known of the British supply base on the Helpmekaar heights. At some point, therefore, the raiders shed small parties who set out to ravage the countryside. Smith could see smoke rising from the European house and African huts as the Zulus put them to the torch. Some quite large groups of warriors even pushed as far forward as the foot of the

Helpmekaar escarpment. As recently as the 1960s, an elderly lady, 'Gogo' Khumalo, who lived in a homestead between Rorke's Drift and Fugitives' Drift, recalled that as a child she hid in an underground grain store to escape the uThulwana, whom she could hear looting her home above her!

Such a dispersal probably reduced the Zulu force to between 3,500 and 4,000 men. These advanced up the valley between Shiyane and kwaSingqindi hill to the south-west, with the iNdluyengwe in the lead and the senior men some way behind. A shoulder of land between the two hills hid the Mission from view, and before they crested the rise and came within sight of the British garrison, the iNdluyengwe paused to make their final preparations. Private Hitch, on the storehouse roof, was the only man among the defenders who could see them:

Left: A Zulu knobkerry picked up at Rorke's Drift by Lieutenant Gonville Bromhead. (Keith Reeves collection)

Right: A typical Zulu powder-horn. This example is believed to have been taken from a dead Zulu at Rorke's Drift. (Keith Reeves collection)

Right: Zulu ordnance: percussion caps, an improvised powder measure (bottom left) and rough lead bullets, typical of the ammunition available to the Zulus. ('SB' Bourquin collection)

Below: This Brown Bess musket, the wood badly damaged by termites, is typical of the firearms in Zulu possession at the beginning of the Anglo-Zulu War. This example had been part of the king's armoury at Ulundi. (kwaZulu Cultural Museum,

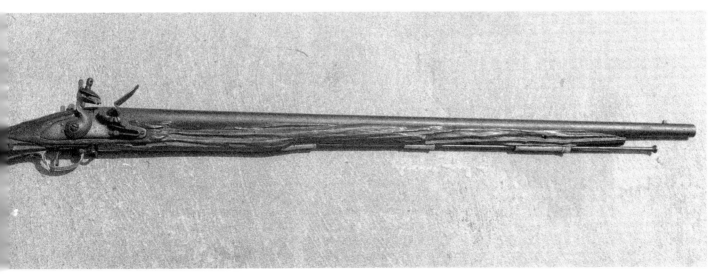

'I saw an advanced guard of the enemy coming over the brow of the hill on our right front ... The big mob of the enemy soon came up, extending from the right, and the column appeared to me, as I watched them from the roof of the house, to be about a mile and a half in length. They were then just beyond gunshot, but were perfectly quiet. They then made a right wheel, and the extreme right moved into the caves on the adjoining hill, and as I was about the only man they could see, being on the roof, they took a pot-shot at me but missed. I reported the movements to my comrades below, and fired three shots, these being the first that were fired at the Zulus at Rorke's Drift; the enemy made a yell and came on at the little front with a rush, and I then got down and took my position with the rest of the company ...'

One wonders if this display of a highly disciplined deployment had suggested to Hitch that the Zulus were a very different fighting force from the Xhosa he had encountered on the Cape Frontier. If not, he would shortly find out.

Left: A modern photograph, taken with a 200mm telephoto lens to duplicate the effect of a telescope, showing Isandlwana from the top of Shiyane. Witt, Reynolds and Smith would have been able to see something of the fighting on the slopes of the hills to the left of the mountain, and the advance of the Zulu right horn, which swept across the valley below the mountain. (Author's photograph)

Left: The Mission, photographed late 1879, at the angle from which the Zulus would have first seen it. Nothing remains of the hospital except the section of high wall on the extreme left; this loop-holed rampart was built after the battle. The graves of the defenders killed in the fight can be seen in the foreground.

4. ACTION!

Just before the Zulus came into view, Harry Lugg heard the command, 'Stay operations and fall in!' and the men took up their posts. The stock of Lugg's carbine was bent, so he found a length of leather rein, tied it up, and fell in with the men of 'B' Company: 'I thought, if I can get somewhere to sit down and pop away I shall be alright, because my knees were much swollen. I was told off in my turn to take a loophole, and defend the roof from fire.'

It is not entirely clear who was issuing these orders, but generally Chard seems to have given over-all instructions while Bromhead and Bourne detailed the men to carry them out. Clearly the men of 'B' Company were deployed by their own officer or NCO, because it seems that the best shots were posted along the barricade at the back wall where the initial attack was likely to fall. Corporal John Lyons of 'B' Company remembered that the men were told not to fire without orders, but Lugg thought that '...no orders were given, every man to act as he thought proper'. In fact, detailed orders would have been inappropriate and Chard probably gave the men no more than a cheering word. Henry Hook recalled that, '...our orders ... were never to say die or surrender', but then surrender was never a practical option.

Gunner Howard recalled that '...boxes of ammunition were placed behind us', and it is interesting — before the first shots are fired — to consider 'B' Company's situation with regard to ammunition. (Following the Isandlwana disaster, the alleged failure of the ammunition supply was a key feature in the recriminations, although there is no reliable evidence that the 24th ran low on ammunition until long after the firing line had collapsed.) Assistant Commissary Dunne also mentioned that ammunition was served out, so 'B' Company had obviously taken precautions. According to Field Force Regulations, the total reserve ammunition was to be 270 rounds, 70 carried by each man on his person, plus a further 200 rounds per man '...to be kept constantly in the possession of regiments and detached companies in the field'. This meant that the necessary boxes were to be kept with the company at all times. The full Company reserve, allowing 270 rounds per man, was 27,000 rounds; each box held 600 rounds, to give a total of 45 boxes, although at any given time a portion of this total should have been in the men's pouches. Since Rorke's Drift was a supply depot it is inconceivable that 'B' Company's reserve was not at hand; it was probably in the storehouse. There may have been a few extra boxes scattered about to supply the various men on detached duty, so there may have been as many as 30,000 rounds on site altogether. It is unlikely that there were significantly more than that, however,

Below: Otto Witt's house today. This building was built on the site of the hospital and much resembles it; it would have had a thatched roof in 1879. This is the back of the building, the view the Zulus would have had when they attacked.

Left: The Mission photographed in about 1884, from the Shiyane terraces to the right of the initial Zulu attack, looking towards kwaSingqindi hill. (Bryan Maggs collection)

Below: Chard's own panoramic sketch of Rorke's Drift, which accompanied his letter to Queen Victoria, is undoubtedly the most comprehensive and accurate representation of the scene. It was drawn looking towards the post , with Shiyane,and the line of the Zulu attack, behind. Chard numbered the features: (1) Oskarberg (Shiyane); (2) rocks and caves occupied by Zulus; (3) the cattle kraal; (4) 'B' Company's camp (tents struck); (5) well-built cattle-kraal or pen ; (6) mealie-bag wall; (7) two heaps of mealie-bags, later made into redoubts; (8) storehouse; (9) cookhouse; (10) ovens; (11) wagons; (12) biscuit-box wall; (13) hospital; (14) stone wall; (15) garden. (Royal Archives, Windsor)

ZULUS FIRST APPEAR

1 Oscarberg.   4 Camp of B Cᵒ 24ᵗʰ
2 Rocks and Caves occupied by Zulus.   9 Cook House. 1020 ovens.
3 Cattle Kraal.   5 Well built Kraal.   8 Commᵗ Store. 11 Wagons. 13 Hospital.   14 Wall 5 ft.
                              7 2 Heaps of Mealies in Sacks
                6 Mealie sack Wall.   12 Wall of Biscuit Boxes.   15 Garden.

because the battalion reserves for both the 1/24th and 2/24th were in the camp at Isandlwana. Indeed, the Zulus were looting them at that very moment. But all in all, the garrison must have opened the battle confidant that ammunition supply, at least, would not be a problem.

At about 4.30 p.m. the first Zulus came into view. A line of skirmishers streamed over the southern shoulder of Shiyane, fed from the rear by small groups of twenty or thirty men who extended 'in section of fours', until they had taken up the traditional 'beast's horns' attack formation. These were the younger men of the iNdluyengwe, and they came on at a fast run, stooping as low as possible, keeping their heads down, with their chins close to the ground. According to Henry Hook, they '... took advantage of every bit of cover there was', ducking behind anthills and boulders, and weaving among the scant protection afforded by the bush and grass on the otherwise bare slope. Corporal Lyons noted that '...the Zulus did not shout, as they generally do; but after extending and forming a half-moon, they steadily advanced and kept up a tremendous fire'. At about 500 yards' range the men along the back wall opened fire in reply, and the battle began in earnest. Lugg had:

'...the satisfaction of seeing the first I fired at roll over at 350, and then my nerves were as steady as a rock. I made sure almost before I pulled the trigger. There was some of the best shooting at 450 yards that I have ever seen.'

According to Gunner Howard, the heavy Martini-Henry bullets had a devastating effect at that range, and as they were hit the Zulus, '...would give a little spring in the air and fall down flat'. They were undaunted nevertheless, and Chard was impressed at the way they pushed forward their attack:

'We opened fire on them, between five and six hundred yards, at first a little wild, but only for a short time ... The men were quite steady, and the Zulus began to fall very thick. However, it did not seem to stop them at all ... It seemed as if nothing would stop them, and they rushed on in spite of their heavy loss to within 50 yards of the wall, when they were taken in the flank by the fire from the end wall of the store building, and met with such a heavy direct fire from the mealie wall, and the Hospital at the same time, that they were checked as if by magic.'

Private Hook, who was apparently a marksman in the Company, remembered that in the first attack he fired three shots at a warrior sheltering behind an anthill. After the third shot, he didn't see the man move again. It was clearly impossible to charge home in the teeth of such a fire, and some

Chard's own sketch maps and panorama (opposite page) drawn as part of an account of the defence of Rorke's Drift by Major J R M Chard, VC RE, submitted to Queen Victoria on 21st February 1880. Copyright reserved. Reproduced by gracious permission of Her Majesty The Queen.

Right: *Chard's own sketch of the area around Rorke's Drift, setting the position of the mission station (left) into the context of Shiyane hill ('Oscarberg', bottom) and the crossing on the Mzinyathi (Buffalo) river (right). Copyright reserved. Reproduced by gracious permission of Her Majesty The Queen.*

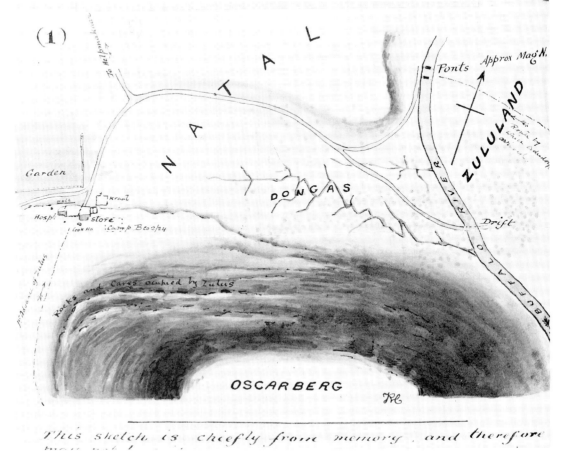

of the Zulus threw themselves down in the grass and tried to wriggle forward to the cover of the cook-house and ovens, while the rest veered off to their left, and poured into the bush and orchard along the front of the post. This offered a greater chance of concealment, at least, and they opened a heavy fire on the garrison and began to creep forward towards the front of the hospital.

It should be remembered that at this stage the Zulu attack had developed without much prior planning. Hitch, from his vantage point on the roof, had seen the iNdluyengwe drawing up in battle formation, but the Zulus had clearly hoped to take the post in the first rush. They were not to be put off by their initial check, but it is doubtful that their commanders had any secondary plan in mind. Moving into the bush was simply the obvious way of escaping the hail of fire while at the same time getting closer to the enemy. In fact, it is debatable whether their officers would have been able to exercise much control over their men once the battle had started. Throughout the Anglo-Zulu War the Zulu army proved that it was not disciplined enough to hold back when it came in sight of the enemy; the warriors were eager to attack regardless of the instructions of their officers, and any tactical subtlety was soon forgotten in the excitement of the moment. The best the *izinduna* could hope for was to try to direct the onrush at the weakest point of the British line.

It is easy to imagine that the Zulus had a fundamental advantage because of their overwhelming numbers. In fact, however, the battle was fought very much on terms favourable to the British. Every Anglo-Zulu battle was a contest between two very different tactical systems, and the extent to which either side was victorious depended on its ability to bring about the circumstance best suited to its own mode of operations. To overcome an enemy possessing a far greater and more terrible firepower capability, the Zulus needed to catch them in the open, where their superior numbers and manoeuvrability could be used to best effect. This is exactly what happened at Isandlwana, and in the other Zulu victories later in the war — Ntombe and Hlobane. The British, however, sought to keep their formations as tight as possible, in order to concentrate their firepower. When they managed that successfully the Zulus never had a chance to come close enough to make their numbers tell. At Rorke's Drift Chard's men could scarcely have been deployed on a narrower front, and were protected by effective barricades. No matter how large the Zulu force, there was a limit to the number they could deploy to contact at any given point; deep formations were of little use to them because the rear ranks could not contribute to the fight. In fact, it is more than likely that most

Below: The hospital building today, showing how the ground slopes away in front of the verandah. The line of stones marks the approximate position of the stone wall in front of the hospital; the mealie-bag barricades were on the slope above it. (Author's photograph)

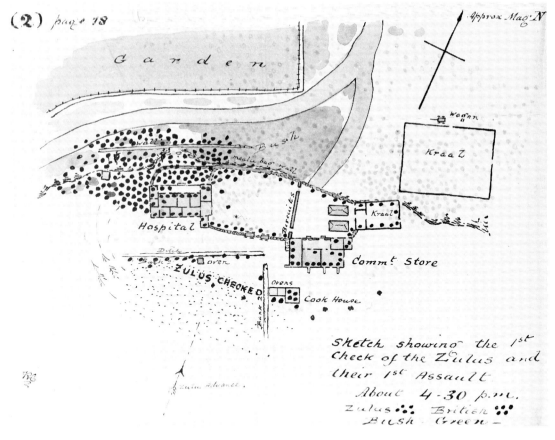

Right: George Edward Orchard, who enlisted under the name of George Edwards. Private Edwards was one of those defending the rear mealie-bag wall. (Orchard family)

of the Zulus spent a major part of the battle lying in the bush and grass at the front of the post, waiting for the chance to do something useful.

But there was a very apparent weakness in Chard's line. The front of the hospital was poorly barricaded, and the Zulus could move up to within a few yards of it, sheltered by the bush growing close to the foot of the slope. The leading warriors did not pause in their attack, but streamed through the bush straight up towards the barricade, and the first of a series of deadly struggles along the front of the building began. Here the defenders could not bring to bear a sufficient volume of fire to stop them, and they rushed up and engaged the defenders hand-to-hand. Private Hitch, who had taken up a position here, recalled:

'I found as they got close to the laager I was out of the fighting so I slid down the thatch roof, dropping into the laager, taking up my position on an open space which we had not time to complete as the deadly work now commenced.

'The Zulus pushing right up to the porch, it was not until the bayonet was freely given that they flinched the least bit. Had the Zulus taken the bayonet as freely as they took the bullets, we could not have stood more than fifteen minutes. They pushed right up to us, and not only got up to the laager, but got in with us, but they seem to have a great dread of the bayonet, which stood to us from beginning to end. During that struggle there was a fine big Zulu — seeing me shoot his mate down — he sprang forward, dropping his rifle and assegais, seizing hold of the muzzle of my rifle with his left hand and the right hand hold of the bayonet. Thinking to disarm me, he pulled and tried hard to get the rifle from me, but I had a firm hold of the small of the butt of the rifle with my left hand. My cartridges [were] on the top of the mealie-bags, which enabled me to load my rifle and [I] shot the poor wretch whilst holding on to his grasp for some few moments. They dropped back into the garden, which served as a great protection for them — had it not been for that garden, dead [ground] and wall, they could not have prolonged the engagement for thirteen hours as they did.'

It is curious that a people accustomed to fighting with stabbing weapons seemed reluctant to face the bayonet, but the same phenomenon was noticed at Isandlwana and elsewhere. The 'lunger' was, it must be said, a particularly terrifying weapon, and it gave a soldier a reach of something over six feet; far more than the three or four feet needed by a warrior to use his stabbing spear effectively. Nor was it always easy to deflect a bayonet thrust with the shield, because the force of the thrust was concentrated on to a narrow point, which could twist a shield out of a warrior's hand, or even punch right through it. The prospect of being transfixed through the throat or chest before there was an opportunity to retaliate no doubt accounted for much of the Zulu reluctance. However, the Zulus tried to rush the verandah three or four times, and each time Bromhead and Colour-Sergeant Bourne led a few men who drove them back with the bayonet. Each time they fell back into the garden they regrouped and came forward again. James Dalton was in the thick of the fight, encouraging the men, and using a rifle to good effect. On one occasion he, '...shot a Zulu who was in the act of assegaiing a corporal of the Army Service Corps, the muzzle of whose rifle he had seized'.

While this desperate struggle was taking place along the front of the post, the second Zulu force, the senior men of the uThulwana, iNdlondlo and uDloko *amabutho*, came up at the back. It seems unlikely that Prince Dabulamanzi had co-ordinated his plan of attack with the iNdluyengwe, but his men would have heard the sound of the firing long before they came round the hill, and by the time they arrived they were effectively committed to supporting those already engaged. It would have been difficult to pass by and leave the fighting to their comrades, and in any case most of them would have been only too keen to get to grips with the enemy. Seeing that the attack along the rear wall had ground to a halt, however, they moved further to the left, past the side of the hospital, and joined the warriors sheltering in the orchard.

As this attack developed it seems that the Zulus lost one of their two senior commanders to British rifle fire. One of those defending the back wall, Private James Dunbar, attracted Chard's attention by the way he coolly shot first a chief on a grey horse, then eight more warriors on the slopes of the hill with as many consecutive shots. Chard in fact suggests that this took place when the first Zulu attack developed, but we know from the Reverend Smith that the mounted chiefs were with the second party. What is less well known is that another soldier also claimed the honour of shooting the chief; Private George Edwards — who had enlisted, like many of pals, under a false name, and whose real name was George Edward Orchard — had spotted the chief because he was mounted and because he was wearing a distinctive shawl. He had taken careful aim, but at the moment he fired, the man next to him also fired, and the chief fell. One assumes that Edwards's neighbour was Private Dunbar, and of course it is impossible to say whose shot actually struck home. In any event the chief was killed. It is often possible to identify an important Zulu killed in battle because the Zulus assessed the destructiveness of a particular engagement by the number of important men they lost; however, there is no tradition that identifies this man by name. It certainly wasn't Dabulamanzi himself; he survived the battle unscathed. The senior son of Masiphula, who had been an enormously influential councillor to King Mpande, was killed in the action, as were three or four other head-men, but none of their deaths is linked specifically to this incident. Perhaps the Zulus were reluctant to remember it because of the stigma of defeat which clung to those who attacked Rorke's Drift.

Whoever he was, the death of this officer did not deter the senior men's attack. Pressure on the front of the hospital became insupportable and the defenders were driven back from the space in front of the verandah. Some boxes and sacks were hastily dragged across to plug the gap between the wing of the hospital and the front barricade so as to prevent the Zulus from outflanking the men on the front wall. The defenders could crouch behind these, or shelter behind the corner of the hospital itself, and lean round to rake the verandah with fire at only a few yards' range. This made it extremely dangerous for any warriors who tried to take advantage of their retreat, but a few were brave enough to risk the fire and hurl themselves up to the verandah. If they made it alive, they might have found some shelter in the lee of the wing, where the defenders' fire couldn't reach them. Chaplain Smith described this phase of the struggle:

'...such a heavy fire was sent along the front of the hospital that, although scores of Zulus jumped over the mealie bags to get into the building, nearly every man perished in that fatal leap: but they rushed to their death like demons, yelling their

Right: *Although of poor quality, and dating from about the turn of the century, this image duplicates the appearance of the hospital at the time of the battle, and gives a good idea of how the front was obscured by bush. (Natal Museums Service)*

Right: *Chard's sketch of between 4.30pm and 6.00pm, the Zulus extend their attack along the front of the post, and drive the 77 defenders back from the barricade in front of the hospital verandah. The fire from the Shiyane terraces begins to cause casualties in the yard.*
Copyright reserved. Reproduced by gracious permission of Her Majesty The Queen.

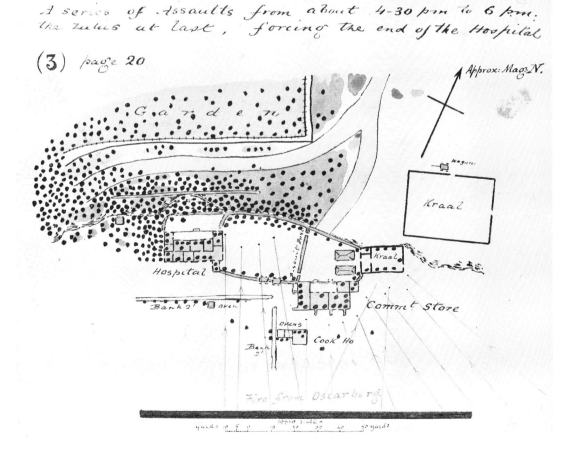

war-cry "Usuto! Usuto!" [*uSuthu!*] ... As long as we held the front wall, the Zulus failed in their repeated attempts to get into the far-end room of the hospital, Lieutenant Bromhead having several times driven them back with a bayonet charge.'

Frank Bourne was impressed by the extraordinary way the Zulus disregarded their own safety:

'To show their fearlessness and their contempt for the red-coats and small numbers, they tried to leap the parapet, and at times seized our bayonets, only to be shot down. Looking back, one cannot but admire their fanatical bravery.'

Raw courage was not enough by itself, however, and the verandah was soon littered with the dead and dying. But as Chard commented, the determination of the Zulu attacks soon led to a situation in which they '...in this part soon held one side of the wall, while we held the other'.

It is interesting to piece together from the glimpses afforded by the accounts of other participants how Chard and Bromhead personally conducted the defence. Chard was constantly on the move, observing the situation around the perimeter, watching for each developing threat and moving men to meet it. Both he and Bromhead carried revolvers, but both at various times took up rifles and fired over the barricade when necessary. It is extremely unlikely that either of them was wearing a sword; in the confused and close-quarter struggle a sword would have been useless and there is no mention of one. Bromhead, together with his NCOs, seems to have led his Company from the front, and to have placed himself conspicuously in the most dangerous positions in order to encourage his men.

Sadly, it is impossible to determine the movements of the Zulu commanders in the same way. After Dabulamanzi was seen to ride up at the head of the senior men, there is no further mention of him whatsoever and, although the defenders' attention was drawn to individual Zulus leading attacks from time to time, there is no evidence to suggest any of them was Dabulamanzi. We simply know nothing of his movements, his tactical intentions or any commands that he issued. There is a local tradition that he took up a position beneath the Shiyane terraces, at a spot where a Mission bell has since been erected. Perhaps he did; Zulu commanders traditionally placed themselves on high ground, where they could see what was going on, and this spot would have been as good as any.

As Hitch had noticed at the beginning of the fight, the Zulus were by now occupying the Shiyane terrace in large numbers, and from there they opened a heavy fire on the back of the post. This terrace, which runs around the foot of the hill, some three or four hundred yards from the back of the buildings, is an exposed reef of stone which the

Below: *The line of broken strata around the foot of Shiyane which provided the Zulu riflemen with so much cover. (Author's photograph)*

Right: *The Mission today, photographed from the shallow caves on the Shiyane terrace where the Zulu riflemen fired down into the compound. The dark trees in the middle distance mark the cemetery; the old hospital was just beyond it. (Author's photograph)*

elements have broken down and eroded. Large slabs of rock have fallen away and lie scattered below it, and rainfall has gouged shallow caves in the sandy soil between the boulders. It was an excellent source of cover which, moreover, looked directly down on the centre of the yard between the buildings. Those men defending the rear barricade, which was the slightly higher of the two, were mostly hidden from sight, but the men along the front wall were completely exposed in their rear to fire from the terrace. A squad of good marksmen, armed with efficient modern weapons — even by 1879 standards — could have cleared that yard in half an hour; the tragedy for the Zulus was that they had no such weapons, and the range was too long for the antiquated weapons at their disposal.

It is interesting to pause and consider how effective the assorted flintlocks and percussion guns with which they were armed really were. Official British tests carried out on the Enfield percussion rifle — which dated from the 1850s and was probably the most modern and efficient of those carried by the Zulus in any quantity — suggested that a well-trained soldier firing under ideal conditions could expect a significant proportion of hits on a man-sized target at 200 yards' range. At 500 yards he would be expected to hit a target six feet square with 50 per cent of his shots. At 1,000 yards he would be expected to achieve the same percentage of hits on a target eight feet square. This sounds impressive, but of course battle conditions are far from ideal and the efficiency of the best-trained soldier of the day would probably

have been impaired when in combat. The distraction of noise and smoke, the unsettling effect of enemy fire, the unsteadiness caused by surges of adrenalin prompted by rage or fear, all made it difficult to retain anything like the level of accuracy achieved in the calm of the firing-range. And the Zulus were not well-trained, their weapons were not in good condition and their ammunition was not of the best quality. Any assessment of their chances of scoring a hit at ranges of 300-400 yards would be purely speculative, but even with the Enfield they must have been low. For the Brown Bess musket, with which the majority were probably armed, the chances were minimal. In 1841 a series of tests conducted by the Royal Engineers found that the Brown Bess fired at ranges between 100 and 700 yards, according to the elevation, produced variations of as much as 100 yards between shots at any given range. At 150 yards, three shots out of four hit a target twelve feet high and three feet wide. When firing at the same target at a greater range, however, not a single hit was scored. Firing at a target six feet wide at a range of 250 yards produced similarly dismal results. Furthermore, the gun missed fire more than once in every six shots. With such weapons, any successful results scored by the Zulus must have been purely fortuitous.

By contrast, the British soldiers returning fire from the rear barricade were doing so at an ideal range for the Martini-Henry. At ranges of more than 450 yards, the marksman has to fire over raised backsights, and it is necessary to crane the neck and hold the butt slightly away from the face to look down the barrel, with a resulting loss of steadiness. At 400 yards the sights can be lowered, however, and the marksman can bring the butt close into his shoulder. Accuracy increases dramatically, and it is no coincidence that it was at this distance that the Zulu charges first faltered in battle after battle throughout the war. Firing from behind the support of a steady barricade, with sufficient time to aim and place each shot, was probably about as ideal as conditions in combat could be. For the good shots like those apparently placed along the back wall, the firefight must have been an unequal contest, with the odds stacked decidedly in their favour. Even if the Zulus were well hidden among the rocks, the thick smoke discharged by their weapons must have given their position away, and in the late afternoon in January, the summer sun falls directly across the Shiyane terrace, and must have lit it up like a spot-light. There is a remarkable story that suggests something of the efficiency of the 24th's fire. Several men had extraordinary escapes at Rorke's Drift, but none more so than Chard's African wagon driver. This man — Chard didn't record his name — had been in charge of the Engineers' wagon during the preparations for the defence. After parking it near the large cattle-pen, he unharnessed the mules and set them free. Then, when the first sounds of firing announced the arrival of the Zulus, he fled to hide among the rocks on the Shiyane terrace. This turned out to be a bad idea:

'He saw the Zulus run by him and, to his horror, some of them entered the cave he was in, and lying down commenced firing at us. The poor wretch was crouching in the darkness, in the far depths of the cave, afraid to speak or move, and our bullets came into the cave, actually killing one of the Zulus. He did not know from whom he was in the most danger, friends or foes ...'

Whatever its limitations, however, the sheer volume of Zulu fire was bound to have some effect. 'They [kept] up a heavy fire', remembered Hitch, 'from front and rear from which we suffered very much.' Indeed, the accounts of survivors suggest that the air above the post was alive with shots humming past from all directions. Most of the fire originating from the garden probably went high, not only because the Zulus invariably fired high, but also because their targets were raised up on the ledge above them; that from Shiyane, however, struck freely down into the yard. Private Thomas Cole, one of the defenders of the hospital, left his post to fight on the front barricade and had no sooner stepped outside than he was killed by a bullet which passed straight through his head and struck the man next to him — Private James Bushe — on the bridge of the nose. Cole was obviously a popular figure, if only because of his inevitable

Above: *Corporal (later Sergeant) William Allen, wounded by a musket ball at Rorke's Drift, and awarded the Victoria Cross. (Royal Archives, Windsor)*

nick-name, and the word went round that, '...poor old King Cole is killed'. In the centre of the yard, a bullet struck Corporal C. Scammell of the NNC through the back of the shoulder and he collapsed. Someone helped him off to the verandah of the hospital, where Surgeon Reynolds was tending the wounded, but he refused to stay there and staggered out again. He spotted Chard firing a rifle over the barricades and crawled over to hand him his cartridges. Chard, incidently, can't have picked up an ammunition belt to go with this rifle, as Scammell wasn't the only man who noticed that he was short of cartridges. Scammell then called out for a drink of water and Acting-Storekeeper Louis Byrne fetched him one. Just as Byrne gave it to him he was shot through the head and fell down dead. On the back wall Corporals John Lyons and William Allen were among those trying to keep the Zulus' riflemen pinned down. Lyons leaned forward over the barricade to try to get a better shot and was struck in the neck by a musket ball:

Right: *Surgeon James Reynolds delivers ammunition to the defenders of the hospital; it was during this incident that a bullet passed through his helmet. Note the water-cart in the background; in fact the cart present at Rorke's Drift was probably a two-wheeled vehicle. (From 'The Bronze Cross')*

'I only turned round once [to see the Zulu attack] and in that brief interval I saw Private Cole shot, and he fell dead. Seeing this, I kept myself more over the bags, knowing that the shot which hit him had come over our heads, and I was determined to check this flank firing as much as possible. I became thus more exposed, and so did Corporal Allen. We fired many shots, and I said to my comrade, "They are falling fast over there," and he replied, "Yes, we are giving it to them." I saw many Zulus killed on the hill. About half-past seven, as near as I can tell, after we had been fighting between two and three hours, I received a shot through the right side of the neck. The ball lodged in the back, striking the spine ... My right arm was partially disabled. I said, "Give it to them, Allen. I am done; I am dying," and he replied, "All right Jack": and while I was speaking to him I saw a hole in the right sleeve of his jacket, and I said, "Allen, you are shot," and he replied, "Yes, goodbye." He walked away with blood running from his arm...'

Lyons must have staggered back from the barricade and twisted slightly as he fell, since Chard saw him lying in one of the gaps between the biscuit box wall which bisected the yard:

'I thought he was killed, but looking up he said, "Oh, Sir! you are not going to leave me here like a dog?" We pulled him in and laid him down behind the biscuit boxes where he was immediately looked to by Reynolds.'

Reynolds himself had something of a lucky escape; at one point he was carrying an armful of ammunition to men inside the hospital when a bullet passed through his helmet. James Dalton also received a severe wound, but it is not entirely clear at what point in the battle this happened; the Reverend Smith implies that it was early on, when the Zulus were assaulting the front of the hospital. Chard, however, suggests that it occurred later, in front of the storehouse. Dalton had been in the thick of the fight, encouraging the men and firing a rifle with considerable accuracy. According to Smith:

'Mr Dalton, who is a tall man, was continually going about the barricades, fearlessly exposing himself, and cheering the men, and using his own rifle most effectively. A Zulu ran up near the barricade. Mr Dalton called out, "Pot that fellow!" and himself aimed over the parapet at another, when his rifle dropped and he turned round, quite pale, and said that he had been shot. The doctor was by his side at once, and found that a bullet had passed quite through above the right shoulder. Unable any longer to use his rifle (although he did not cease to direct the fire of the men who were near him) he handed it to Mr Byrne, who used it well.'

According to Chard, it was he who took Dalton's rifle:

'I was standing near him at the time, and he handed me his rifle so coolly that I had no idea until afterwards of how severely he was wounded. He waited quite quietly for me to take the

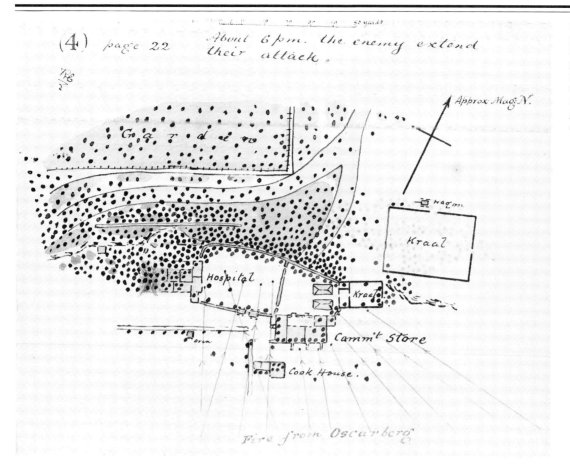

(4) page 22   About 6pm. the enemy extend their attack.

Approx Mag: N.

wagon

Garden

Kraal

Hospital

Kraal

Comm't Store

Oven

Cook House.

Fire from Oscarberg

cartridges he had left out of his pockets. We put him inside our mealie sack redoubt, building it up around him.'

These casualties must have been worrying to Chard who clearly could not afford to lose men at such a rate. He must already have been considering abandoning the yard and withdrawing behind the more secure biscuit-box line in front of the storehouse when a fresh Zulu attack decided him. At about 6 p.m., having failed to carry the front of the hospital, about the Zulus extended their attacks a little to their left, advancing through the bush to strike at the centre of the front wall and along beyond the road. This was a relatively secure position because the barricades were built on top of the 4-foot rocky ledge. Nevertheless:

'I feared seriously [that they] would get over our wall behind the biscuit boxes. I ran back with 2 or 3 men to this part of the wall and was immediately joined by Bromhead with 2 or 3 more. The enemy stuck to this assault most tenaciously, and on their repulse, and retiring to the bush, I called all the men inside our retrenchment — and the enemy immediately occupied the wall we had abandoned and used it as breastwork to fire by.'

One wonders how easily that withdrawal was accomplished given that the Zulus were so close; there must have been a danger of the Zulus getting in among the men as they fell back, unprotected by

the barricade. But nothing of the sort seems to have happened so presumably Chard must have found a way to cover the retreat.

The position in front of the storehouse was much more secure. For one thing, the store itself sheltered the men in front of it from the fire from the Shiyane terraces, which was immediately rendered ineffective. Secondly Chard's men were much more concentrated in the confined space and must have met each attack literally shoulder to shoulder. But there were disadvantages because, as Chard said, the Zulus immediately occupied the outside of the barricades which the defenders had just vacated, and opened a tremendous fire from only thirty or forty yards' range. Indeed, along the front of the post the Zulus could by now move up from the bush to crouch beneath the rocky ledge which, masked by the abandoned barricade, had become dead ground. The boldest warriors crept along and nestled in the crevices of the ledge just out of reach of the defenders' fire, and snatched shots at the redcoats above them whenever they exposed themselves, and from time to time attempted a desperate charge.

In an endeavour to check this threat Bromhead, Private Hitch and a handful of others took up a position on the right of the line of biscuit boxes, by the dangerous angle where it joined the front barricade. Here they were very exposed to crossfire from the Zulus now occupying the back barricade, and from those in the garden. Hitch takes up the story:

'Bromhead and myself and five others took up the position on the right of the second line of defence where we were exposed to the cross fire. Bromhead took the centre and was the only one that did not get wounded. There was four killed and two wounded, myself was the last of the six shot. Bromhead and myself had it to ourselves about an hour and a half, Bromhead using his rifle and revolver with deadly aim. Bromhead kept telling the men not to waste one round ... They seemed determined to move Bromhead and myself. We were so busy that one had [got] inside and was in the act of assegaiing Bromhead. Bromhead, not knowing he was there, I put my rifle on him knowing at the same time it was empty, instead of him delivering the assegai, which no doubt would

Below: A reconstructed section of the mealie-bag barricade on the front wall, displayed in the battlefield museum. (Natal Museums Service/Author)

have been fatal, he dodged down and hopped out of the laager...

'They rushed up madly, not withstanding the heavy loss they had already suffered. It was in this struggle that I was shot. They pressed us very hard, several of them mounting the barricade. I knew this one had got his rifle presented at me, but at the same time I had got my hands full in front, and I was at the present when he shot me through the right shoulder blade and passed through my shoulder which splintered the shoulder bone very much, as I have had in all 39 pieces of broken bone taken from my shoulder. I tried to keep my feet but could not, he could have assegaied me had not Bromhead shot him with his revolver. Bromhead seemed sorry when he saw me down bleeding so freely, saying, "Mate, I am very sorry to see you down." I was not down more than a few minutes, stripping (to) my shirt-sleeves with my waist-belt on and valise straps I put my wounded arm under my waist-belt. I was able to make another stand, getting Bromhead's revolver, and with his assistance loading it, I managed very well with it.'

It would be interesting to know just who the killed and wounded were on this occasion. Hitch gives us a clue: in another account, speaking of Private Edward Nicholas, of the 1/24th, who had been a patient in the hospital, he says, 'I saw one of my comrades — Private Nicholas — killed; he was shot through the head, his brains being scattered all about us!' If Hitch was being literal when he said four men were killed, there is a limited choice for the remaining three. Of all of those killed on the British side, the deaths of only three — Private James Chick, of 'D' Company, 2/24th, Private John Fagan of 'B' Company, and John Scanlon of 'A' Company — are not described in one or other of the accounts. In addition, Lance-Sergeant Thomas Williams — who had been in charge of the detachment of the 24th at the ponts earlier in the day — was mortally wounded. Under the circumstances Hitch might easily have mistaken a mortally wounded man for a fatality; he might equally, of course, have got the number wrong. At least one of these men must have been killed earlier in the fight because his body had been left slumped forward against the barricade. It is, of course, notoriously difficult to decide such matters when relying on the accounts of men who were recalling what can only have been a terrifying and confusing situation at the time.

It is rather easier to work out who the other wounded man was; Hitch says, 'another, Corporal Sheath of the Native Contingent, was shot on my left'. Corporal Friedrich Schiess, who had been a patient in the hospital, suffering from blisters, was wounded by a bullet which tore open the instep of his foot. According to Chaplain Smith, '...he would not allow that his wound was sufficient reason for leaving his post, though he has suffered most

acutely from it since'. Chard describes an incident which can only have happened at about this time:

'Corporal Schiess, Natal Native Contingent, who was a patient in the Hospital with a wound in the foot [sic], which caused him great pain, behaved with the greatest coolness and gallantry throughout the attack, and at this time creeping out a short distance along the wall which we had abandoned, and slowly raising himself, to get a shot at some of the enemy who had been particularly annoying, his hat was blown off by a shot from a Zulu on the other side of the wall. He immediately jumped up, bayonetted the Zulu and shot a second, and bayonetted a third who came to their assistance.'

Curiously enough, when an archaeological survey of part of the Rorke's Drift site was undertaken in 1988-9, a handful of unexpended percussion caps were found beneath the ledge where this incident must have occurred. Were they dropped by one of Schiess's victims?

Not long after the men had fallen back to the line of biscuit boxes, a rumour went round that a cloud of dust could be seen on the road towards Helpmekaar. Dunne himself, who had been keeping a look-out, saw it, though Chard, '...could see nothing of the sort myself. A cheer was raised, and the enemy seemed to pause, to know what it

meant, but there was no answer to it.' The garrison hoped it was Rainforth's Company, coming down at last to their aid and, curiously, both Rainforth's and Upcher's Companies had marched out down the road in the early evening. The first survivors from Isandlwana had trickled in to Helpmekaar in the late afternoon, exhausted and terror-struck, just as they had been at Rorke's Drift. Upcher, the senior officer, decided to move down to reinforce the garrison at the Drift and to try to prevent any Zulus getting across the river. On the way they met Spalding heading in the opposite direction. Spalding — who must have been taking his journey easily — had not yet heard of the disaster. He promptly turned around and, with a man named Dickson of the Buffalo Border Guard, rode on ahead of the infantry to find out what was happening. Along the road they met fugitives — probably the same men who had ridden past Rorke's Drift —streaming past; Spalding tried to persuade them to stand by him, but they would not, all of them assuring Spalding that Rorke's Drift had already fallen. When Spalding and Dickson were about three miles from the Drift a group of warriors suddenly rose across the road fifty yards in front of them, and threw out horns to surround them. The identity of these Zulus is intriguing, since this is the only mention of their

Above: The rocky ledge along the front of the post today, looking toward's Witt's house. The barricade was built along the top of this natural obstacle, but after the front wall was abandoned it became dead ground and the Zulus could crouch there unobserved. The incident which won Schiess the VC must have occurred at about this spot. (Author's photograph)

Right: The ferocity of the hand-to-hand fighting is captured in this contemporary engraving of the assault on the barricade. (Author's collection)

existence; presumably they were one of the parties that had broken away from the main body to raid the deserted homesteads between the Mzinyathi and the Helpmekaar escarpment. If so, they were several miles inside Natal territory, and one wonders if they had been contemplating an attack on Helpmekaar. It was clearly impossible for Spalding to proceed further and the two men rode back to join the infantry. Convinced that Rorke's

Drift had already fallen, they hurried back to Helpmekaar to prepare to defend the stores accumulated there. Chard was probably correct when he said that '...two companies from the 24th at Helpmekaar did come down to the foot of the hill, but not, I believe, within sight of us', but it seems too much of a coincidence that dust was spotted at about the time that there was movement on the road; it may be that it was thrown up by the

Zulus encountered by Spalding.

The fire from the line of biscuit boxes effectively kept the yard clear of Zulus, but the pressure on the front wall continued unabated, and Chard cast about for a way of giving himself an extra line of fire. By his own account, he was worried that the Zulus might force a way into the storehouse. If this had happened it is difficult to see how the garrison could have survived, but Chard needed one last stronghold on which to fall back. There had not been time to drag all the mealie-bags out on to the perimeter, and two large piles were still heaped up in front of the store. They offered the raw material for a makeshift redoubt, and Walter Dunne set about dragging them into shape. According to Chard:

'Assistant Commissary Dunne worked hard at this, and from his height, being a tall man, he was much exposed, in addition to the fact that the heaps were high above our walls, and that most of the Zulu bullets went high.'

Dunne's own account modestly plays down the danger, but suggests something of the physical effort involved, and ends on a finely observed reminder that the universe of battle wrought havoc not just to its active participants:

'...Chard decided to form a sort of redoubt of mealie bags, where a last stand could be made. We laboured at this 'til we dropped from exhaustion; but succeeded in building it up to about eight feet on the outside, and here the wounded were brought for protection. It was hard work, for the bags of mealies weighed 200 lbs. Overhead, the small birds, disturbed from their nests by the turmoil and smoke, flew hither and thither confusedly.'

By now it was getting dark. Summer evenings in Zululand can be beautiful, the sky working through subtle shades of pink and mauve in the warm, still air, giving way to a flare of red and orange as the sun sets. When the sun went down at about 7 o'clock on the evening of Wednesday, 22 January 1879, however, no one was concerned with the skyscape. The Battle of Rorke's Drift had been under way for two and a half hours and both sides had expended tremendous reserves of physical and emotional energy. To sustain any struggle for that length of time would be exhausting, but the close-quarter fire-fights and ferocious bouts of hand-to hand combat, repeated over and over again, must have pushed men on both sides to the brink of endurance. As the shadows lengthened the Zulus took advantage of the gloom to push forward into areas previously out of reach. Chard says:

'As darkness came on we were completely surrounded. The Zulus wrecked the camp of the

Above: *A dramatic engraving of the attack on Rorke's Drift published in The Graphic; although the terrain is fairly accurate, the layout of the buildings is incorrect. (Author's collection)*

Right: *A late Victorian painting of the battle by W.H. Dugan. This painting is unusual in that it gives both combatants equal emphasis, although there are some inaccuracies of costume on both sides — notably the shield of the warrior centre — and the composition suggests nothing of the significant terrain features. (RRW Museum, Brecon)*

24th Company and my wagon which had been left outside, in spite of the efforts of my batman, Driver Robson (the only man of the Royal Engineers with us), who had directed his particular attention to keeping the Zulus off this wagon in which were, as he described it, "Our things".'

It is interesting to note that two separate witnesses, Commandant Hamilton-Browne and Lieutenant Henry Harford, both of the 3rd NNC, visiting the field next morning, commented on the presence of a large stack of forage which was apparently lying somewhere between the struck tents of 'B' Company and the walls of the storehouse. They marvelled that the Zulus had not set it ablaze, speculating on the havoc that might have been caused if they had done so. They had a point; indeed, it was such an obvious move that one wonders whether this pile was forage at all, or whether it was merely the thatch removed from the roof of the store by the garrison on the morning of the 23rd.

At the back of the post, 'B' Company's marksmen, Privates James Dunbar, George Edwards and their like, had long since been withdrawn inside the new perimeter, and only the fire from the storehouse loop-holes was keeping the Zulus at bay. One warrior ran right up to the wall and tried to set fire to the roof, but was shot dead as he did so. Chard thought that Adendorff was the man responsible, although another account suggests that it was Attwood; no doubt both of

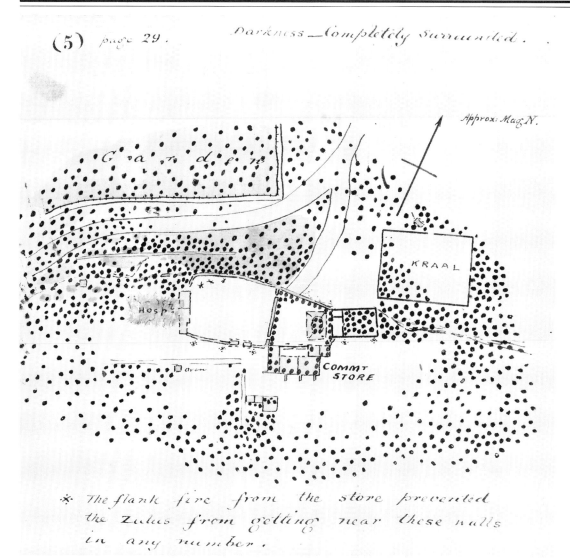

(5) page 29.

Darkness — Completely Surrounded.

Approx: Mag: N.

The flank fire from the store prevented the Zulus from getting near these walls in any number.

them were fully employed. Harry Lugg told a strange story about the fighting along the back wall at this time: as it was getting dark he noticed a warrior sneak into the deserted cook-house and surreptitiously light his *gudu* (a large horn usually used for smoking *dagga* (cannabis)), from the embers still glowing in the stove. Lugg shot him dead. Years later, in 1902, Lugg, who was still involved with the Natal Volunteer movement, was carrying out an inspection of the graves at Isandlwana, when he met an elderly Zulu who had sustained a number of wounds at Rorke's Drift. One bullet had creased his scalp, another had hit his left shoulder and two had passed through the calf of his leg — a revealing insight, incidentally, into the price paid by the Zulus for their persistence. Without revealing his own involvement in the fight, Lugg asked the old warrior to tell his story. The man was an eloquent speaker and conjured up the sounds of the action: the crashing of the rifles, the groans of the injured and the yelling war-cries of the Zulus. When he had come

to the end of his tale, Lugg asked him casually who the man was that had been killed in the cook-house. *'Kanti nawe wawukhena?'* ('And were you there also?') cried the old man in astonishment. *'Wafa uMngumule! Sizinja ngaphansi kwezinyao zenu.'* ('And so perished Mngamule! We were merely dogs under your feet').

Of course, when Chard ordered his men to fall back to the inner retrenchment, he effectively abandoned the defenders in the hospital to take their own chances with the Zulus. The bitterest, and perhaps most celebrated, part of the battle was taking place unseen by the men manning the final perimeter.

Indeed, the fight for the hospital has become such an epic part of the legend of Rorke's Drift that it is worth sounding a note of caution before describing it. It is difficult enough to reconstruct any battle from the fragmentary descriptions of participants, because the focus of men in action is limited almost entirely to their immediate front. Finer points of tactical significance tend to be

overlooked when the man next to one collapses screaming hysterically because half his head has been blown away, or when a Zulu warrior is rushing down on one with a stabbing spear from only a few yards away. We know less about the fight for the hospital at Rorke's Drift than is often supposed, partly because this natural tendency towards tunnel vision was exaggerated in the extraordinary, claustrophobic confusion, and partly because only one of the participants left an account that is anything like detailed. And that account, by Private Henry Hook, was written nearly thirty years later, at the end of his life, when the exact details of the hospital's internal geography must have been beginning to fade from his memory. There is an inevitable temptation to try to work out exactly what happened in each room during the epic struggle, but it is unlikely to be achieved to a satisfying degree. Hook's account is fuzzy round the edges, and his references to doors and windows do not entirely tie in with Lieutenant Chard's plan of the building — although it must be said that this was probably completed from memory after the place had burned down. So, in short, any reconstruction of events must embrace a significant element of speculation.

Most accounts agree that there were about thirty patients in the hospital, of whom about nine were men like Private Connolly who, with his dislocated knee, could not easily walk without assistance. Surgeon Reynolds mentioned that only two men, Sergeant Robert Maxfield, of 'G' Company, 2/24th and Private James Jenkins, both of whom were 'debilitated by fever', were seriously incapacitated. The rest were able to defend themselves to some degree, and were issued with rifles. Not all of them remained in the hospital, however; we know that

Above: Private Fred Hitch, who was severely wounded in the defence; his arm is still strapped up in this photograph which was taken after the award of his VC. (Keith Reeves collection)

Right: Sergeant (later Colour-Sergeant) Edward Wilson, 1/24th. Wilson was a patient in the hospital and took part in the defence. In 1880 he was one of the party that presented the Queen's Colour of the 1st Battalion to Queen Victoria at Osborne House. (RRW Museum, Brecon)

Far right: Trooper Henry — known as 'Harry' — Lugg of the Natal Mounted Police. (Xhawulisa collection)

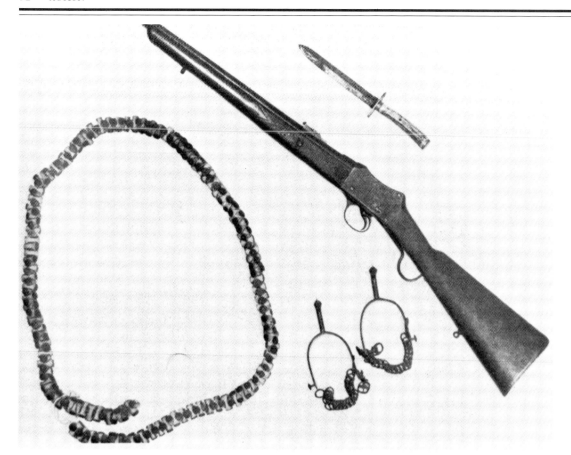

Left: Harry Lugg's Swinburne-Henry carbine, which he carried at Rorke's Drift, his hunting-knife and a Zulu iziqu necklace of willow-wood, a decoration for bravery. (Xhawulisa collection)

Left: A woollen cap worn during the battle by Trooper Lugg of the Natal Mounted Police. (Warriors' Gate Museum)

both Lugg and Schiess took up a position elsewhere on the perimeter at the beginning of the fight, so the precise number of men actually in the building when the Zulus attacked remains unknown. Only seventeen or eighteen patients are mentioned by name, which leaves nearly half unaccounted for. Six fit men from 'B' Company had been detailed to assist them, but there was no NCO in charge, nor does anyone appear to have been appointed to over-all command of the building. Presumably, since many of the rooms didn't connect with one another, this was thought

Right. The hunting-knife with which Lugg killed a Zulu on the morning after the battle. (Warriors' Gate Museum)

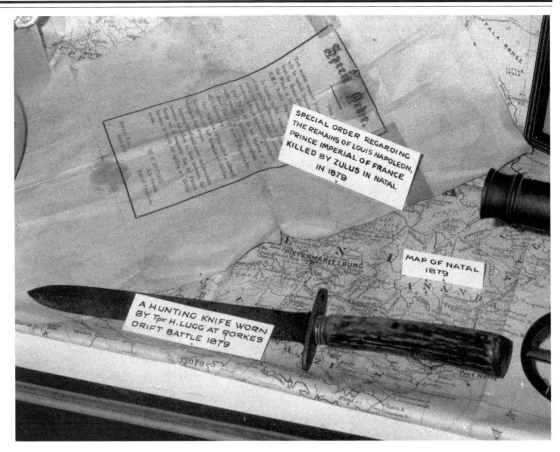

to be unnecessary. Nevertheless the men had knocked loop-holes through the outside walls, and had blocked up the doors and windows with mealie-bags and mattresses. Chard:

'...had tried to impress upon the men in the Hospital the necessity for making a communication right through the building — unfortunately this was not done. Probably at the time the men could not see the necessity, and doubtless also there was no time to do it. Without in the least detracting from the gallant fellows who defended the Hospital, and I hope I shall not be misunderstood in saying so, I have always regretted, as I did then, the absence of my poor sappers, who had only just left that morning for Isandhlwana and arrived there just in time to be killed.'

It is impossible to tell with any certainty which rooms the defenders were in. Chard's careful maps, drawn at Queen Victoria's request, show defenders evenly spaced throughout the rooms; this seems to be logical, although it must be said that Chard probably didn't see the men placed himself, and their own accounts are vague when it comes to who was in which room. Hook says nothing more than that he was in 'a small room', while he says that Privates William Jones and Robert Jones were in '...another ward which faced the hill' with seven patients. This implies that Hook's own room did not face the hill, although he may not have intended to imply this. Hook had with him Private

Cole and the wounded NNC man from Mkhungo's people. Privates Joseph Williams and John Williams were in another room with Private William Horrigan and two other patients. Gunner Howard was in another room, presumably on his own, while Privates William Beckett and John Waters, both of the 1/24th, were together in another small room. Another patient, Private William Roy, 1/24th, was in yet another room with a man he identifies only as 'an old soldier'. Where accounts from these men survive, they do not always mention one another, which confirms the isolated nature of the fighting.

From the very beginning, it will be recalled, the Zulus launched their fiercest attacks on the front of the hospital. They were driven back time and again by Bromhead's bayonet charges, and even when the defenders had been forced to abandon the verandah, the close-range fire from the improvised barricade on the right-front corner had kept them at bay. Private Cole, Hook's companion, was apparently claustrophobic, for the battle had not been long under way when he declared that he could stand it no longer and went outside. According to Hook, only one door out of the hospital had been left open, and that opened on to the verandah; Cole must have walked straight out into the middle of the fight raging there. Perhaps he had time to join in the defence — several men remembered seeing him there — but shortly

Left and above: A chair recovered from the hospital at Rorke's Drift on the morning of the 23rd by Colonel Henry Degacher who commanded the 2nd Battalion. (RRW Museum, Brecon)

afterwards he was shot dead. Once the garrison had abandoned the yard in the face of this pressure, there was nothing to prevent the Zulus bursting in through that same door. 'While I and another old soldier were inside at the back window', recalled Private Roy, 'we did not know they had taken it at the front.' None of the defenders seems to have been stationed in the two large rooms in the centre of the building, which face on to the verandah. This seems odd, especially since the building's vulnerability from this quarter was soon made apparent. Perhaps it was a matter of perception; it may be that all these rooms seemed small to the defenders, and individual incidents were simply telescoped into the over-all story of the fight. All the same, it must have been through these rooms that the Zulus first entered the building, and they had not long done so when they set the place on fire with the intention of driving the defenders out. This added an horrific new twist to an already nightmarish situation; as Hook succinctly has it, '...this put us in a terrible plight, because it meant that we were either to be massacred or burnt alive'. The thatch on the storehouse must have been very damp after weeks of rain, and it apparently took some time for the fire to take hold. In the meantime, however, the rooms began to fill with smoke.

In their room, Privates Waters and Beckett became involved in a bizarre little fight which centred upon a large cupboard belonging to the Reverend Witt. When they saw that the Zulus had entered the building, Waters and Beckett both

dodged inside the cupboard and hid among some of Witt's clothes which were still hanging inside. One wonders if they were perhaps in the room on the far left of the verandah; certainly when Witt rebuilt his home, this was the minister's room. If this was where they were hiding, they were probably overlooked because the attention of the Zulus was distracted by the fighting at the other end of the verandah. If they were not it is difficult to understand why the Zulus did not search the place more thoroughly. At one point, they must have been discovered, as Waters shot several warriors who came into the room, and was wounded twice himself, once in the shoulder and once in the knee. If these Zulu dead had fallen back on to the verandah, it is quite possible that the direction from which the shots came would not have been apparent. It seems very unlikely that the two men could have remained hidden in a cupboard, which must have been fairly conspicuous, in an isolated room in the middle of the house, with dead Zulus littering the floor. The tension must have been unbearable, and after a while Beckett could stand it no longer and made a break for the outside. As he ran out, however, a warrior spotted him and stabbed him through the stomach, and he staggered off and collapsed in the bush.

Waters stayed hidden for as long as he dared, until the room filled with smoke and the heat became unbearable. Then:

'I put on a black cloak which I found in the cupboard, and which must have belonged to Mr Witt, and ran out into the long grass and lay down. The Zulus must have thought I was one of their dead comrades, as they were all round me, and some trod on me.'

Although it was dark, the prospect of spending the entire night lying out in the bush, awaiting the moment when he would be identified, clearly did not appeal to Waters so he worked his way round

to the back of the post, creeping towards the cookhouse. This was only a few yards from the corner of the storehouse, and he no doubt hoped to get back inside the perimeter. To his horror, however, he found that the cook-house was full of Zulus who were firing at the defenders. It was too late to turn back so he, '...crept softly to the fireplace and,

standing up in the chimney, blacked his face and hands with the soot. He remained there until the Zulus left.' That was a moment that defies the imagination; in the darkness of the cramped little out-building, lit only by the guttering light from the burning hospital, Waters must have been close enough to touch those warriors. The flash as they

discharged their muskets must have been dazzling and the noise must have boomed around the walls. No doubt the fire from the defenders was as much of a danger as discovery itself. That he remained there and survived surely indicates a reserve of courage born of desperation.

Gunner Howard, too, escaped from the hospital into the darkness. He had been defending a room with a rifle '...belonging to a sergeant who was too ill to use it' — Maxfield, presumably, since Howard adds, 'The Zulus made short work of him.' His own account doesn't mention his escape, but according to Chard:

'...[he] ran out through the enemy, and lay down on the upper side of the wall in front of our N. Parapet. The bodies of several horses that were killed early in the evening were lying here, and concealed by these and by the Zulu bodies and the low grass and bushes, he remained unseen with the Zulus all around him.'

If Howard were wearing his dark-blue Artillery uniform, no doubt this would have helped make him less conspicuous. At one point a stray pig was shot and lay squealing nearby, but Howard remained unnoticed. The most desperate struggle took place along the row of small rooms at the back of the hospital, and one can do no better than quote Hook's own account. After Cole went outside:

'I was left alone with a patient, a native whose leg was broken and who kept crying out, "Take my bandage off, so that I can come." But it was impossible to do anything but fight, and I blazed away as hard as I could. By this time I was the only defender in my room. Poor Old King Cole was lying dead outside and the helpless patient was crying and groaning near me. The Zulus were swarming round us, and there was an extraordinary rattle as the bullets struck the biscuit boxes, and queer thuds as they plumped into the bags of mealies. Then there was the whizz and rip of the assegais, of which I had experience in the [Cape

Frontier] campaign of 1877-8. We had plenty of ammunition, but we were told to save it and so we took careful aim at every shot, and hardly a cartridge was wasted ... My own little room communicated with another by means of a frail door like a bedroom door. Fire and dense choking smoke forced me to get out and go into the other room. It was impossible to take the native patient with me, and I had to leave him to an awful fate. But his death was, at any rate, a merciful one. I heard the Zulus asking him questions, and he tried to tear off his bandages and escape.

'In the room where I now was there were nine sick men, and I alone to look after them for some time. Suddenly in the thick of the smoke I saw John Williams, and above the dim of battle I heard him shout, "The Zulus are swarming all over the place. They've dragged Joseph Williams out and killed him." John Williams had held the other room with Private William Horrigan for more than an hour, until they had not a cartridge left. The Zulus

then burst in and dragged out Joseph Williams and two of the patients, and assegaied them. It was only because they were so busy with this slaughtering that John Williams and two of the patients were able to knock a hole into the partition and get into the room where I was posted. Horrigan was killed.'

The fighting in this 'other room' — it is of course quite impossible to say which one — requires further comment. Joseph Williams was a young soldier with less than two years' service behind him, but he seems to have acquitted himself very well; no fewer than fourteen dead Zulus were found outside the window in his line of fire next morning. Lieutenant William Weallans, who was at Rorke's Drift the morning after the fight, gave a different account of Williams's death in a letter dated 2 February:

'One man, named Williams, did a very plucky thing; he got into a small room by himself, and from a window fired away all the ammunition he had. He then tried to make a bolt for it into the fort, but unfortunately fell in getting out of the window. He got up, however, and tried to join the fort, when he was wounded by an assegai. He was caught by the Zulus and literally cut to pieces, as they were so infuriated at the number of them that he had killed. He had only about six yards to run to get into the fort, as the hospital was in the same line of defence. It seems very hard that he should have lost his life after fighting so well.'

Unfortunately, John Williams seem to have left no account of the fight, so we have only these two hearsay accounts with which to reconstruct Joseph Williams's death. However, it should be noted that they are not necessarily incompatible; Weallans says that Joseph Williams was trying to escape, and John Williams — who would hardly have had time to go into greater detail —told Hook that he had been 'dragged out'. In either case, he was overwhelmed by the Zulus outside the building itself, and the escape story seems marginally the more credible — why would the Zulus have dragged him out when they were content to kill any others they could catch within the building itself? Too much has been made of Weallans's suggestion

Left: *This contemporary image from* The Penny Illustrated *is unusual in that it depicts the attack from the Zulu viewpoint. (Rai England collection)*

Right: *Private Alfred Henry Hook, generally known as Henry or Harry Hook. (Keith Reeves collection)*

Right: *John Fielding, who enlisted under the name of John Williams, so that his father couldn't trace him; Williams was one of the defenders of the hospital. (Keith Reeves collection)*

that Williams was 'literally cut to pieces'; this is a very subjective phrase and merely suggests the horror the British experienced on seeing the bodies of men killed by the Zulus. Most had been repeatedly stabbed and the corpses had usually been disembowelled. This was done in accordance with a Zulu spiritual belief which held that the dark spiritual forces, *umnyama*, which lingered near a body after death, attached themselves to the slayer unless they were allowed to escape through the stomach cavity. On occasions, in the frenzy of battle, many dead soldiers were badly mutilated, but there is no evidence whatsoever that the Zulus indulged in torture at any time, and there is no reason to suppose that Williams was deliberately dismembered as a form of revenge, which would have been quite contrary to normal Zulu practice.

We must presume that the other two patients were Privates Garret Hayden and Robert Adams. Hayden's body was found in the hospital ruins after the battle; according to Sergeant George Smith of 'B' Company, he had been, '...stabbed in ... sixteen places, and his belly cut right up in two places, and part of his cheek was cut off'. His death is not described in detail by any of the surviving defenders however, and nor is that of Adams. According to Reynolds, Adams (of 'D' Company 2/24th), was, '... well able to move about but could not be persuaded to leave his temporary refuge in a small room, and face the danger of an attempt to escape to the laager'. One wonders if these two had in fact been defending another room, perhaps one of those opening on to the verandah, and been killed when the Zulus burst in; after all, Williams seems to have given Hook no more than a precis of their deaths.

Whatever may or may not have happened in the warren of close, dark little rooms in Mr Witt's house, a deadly game of chase now began as the survivors retreated from room to room. According to Hook, '...the ends of the building were of stone, and the side walls of ordinary bricks, and the inside walls or partitions of sun-dried bricks of mud. These shoddy inside bricks were our salvation.' Modern archaeological evidence has supported Hook's account; the interior walls were apparently built of bricks of mud mixed with *dagga*, plastered over and either papered or painted. They were certainly not particularly strong. Now Hook and Williams were in the same room, but the Zulus were already trying to burst through the doorway. 'What', asked Hook, 'were we to do? We were pinned like rats in a trap.'

'The only way of escape was with the wall itself, by making a hole big enough for a man to crawl through into an adjoining room, and so on until he got to our innermost entrenchment outside. Williams worked desperately at the wall with the navvy's pick, which I had been using to make some of the loopholes with.

'All this time the Zulus were trying to get into the room. Their assegais kept whizzing towards us, and one struck me on the front of the helmet. We were wearing the white tropical helmets then. But the helmet tilted back under the blow and made the spear lose its power so that I escaped with a scalp wound which did not trouble me much then, although it has often caused me illness since. Only one man at a time could get in at the door. A big Zulu sprang forward and seized my rifle, but I tore it free and, slipping a cartridge in, I shot him point blank. Time after time the Zulus gripped the muzzle and tried to tear the rifle from my grasp, and time after time I wrenched it back, because I had a better grip than they had. All this time Williams was getting the sick through the hole into the next room, all except one, a soldier of the 24th named Conley, who could not move because of a broken leg [sic]. Watching for my chance, I dashed from the doorway and, grabbing Conley, I pulled him after me through the hole. His leg got broken again, but there was no help for it. As soon as we left the room, the Zulus burst in with such furious cries of disappointment and rage.

'Now there was a repetition of the work of holding the door-way, except that I had to stand by a hole instead of a door, while Williams picked away at the far wall to make an opening for escape into the next room. There was more desperate and almost hopeless fighting, as it seemed, but most of the poor fellows were got through the hole. Again I had to drag Conley through, a terrific task because he was a very heavy man. We were now all in a little room that gave upon the inner line of defence that had been made. We (Williams and Robert Jones and William Jones and myself) were the last men to leave the hospital, after most of the poor fellows had already got through the hole.'

The two Joneses had apparently been defending this room for some time, and had already passed most of their patients out through the window. Robert Jones had been slightly wounded in the fight, a spear-scrape on the abdomen — a particularly close shave. When all the patients were out, Hook, Williams and the two Joneses

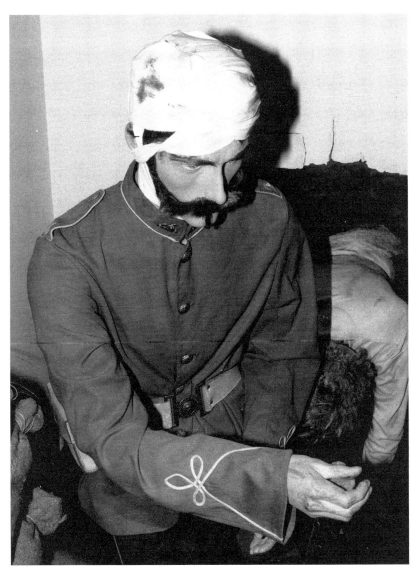

Below: The claustrophobic struggle for the hospital is captured in this display in the on-site museum. (Natal Museums Service/Author)

clambered through the window after them. The last patient, Sergeant Maxfield, was delirious, '...and although they dressed him, he refused to move. Robert Jones made a last rush to try and get him away, but when he got back into the room he saw that Maxfield was being stabbed by the Zulus as he lay on the bed.'

Having escaped from the building, the men's ordeal was by no means over; dropping into the yard, they found that they were in a dangerous no man's land, with their comrades thirty yards away behind the biscuit-box barricade in front, and the Zulus massing behind the abandoned mealie-bag walls on each side. The fire from the garrison made any attempt by the Zulus to enter the yard almost suicidal, but from time to time a warrior would risk it to try to intercept the patients as they crossed the open ground. According to Chard, one of the first patients out:

'Trooper Hunter, Natal Mounted Police, escaping from the hospital, stood still for a moment, hesitating which way to go, dazed by the glare of the burning hospital, and the firing that was going on all around. He was assegaied before our eyes, the Zulu who killed him immediately afterwards falling.'

Private Roy recalled that, '...my rifle got disabled, so I fixed my bayonet and charged out of the house. While we were charging out, the old soldier [his companion] got wounded in the ear. There were about thirty Zulus chasing us, but the men inside the fort shot them before they could harm us.' According to Chaplain Smith, '...one poor fellow [Jenkins] venturing through one of these [holes] was also seized and dragged away'. This is odd because Chard mentions that during the fight Private Jenkins '...saying "Look out, Sir!" [and] gave my head a duck down just as a bullet whizzed over it. He had noticed a Zulu who was quite near in another direction taking a deliberate aim at me. For all the man could have known, the shot might have been aimed at himself.' There was only one Jenkins — Private James Jenkins, 1/24th — at Rorke's Drift, and clearly he cannot have been in the hospital and on the wall with Chard. Wherever he was, however, he was killed during the fight. Corporal Allen and Private Hitch did their best to help the patients across the space and into the final perimeter. Hitch's resilience was extraordinary. He had continued to assist in the defence of the biscuit-box line until his injury at last got the better of him:

'I was serving out ammunition myself when I became thirsty and faint. I got worse, a chum tore out the lining of Mr Dunne's coat and tied it around my shoulder. I got so thirsty that I could not do much, in fact we were all exhausted and the ammunition being counted.

'Deakin, a comrade, said to me when I was leaning back against the biscuit boxes, "Fred, when

it comes to the last shall I shoot you?" I declined. "No, they have very nearly done for me and they can finish me right out when it comes to the last." I don't remember much after that.'

Once all the men who were going to get out of the hospital had done so and the wounded had been taken to Surgeon Reynolds's makeshift hospital on the storehouse verandah, the garrison settled in to defend the painfully small area of ground remaining. But, appallingly vulnerable as their position must have seemed, the Zulus had gained little by their successes so far, and the options open to them were now more limited than before. As the roof of the hospital flared up, it illuminated the whole of that side of the battlefield, highlighting the Zulus as they surged out of the darkness long before they could charge home. Gunner Howard recalled:

'When the flames burst out it was all the better for us, for we could see the [Zulus] and they could not see us. Didn't we give it to them anyhow! They sheered off...'

Lugg agreed:

'The thatch roof burst out into flames, and made it as light as day, and before they had time to retreat we were pouring bullets into them like hail. We could see them falling in scores. Then you could hear suppressed British cheers. They kept up the attack all night with no better luck. We knocked them down as fast as they came.'

Dunne recalled:

'As the night wore on the attack slackened from time to time; all firing ceased for the moment, and profound silence reigned, broken only by the words of command of the Zulu leaders, which sounded strangely close. How we longed to know what they said! Every man was then on the alert straining eyes and ears to detect the rush which was sure to follow, only to be checked each time by a withering volley. Luckily the supply of ammunition was very plentiful and it was served out as required, the Chaplain, the Rev. George Smith, being very active in helping to distribute it.'

Smith, indeed, earned himself something of a reputation during the fight. Adendorff told Walter Stafford that:

'You will always find that in a tight corner there is a hard case and there was one at Rorke's Drift. This man was cussing all the time. The Rev. Smith went to him and said, "Please, my good man, stop that cussing. We may shortly have to answer for our sins." The reply he got was, "All right Mister, you do the praying and I will send the black Bs to Hell as fast as I can.'

Sir Garnet Wolseley heard it said that Smith was exhorting the men with the cry, 'Don't swear boys, and shoot them!' Private John Jobbins of 'B' Company thought that Smith's prayers were answered; 'All that night a minister was praying in the fort that they would go away. God helped us and gave us the victory.'

After dark, the Zulus turned their attention to the line at the far end of the storehouse. Here the barricades tended to obscure the glare from the burning building, and the Zulus could muster in a relative degree of safety. They launched a series of desperate attacks on the stone cattle-kraal and gradually forced the defenders back, first to the interior partition, and then to the inside wall. But the results of this success were limited, as Chard explained:

'They also attacked the eastern end of our position, and after being several times repulsed, eventually got into the kraal, which was strongly built with high walls, and drove us to the middle, and then to the inner wall of the Kraal — the enemy occupying the middle wall as we abandoned it. This wall was too high for them to use it

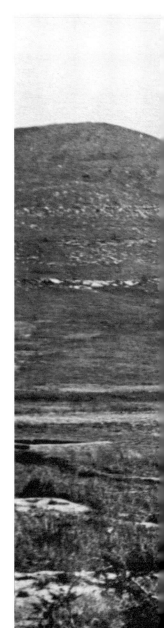

Left: Private William Roy, 1/24th, a patient in the hospital who was awarded the DCM for his part in its defence. (Author's collection)

Right: As darkness falls, the Zulus completely surround the post, and the struggle is illuminated by the flames of the burning hospital. A very accurate rendition of the scene from a drawing by Bourne which accompanied his account of the battle. (RRW Museum, Brecon)

Below: The storehouse and walls of Fort Bromhead, abandoned at the end of the war; photographed from the foot of Shiyane, looking towards kwaSingqindi hill to the south-west. (Keith Reeves collection)

effectively to fire over, and a Zulu no sooner showed his head over it than he was dropped, being so close that it was almost impossible to miss him.'

During this struggle Private Michael Minehan of 'B' Company felt something clutching at his leg, and looking down saw a hand grabbing at him from out of the straw; he 'prodded' the straw with his bayonet and transfixed a Zulu who had crawled through to get at him.

After the assault on the cattle-kraal failed, the Zulu attacks became increasingly erratic. Henry Hook, as eloquent as ever, gave an evocative impression of their last rushes:

'They could not get at us, so they went away, and had ten or fifteen minutes of a war-dance. This roused them up again, and their excitement was so intense that the ground fairly seemed to shake. Then, when they were goaded to the highest pitch, they would hurl themselves at us.'

Chard described how the attacks gradually burnt themselves out, and how the rest of the weary night passed:

'...every now and then a confused shout of 'Usutu!' [uSuthu!] from many voices seemed to show that they were going to attack from one side, and immediately the same thing would happen on the other, leaving us in doubt as to where they meant to attack. About midnight or a little after the fire slackened, and after that, although they kept us constantly on the alert, by feigning, as before, to come on at different points, the fire was of a desultory character. Our men were careful, and only fired when they could get a chance. The flame of the burning Hospital was now getting low, and as pieces of the roof fell in, or hitherto unburnt parts of the thatch ignited, the flames would blaze up illuminating our helmets and faces. A few shots from the Zulus, replied to by our men — again silence, broken only by the same thing repeatedly happening. This sort of thing went on until about 4 a.m. and we were anxiously waiting for daybreak and the renewal of the attack, which their comparative, and at length complete silence, led us to expect.'

By now the men in the garrison must have been completely spent. Their emotions had been stretched to the limit of endurance in hour after hour of fierce close-quarters fighting, and images of violent death were literally piled up around them. They were physically exhausted by the prodigious expenditure of energy needed to sustain the desperate, primeval nature of the fighting, and by the continual handling of their own weapons. According to Henry Hook:

'...we did so much firing that [the rifles] became hot, and the brass of the cartridges softened, the result being that the barrels got very foul and the cartridge-chamber jammed. My own rifle was jammed several times, and I had to work

Left: Private John Jobbins, a member of 'B' Company, who served in the defence. (Tim Day)

Below: Chaplain George Smith, sketched by J.N. Crealock, in the long black coat, faded green, which served as his campaign kit. (Sherwood Foresters Museum)

away with the ram-rod 'til I cleared it. We used the old three-sided bayonet, and ... They were very fine weapons too, but some were very poor in quality, and either twisted or badly bent. Several were like that after the fight; but some terrible thrusts were given, and I saw dead Zulus pinned to the ground by the bayonets going through them.

'All this time the sick and wounded were crying out for water. We had a water-cart full of water, but it was just by the deserted hospital, and we could not hope to get it until day broke, when the Zulus might begin to lose heart and stop their mad rushes. But we could not bear the cries any longer, and three or four of us jumped over the boxes and ran and fetched some water in.'

Much has been written about the recoil of the Martini-Henry; in fact it was not as heavy as some accounts have suggested, just a steady thump in the shoulder as the shot was fired. After ten rounds, however, there came the first trace of an ache in the shoulder muscles, and after twenty it was difficult not to flinch when pulling the trigger. As Hook suggests, the recoil became more and more pronounced as the chamber and barrel became

fouled Many men must have suffered severe headaches as a result. After a hundred rounds, it is difficult to imagine that anyone could fire the rifle efficiently. By then the barrel would have been so hot as to burn one's hands.

Under these circumstances, one wonders how well Chard's men would have coped with a fresh Zulu onslaught in the morning. Furthermore, Chard noted that although, '...each man had a good supply of ammunition in his pouches, we had only about a box and a half besides'. It was fortunate for the garrison that the attackers were in an even worse state.

The battle of Rorke's Drift proved also a terrible ordeal for the attackers, most of whom were middle-aged men who had run fifteen or twenty miles across country and forded the Mzinyathi before the battle began. They had sustained several hours of hand-to-hand fighting while completely exposed to the most appalling close-range fire from which they had no protection whatsoever. They had clambered over the barricades — a demanding feat in itself — and had faced the terrible bayonets time and again. Seized by the burning thirst which

Below: Chaplain Smith photographed as a member of the Army Chaplains' Department. He is wearing his South Africa 1879 medal, Egypt Medal and Khedive's Star. (Army Chaplains' Department Museum)
Below right: A folding chair which apparently belonged to Chaplain Smith, and which he had with him at Rorke's Drift. (RRW Museum, Brecon)

so often afflicts men in the psychic stress of combat, they had no water-bottles and no water-carts. Wounded, there was no doctor on hand to tend them; they simply lay out in the open and bled until they died, unless they managed to crawl away, or a friend or kinsman braved the fire to drag them off. And — which must have been all the more disheartening it had all been to no avail. Each time some limited success offered them a promise of victory, it proved illusory, and the British remained as firmly entrenched as ever. Muziwento, a Zulu boy whose father had fought at Isandlwana, remembered Rorke's Drift as it was described to him by those who took part. Their account was short but to the point, and suggests the extent to which the two sides had fought each other to a standstill:

'The Zulus arrived at Jim's house. They fought, they yelled, they shouted, "It dies at the entrance! It dies in the door-way! It dies in the entrance! It dies in the doorway!" They stabbed the sacks; they dug with their assegais. They were struck; they died. They set fire to the house. It was no longer

fighting; they were now exchanging salutations merely.'

The fact is that to many of the Zulus the fight must have seemed hopeless after the attacks on the cattle-kraal failed. They had now assaulted every side of the post in conditions that suited them best. They had set fire to the hospital, they had shot at the defenders, they had rushed them with their spears; there was nothing left to try. Under normal circumstances the Zulus did not favour night attacks, and it says much for their extraordinary determination that they continued the battle long after dark. By about 9 or 10 o'clock, however, they had begun to drift away. Many no doubt slipped off of their own accord, but for the most part the retreat was orderly. Some crossed back into Zululand via Rorke's Drift, but the majority went back the way they had come. Some even wandered farther down stream on the Natal bank before returning to their homes; there is a tradition among the descendants of the missionary families who lived at Eland's Kraal, a few miles south of Fugitives' Drift, that on the morning of the 23rd exhausted Zulus retreating from Rorke's Drift

Above: After dark, the Zulu attacks shifted to the area of the cattle-kraal. The kraal seen here has been reconstructed approximately on the site of the original; the church behind it was built on the site of the store. Note how the rocky ledge gave the defenders a distinct height advantage. (Ian Castle)

crossed through the Mission lands, dragging their shields behind them.

For the defenders of Rorke's Drift, the first cold, grey light of dawn, just after 5.20 on the 23rd, brought a sight of utter devastation. A heavy pall of smoke hung over the post, carrying with it the acrid smell of roasted flesh. Hundreds of Zulu dead were sprawled around the post, piled up, in places where the attack had been fiercest, almost to the top of the barricade. Not all the Zulu wounded had been evacuated, and there must have been dozens lying about, flopping grotesquely and groaning in agony.

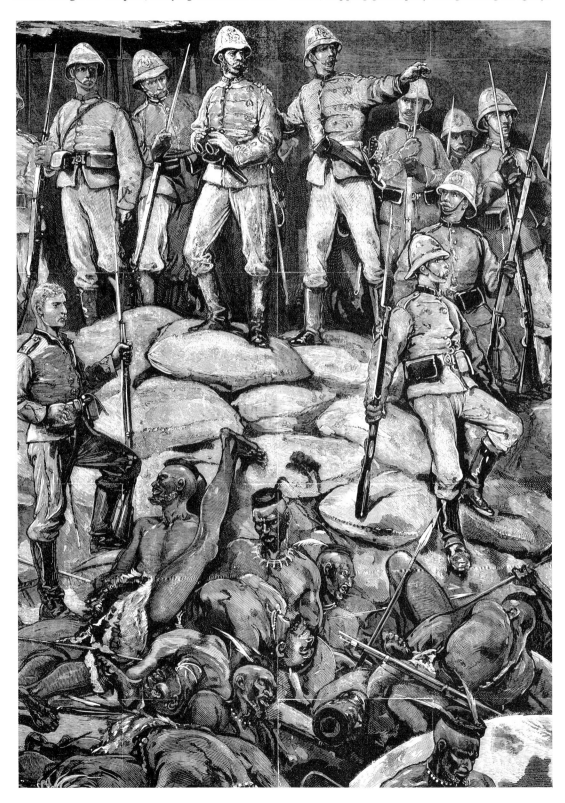

Right: *A grim illustration from* The Graphic *which suggests something of the carnage revealed on the morning of the 23rd. In places the Zulu bodies were heaped to the top of the mealie-bag ramparts. Curiously, the artist has accurately represented the Zulus as middle-aged men wearing the headring, but some of the details of the soldiers' uniforms are incorrect.*

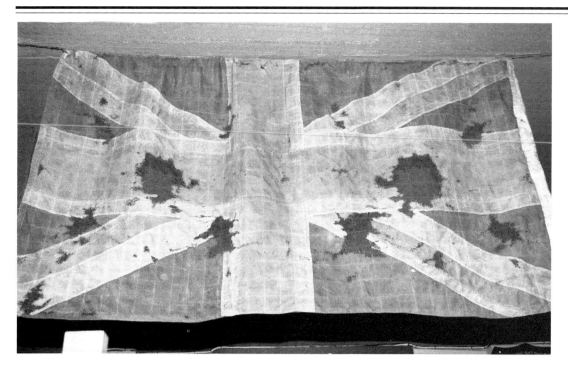

Shields, spears and firearms littered the field, and the yard was carpeted with spilt grain from the mealie-bags, cartridge cases and the brown paper wrappers from the cartridge packets, battered helmets and discarded pieces of equipment. The men of the garrison must have been an awful sight; blackened by grime, battered, bloody.

Two of the men who had spent the night outside the perimeter stood up and identified themselves. Private Waters, with his blackened features, '... was very nearly shot in coming out, one of our men at the wall raising his rifle to do so at the sight of his black face and strange costume, but Waters cried out just in time to save himself.'

Gunner Howard emerged from among the dead horses in the bush at the front of the hospital. Then, to the garrison's surprise, a solitary Zulu stood up among the dead in the cattle-kraal, fired at the defenders — missed — and made off towards the river. Walter Dunne thought that he actually walked, which seems unlikely, but he was certainly unhurried. Several of the garrison fired shots after him, but Chard was rather pleased to note that 'the plucky fellow got off'.

There was no sign of the Zulu *impi*, but Chard was only too aware that his position was still precarious. He fully expected the Zulus to return to the attack at any moment, and there was no prospect of relief. The fugitives from Isandlwana had been convinced that Lord Chelmsford's Column had shared the same fate as the camp, and the only other nearby garrison was at Helpmekaar. If the Zulus had made a major strike into Natal, Helpmekaar might already have fallen and Zulus might well be half-way to Pietermaritzburg by now. Chard cautiously ordered out patrols to collect up

the Zulu weapons, and to remove the thatch from the storehouse. Then, '...we increased the strength of the defences as much as possible, strengthening and raising our walls, putting sacks on the biscuit boxes, etc.'

Patrolling the battlefield was a grisly business. The bodies of the British dead that had fallen near the hospital lay out in the open, badly cut about. Many of the Zulus had suffered the most ghastly wounds, and in places, in front of the hospital, where the assault had been fiercest and the dead lay thickest, their limbs seemed to have become tightly entwined with one another in the grotesque attitudes of violent death. Dunne noted that the Zulus were, '...all "ring-kop", that is, married men, who alone wear a black ring woven into the hair of the head'. Henry Hook went out to see if he had hit the man he had fired at early in the fight the previous afternoon — 'he was lying behind an anthill with a hole in his skull. I'd clipped him'. George Edwards sought out the body of the Zulu commander who had fallen earlier in the fight, in the hope of procuring his cloak as a souvenir. He was disappointed to find that someone had beaten him to it. Chard was impressed by the extraordinary wounds inflicted on some of the Zulus:

'One man's head was split open, exactly as if done with an axe. Another had been hit just between the eyes, the bullet carrying away the whole of the back of his head, leaving his face perfect, as though it were a mask, only disfigured by the small hole made by the bullet passing through. One of the wretches we found, one hand grasping a bench which had been dragged from the hospital, and sustained thus in the position we found him in, while in the other hand he clutched the knife with which he had mutilated one of our poor fellows, over whom he was still leaning.'

Not all the dead were Zulus, Hook recalls:

'One of the first things I did was to go up to the man who was still looking over our breastworks with his rifle presented to the spot where so many of the Zulus had been. I went up to him, and saw that he did not move, and that he looked very quiet. I went nearer and said, "Hello, what are you doing here?" He made no answer, and did not stir. I went still closer, and something made me tilt his helmet back, as you sometimes tilt back a hat when you want to look closely into a face. As I did so I saw a bullet-mark in his forehead, and knew that he was dead.'

This patrolling was dangerous work, and both Lugg and Hook had narrow escapes. Lugg had left the perimeter when a warrior suddenly sprang up and jammed the muzzle of his musket against him, but the gun misfired and Lugg snatched a hunting-knife from his belt and killed his assailant. This incident earned Lugg the African name of 'Gwazamazulu' ('the stabber of Zulus'). Hook, meanwhile, had wandered further from the buildings:

'I went away, and was walking in the dry bed of a little stream near the drift with my own rifle in my right hand and a bunch of assegais over my shoulder. Suddenly I came across an unarmed Zulu lying on the ground, apparently dead but bleeding from the leg. Thinking it strange that a dead man should bleed, I hesitated, and wondered whether I should go on, as other Zulus might be lurking about. But I resumed my task. Just as I was passing, the supposed dead man seized the butt of my rifle and tried to drag it away. The bunch of assegais rattled to earth.

'The Zulu suddenly released his grasp of the rifle with one hand, and with the other fiercely endeavoured to drag me down. The fight was short and sharp; but it ended by the Zulu being struck in the chest with the butt and knocked to the ground. The rest was quickly over.'

The roof of the hospital had fallen in, but the walls were still standing, and Chard ordered some of the men to demolish them as best they could to clear the field of fire. The ubiquitous Hook again:

'We were ordered to put ropes through the loopholes of the walls of the hospital and pull them

Below: Although this sketch was made by J.N. Crealock after the battle of Ulundi, it gives some impression of how the garden in front of the hospital must have looked on the morning of the 23rd. The curious crouching position of many of the corpses (right) was commented on by several observers. (Sherwood Foresters Museum)

Above: *This photograph purports to show a burial detail of the 2/24th; in fact, it is clearly posed (the 'dead' Zulus have spears tucked under their arms), and was probably taken at Pinetown at the end of the War ('SB' Bourquin)*

down. This we did, and the walls, which had already been weakened by our picks, partially collapsed.'

While this work was going on, Private Beckett was found lying out in the ditch in front of the hospital. His stomach injury was severe, and, although he was taken into the fort and Surgeon Reynolds did his best to save him, he died shortly afterwards. Two African survivors also made themselves known to the post; one was Chard's wagon driver, who came down from the Shiyane terraces, '...looking more dead than alive' after his ordeal. The other was a private of the NNC who had survived Isandlwana. Chard was obviously suspicious of this man, and:

'...sent for Daniells the Pontman, who could speak Zulu a little, to interview him. Daniells had armed himself with Spalding's sword, which he flourished in so wild and eccentric a manner that the poor wretch thought his last hour had come. He professed to be a friendly and to have escaped

from Isandhlwana, and I sent him with a note to the Officer Commanding at Helpmekaar, explaining our situation and asking for help.'

Then, at about 7 a.m. a large body of Zulus suddenly appeared along the shoulder of kwaSingqindi hill, to the south-west, and Chard quickly called in his patrols:

'A large body of the enemy (I believe the same who attacked us) appeared on the hills to the south-west. I thought at the time that they were going to attack us, but from what I now know from Zulus, and also of the numbers we put *hors de combat*, I do not think so.'

This assessment was probably correct. The Zulus had carefully taken up a position out of rifle-range, and there is no suggestion that at any point they deployed to attack. From the slopes of kwaSingqindi, which look out over the sloping flats running down to the Drift, they could see what Chard could not; that there was another body of armed men approaching the Drift. Assistant

Commissary Dunne wrote:

'We all scanned them anxiously, fearing that they might be a fresh body of the enemy, and we felt, and said to each other, that in that case our doom was sealed. Even at that distance there was something strangely silent and solemn about them which depressed our hearts.'

A large part of this new force was clearly black, and the red-coats seemed so few that many at Rorke's Drift thought they were the victorious Zulu army coming on from looting the camp at Isandlwana. According to Chard, '...we improvised a flag', and men were sent up on to the storehouse roof and the high-points of the barricade to see if they could identify the approaching force. It is interesting, incidentally, that Chard talks of an improvised flag; there is no evidence that the Union flag was flown at Rorke's Drift during the fight — indeed it is highly unlikely because it was being used to identify Lord Chelmsford's Headquarters' tent. There exists a Union flag said to have been flown at Rorke's Drift, but it is almost certain that the connection is apocryphal and dates from some years after the Battle. According to Hook:

'Two of our men had been sent on to the roof of the storehouse signalling with flags when the Zulus meant to attack us. This gave us time to be ready for them. The signallers were still able to stand above the ground, so that they could see a good distance. We saw their flags going wildly. What was it? Everybody was mad with anxiety to know whether it could be friends to relieve us, or more Zulus to destroy us. We watched the flags flapping, and then learnt that signals were being made in reply. We knew we were safe and that friends were marching up to us.'

The column down at the Drift was Lord Chelmsford's force, and, as its advanced guard came up, the Zulus of kwaSingqindi quietly disappeared, heading back behind Shiyane and down towards the Mzinyathi valley. For Chelmsford's troops, also, the relief march had been an anxious time. It will be remembered that the force was some miles away from Isandlwana when it was attacked the previous noon, and Chelmsford was blissfully unaware of the dramatic events unfolding there. When, at last, a stream of messages alerted him to the possibility of something at the camp having gone wrong, he marched back as quickly as possible, only to find that the *impi* had already withdrawn, leaving the camp ransacked and the defenders slaughtered. It was impossible to march back to Rorke's Drift immediately so Chelmsford bivouacked that night on the battlefield. The men under his command had the harrowing experience of sleeping among the dead. Many awoke next morning to find that they had been lying next to the disembowelled bodies of comrades to whom they had bade

farewell the day before. Chelmsford moved out before dawn, sparing his men a full view of the horrors around them, and marched them back to Rorke's Drift as quickly as possible. As they crossed the valley of the Manzimyama, the stream which flows behind Isandlwana mountain, a large group of Zulus suddenly loomed up from the valleys on their left, and moved across their front, disappearing into the hills to the north of Isandlwana. From the direction of their march, they must have crossed the Mzinyathi downstream of the Drift, perhaps near its junction with the Batshe, and they must have left the battlefield two or three hours before dawn. The two forces passed quite close to each other, and some of the NNC and Zulu speakers on Chelmsford's staff called across to them. The men said that they were the uThulwana, and that they were returning from 'the other side of the river there-away'.

There was something dream-like, almost surreal, about this incident, and it wasn't merely a product of the overwrought nerves of the men who witnessed and described it. Two armies that had spent the previous day endeavouring to destroy each other, passed by close enough to converse with each other, yet neither felt able to renew the struggle. Men on both sides were struck by the strangeness of it. Nothing reveals more clearly how both sides had been utterly spent by their exertions. Yet it should be noted that even in defeat the Zulus were retiring in good order, grouped under their officers; for them Rorke's Drift was certainly not a rout. For Lord Chelmsford, the news that the Zulus had crossed the Mzinyathi was not reassuring.

When his force arrived at the Drift, Chelmsford was relieved to find that the ponts had not been damaged. The sunken hawsers were recovered, and the infantry were ferried across while the NNC and mounted volunteers plunged into the water. They had crossed into Zululand at exactly the same spot just thirteen days before. It was not at all clear to Chelmsford whether Rorke's Drift had held; a cloud of smoke hung over the post and the Zulus could still be seen on the slopes of kwaSingqindi opposite. The Volunteers were deployed along the bank to cover any attack, while Lieutenant-Colonel F.C. Russell and Lieutenant Walsh of the Mounted Infantry were sent up with a few men to investigate. Even down at the Drift, however, Chelmsford's men could hear the ringing cheers of the garrison when they realized that relief was at hand. 'We broke into roar after roar of cheering,' recalled Hook with elation, 'waving red coats and white helmets, and we cheered again and again.' But it was a time of mixed emotions for the relieving column, as Dunne describes:

'Approaching cautiously at first, a mounted officer, when reassured, galloped up and anxiously enquired if any of the men from Isandlwana had

escaped and joined us. Sadly we answered "No!" Overcome by emotion at the terrible certainty conveyed by that short word, he bent down to his horse's neck trying in vain to stifle the sobs which broke from his overcharged heart. ... Lord Chelmsford next rode up. No one could envy him then, for in defeat, as in success, all thoughts centre on the commander. His first words were, "I thank you all for your gallant defence." Then the main body of the Column began to arrive. Strange arrival! No train of waggons to park — no tents to pitch — weary and sad they looked from fatigue, hunger and anxiety. Fortunate it was that we were able to provide them with food, for they had been without for eighteen hours.'

It is ironic that the defenders of Rorke's Drift should be in a position to offer comfort to the much stronger force led by Chelmsford himself. The arrival of Chelmsford's men meant that the immediate danger had passed and the defenders could at last try to rid themselves of the after effects of the night. Chard was:

'... glad to seize the opportunity to wash my face in a muddy puddle, in company with Private Bush of the 24th, whose face was covered with blood from a wound in the nose caused by the bullet which had passed through and killed Private Cole 24th. With the politeness of a soldier, he lent me his towel, or, rather, a very dirty half of one, before using it himself, and I was glad to accept it.

'In wrecking the stores in my wagon, the Zulus had brought to light a forgotten bottle of beer, and Bromhead and I drank it with mutual congratulations on having come safely out of so much danger.'

As the column came up, the men wandered about together, talking over the details of the fight. Evidence of the garrison's exhaustion was everywhere. Captain W. Penn Symons of the 24th found Private Minehan still in the cattle-kraal, struck dumb with fatigue. Minehan pointed out to him the body of the Zulu under the straw, and told the story of the incident by gesture. Lieutenant John Maxwell of the NNC met two of the 24th who:

'...bared their shoulders and I saw that they were black and blue and swollen, caused by the recoil or kicking of their Martinis, proving to what extent they had been firing. In fact they told me that towards daylight they were unable to place the rifle to the shoulder, but held it pointing out to the front and firing. They had during the night to change shoulder constantly, which caused both being in this state.'

Fifteen of Chard's men had been killed outright and two more — Lance-Sergeant Williams

Above and opposite page: John North Crealock's original sketch of the Mounted Infantry galloping up to the relief of Rorke's Drift on the morning of the 23rd. The storehouse with the mealie-bag redoubt in front is on the left, the ruins of the hospital are on the right. It is interesting to compare the original sketch with the engraved version which appeared in a supplement to The Illustrated London News on 8 March 1879. Crealock's expressive rendition of the Shiyane terraces has been further exaggerated by the engravers. (Crealock's sketch; Sherwood Foresters Museum)

and Private Beckett — were mortally wounded. Lieutenant Maxwell saw five bodies laid out in the cattle-kraal. Fifteen men were suffering from wounds of various degrees of severity, and most of the other survivors had nicks, cuts, grazes and bruises. Almost all the badly wounded had been hit in the upper part of the body, mostly by gun-shots, which shows the how effectively the Zulus had been kept at bay.

Dead and wounded Zulus lay everywhere. Later, during the afternoon, it was found that a large number of wounded Zulus had hidden in the orchard and garden in front of the hospital. Two companies of the 3rd NNC and a few of the 24th, '...quickly drew these fields and killed them with bayonet, butt and assegai'. The 24th were in no mood to be merciful, and during the next few days there were a number of incidents of retribution.

The British noted that the uThulwana and its incorporated *amabutho* had suffered heaviest in the battle. Most of the dead were observed to be old men, some of them 'quite wizened', suggesting how far the rigours of the campaign had already taken their toll. According to one account, '...many of the bodies by their shields and other distinctive marks, such as plumes, head-gear, rings, etc., were identified as belonging to the king's chief and favourite regiments.' Most, the British observed

with some disappointment, were quite short, with only a few reaching to six feet or more, although:

'One huge fellow, who must have been, in life, quite 7 feet high lay on his back with his heels on the top of the parapet and his head nearly touching the ground, the rest of his body supported by a heap of his dead comrades.'

Curiously, a large number seem to have fallen in the same position, hunched forward on their elbows, their knees drawn up to their chins. Burying the bodies was obviously a priority. The NNC, whose fear of *umnyama*, would not allow them to touch the corpses, were employed in digging pits around the post. Both Hook and Dunne suggest that two large trenches were dug in front of the hospital. The location of one of these — to the left front of the post — was first marked many years ago, but the exact site of the other is uncertain. Photographs of the battlefield taken at the end of 1879 show a large, sunken, rectangular area out near the road, and this may well be a burial pit; it is still visible today, although its exact function has yet to be determined. The men of the 24th used reins to drag the bodies away from the ruins and dumped them in the graves.

How many Zulus died at Rorke's Drift? According to Chard's careful account, 351 were buried on the first day after the fight, and many more had crawled off to die in the surrounding countryside. About fifty blood-stained shields were found down by the river, and the British believed that the Zulus had dragged their badly wounded comrades off and tipped them into the Drift. Perhaps they had; if these men were critically injured, their prospects for survival were minimal, and a quick death by drowning was merciful. It is equally feasible that the wounded were carried down to the river on shields, and then helped across by friends and kinsmen. Dead Zulus were come across for months afterwards. There were many lying out along the line of retreat, and when fatigue parties went up to the Shiyane terraces to collect stone to reinforce the defences, they found many bodies hidden in the nooks and crannies between the boulders. Some had undoubtedly crawled there to die; others had probably been given a makeshift burial. If it were impossible to remove all their dead, the Zulus customarily hid them in rocks and covered them with a shield. Lieutenant Henry Harford, the Staff Officer of the 3rd NNC, found a skeleton lying some distance from the post a few weeks after the battle. He took Surgeon Reynolds to see it, and they both admired the man's physique, as if he were a hunting trophy. Well, this was the age of unfettered scientific curiosity, and both Reynolds and Harford took away a few bones with a view to donating them to a museum; Harford was particularly fascinated by the soles of the feet which were of thick, horny skin, and which were the only part of him other than bones that had not decomposed. As late as March, Lieutenant Maxwell and two colleagues were climbing the Shiyane when they found, '...in a cave near the summit three bodies, which were quite hard and sound'. Maxwell thought they had been wounded and crawled thus far to die, but it seems odd that three men should have made for such an out of the way spot; they had probably been placed there by their friends.

On reflection, Chard admitted that the number of 351 dead was a considerable underestimate. One Zulu source later suggested that as many as 600 had been killed, which seems quite plausible. It is impossible to say how many were wounded; normally, in any given battle, more men are wounded than are killed, but it may be that the figures would have been different at Rorke's Drift because, by and large, the fighting was confined to a narrow but extremely destructive zone around the barricades. At close range, where accuracy of fire was much greater, and where any wounded who still looked dangerous might have been shot again or bayoneted, the proportion of killed to wounded must have risen;. indeed many of the wounded that had not managed to escape, were finished off on the 23rd. Nevertheless, the wounded must have numbered several hundred. Some of these would have made the long journey home only to die days or even weeks later from shock or gangrene. The *izinyanga*, the medicine doctors, were skilled at treating everyday injuries with herbal concoctions and poultices. The clean wound caused by a

Below: *The site of the post photographed in late 1879. This picture shows very clearly the Shiyane terrace; the depression in the foreground is believed to be a mass grave of the Zulu dead. (Africana Museum, Johannesburg)*

bayonet thrust healed easily if no vital organ had been damaged, as did a flesh wound caused by a Martini-Henry bullet. If the bullet struck bone, however, the bone shattered into splinters and the appalling wound was beyond the powers of the *izinyanga*.

If as many as 600 Zulus were killed at Rorke's Drift and a further 400 wounded — a purely arbitrary figure — then perhaps one man in four of the attacking force suffered an injury of some kind. In most armies a casualty rate of 10 per cent is often considered sufficient to have an adverse effect on the unit's morale. The Zulus suffered 15 per cent of their men dead and as many as 25 per cent wounded. That they continued to press home their attack in these circumstances is quite extraordinary. Small wonder that it was generally

thought throughout Zululand that the uThulwana '...was finished up at Jim's'. Small wonder that after the day's toll was counted, one Zulu commented, 'The dead are not to be counted, there are so many. The whole Zulu nation is weeping and mourning.'

Finally, before leaving the question of casualties at Rorke's Drift, it is interesting to note that an extraordinary amount of ammunition was expended. According to Chard, although the men had quite a few rounds in their pouches, there was only '...a box and a half besides'. Granting that about 120 men were still fighting, and allowing a high level of rounds remaining, say 40 rounds each, and including the rounds remaining in the boxes, that left a maximum of only 5,700 rounds among the garrison, out of an initial supply of more than

20,000. The men had expended at least 15,000 rounds, probably nearer 20,000, or between approximately 115 and 150 each on average. Many individuals in the thick of the fight no doubt fired off far more. This adds up to an extraordinary volume of fire, although the proportion of shots to hits was low — only one hit for every fifteen or twenty shots fired, and of those hits only one in two or three was fatal. No doubt the figures are distorted because much of the fighting took place in the dark, and presumably the fire was far more effective in the evening than at night. Nor is there any reason to suppose that 'B' Company were poor or unsteady shots; in fact, many of them seem to have been good shots, and their officers exercised a tight fire control. The realization that so much fire in any battle was inevitably ineffectual comes as something of a surprise, but it makes the fact that the Zulus endured it for so long all the more remarkable.

Left: A monument to the Zulu dead in front of the post, unveiled by King Goodwill Zwelithini in 1979. (Author's photograph)

Left: Regimental numerals carved into the rock on the flats below the Shiyane terrace; it is thought that they were put there by men collecting stone to build Fort Bromhead in the weeks after the battle. (Author's collection)

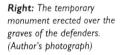

5. AWARDS AND SEQUALS

When the initial euphoria of the relief had subsided, Lord Chelmsford's Column had a busy time of it on Thursday, 22 January 1879. Although the arrival of Chelmsford's men effectively ended the garrison's ordeal, strategically the entire Column remained highly vulnerable. All the signs of the Zulu retreat suggested that they would not renew their attack immediately, but nothing was known of their intentions or whereabouts, and it was quite possible that they might return when they had regrouped. As a consequence, as Chard put it, '…we then had a very busy time making a strong position for the night'. While the Zulu dead were being dragged away, the ruins of the hospital were demolished and fresh loop-holes were knocked through the walls of the store. The mealie-bags were heaped up in new embrasures to accommodate the Column's guns, so that by nightfall the post was comparatively secure.

Chelmsford was keen to learn the details of the fight, and Hitch remembered that Lieutenant Bromhead brought the General to see him while Surgeon Reynolds was dressing his wounds later that morning. Hook found himself called to report in rather embarrassing circumstances:

'There was no time to sit and mope, and there were the sick and wounded as well as the rest to look after. So when the Commander-in-Chief arrived I was back at my cooking in my shirt-sleeves, making tea for the sick. A Sergeant ran up and said, "Lieutenant Bromhead wants you." "Wait 'til I put my coat on," I said. "Come as you are, straight away," he ordered, and with my braces hanging about me, I went into the midst of the officers. Lord Chelmsford asked me all about the defence of the hospital, as I was the last to leave the building.'

Once the living had been congratulated, the dead had to be buried and this, according to Hook, also took place on the 23rd:

'As for our own comrades, we buried them. This was done the day after the fight, not far from the place where they fell, and at the foot of the hill.'

Within a few days half of Chard's own No. 5 Company, Royal Engineers arrived at the post, and the graveyard was fenced off and a wooden cross placed on the site. Hook again:

'Soon afterwards the cemetery was walled in, and a monument was put up in the middle. The lettering was cut on it by a bandsman named Mellsop, who used bits of broken bayonets as chisels. He drew a capital picture of the fight. Those who had been killed in action were buried on one side of the cemetery, and those who had died of disease on the other. A curious thing was that a civilian named Byrne, who had taken part in

Right: The temporary monument erected over the graves of the defenders. (Author's photograph)

the defence and was killed, was buried outside the cemetery wall. I don't know why, except that he was not a regular soldier.'

This last comment is, indeed, curious because there is no indication today that any of the defenders lie outside the cemetery, and Byrne's name appears on the monument. Private Mellsop, who was not one of the defenders, seems to have been quite an artist, since he also contributed a sketch of the graves to *The Illustrated London News*. It is not entirely clear whether he actually designed and constructed the monument itself; if he did, he had obviously been a skilled stonemason in civilian life. Presumably he had other tools to hand, since it would have been almost impossible to construct the monument with nothing more than broken bayonets for chisels.

During the morning Major Spalding rode down from Helpmekaar with two or three volunteers from the garrison there, and they were shocked and appalled by the apocalyptic appearance of the post. The garrison at Helpmekaar had had an unpleasant night of it, cooped up in a similarly improvised laager of mealie-bags, and expecting the victorious Zulus to attack at any moment. Most of the survivors from Isandlwana had passed them by, too, but a few had stayed to help; one or two were so badly shaken by their experiences that they cried out throughout the night, 'Are they coming yet?' The glow of the burning hospital could clearly be seen in the distance at the foot of Shiyane, and long after dark the garrison heard the dull, flat sound of guns firing in the distance. This was Chelmsford's gunners, throwing shells into the camp at Isandlwana before retaking it, but to the men at

Above: *A private of the 24th, tentatively identified as Mellsop, the man who carved the names of the dead on the stone monument at the graves site. (Keith Reeves collection)*

Left: *An engraving of the cemetery, from a sketch by Mellsop. (Author's collection)*

Right: The monument at the grave site today; this wreath was laid on the occasion of the opening of the museum in January 1992. (Author's photograph)

Right: The monument at the grave site today; this wreath was laid on the occasion of the opening of the museum in January 1992. (Author's photograph)

Helpmekaar it suggested further heavy fighting far off in the night. At dawn next day, a heavy mist lay on the ridge, and at first a party of fleeing NNC were mistaken for Zulus, and almost fired upon. Then Chard's messenger arrived with the extraordinary news that Rorke's Drift had held.

The first night spent at Rorke's Drift after the battle was not a cheerful one, either. The Natal Volunteers were deployed in the cattle-kraal, and after an uncomfortable night awoke next morning to find the puffed-up bodies of several dead Zulus in the straw in which they had slept. The white troops had all been deployed inside the fort, while the 3rd NNC were posted on the slopes of Shiyane, to give advance warning of any Zulu approach. Their European officers and NCOs severely resented being left outside the defences; they had no regard for their own troops, and felt they would be caught between the fires of the garrison and the enemy if the Zulus attacked. When a false alarm was raised during the night, the NNC officers bolted for the fort, leaving their men to their fate. By morning the 3rd NNC had lost whatever faith they might once have had in their officers, and in the fighting mettle of the British Army. When this was reported to Lord Chelmsford, he ordered the regiment to parade, and directed its officers to ask the men whether they would stick by them and return to Zululand. Most said that they would not. They were worried that the Zulus might already be raiding their locations, and that their families and homes were at risk. Chelmsford ordered the officers to collect the NNCs' rifles and distinguishing red head-bands, and then dismissed the regiment. The warriors hurried off down the road to Helpmekaar, keen to get away from the war as fast as they could.

Chelmsford did not stay long either. However gallant the defence of Rorke's Drift, it could not disguise the fact that he had been utterly defeated. The Zulus had inflicted upon him one of the worst disasters suffered by the British Army during the colonial era. Not only had the camp at Isandlwana been taken, but 1,700 men lay dead in the green

Below: *Fort Bromhead; the impressive stone walls surrounding Rorke's old store, probably photographed in June 1879, when the post had been abandoned. ('SB' Bourquin)*

grass at the foot of the mountain; the survivors had been ignominiously chased out and were now cooped-up in a squalid little fort from which they had departed in high spirits less than a fortnight before. Chelmsford's entire invasion plan had been crushed and his surviving columns could expect to receive similar treatment at any point. He had to get back to Pietermaritzburg to re-assure the civil authorities, to shore up defence arrangements — which had been woefully neglected, and whose shortcomings were now painfully apparent — and to break the news to the Home Government, who had not wanted the war in the first place. Then, if the Zulus gave him a few days' grace, he would have to rethink the entire campaign. On the morning of the 24th Chelmsford thanked the men of his Column for their support, and with his Staff

rode off to Helpmekaar and thence to Pietermaritzburg. The Mounted Volunteers and Artillery went with him.

Rorke's Drift was now under the command of Colonel Richard Glyn of the 1/24th. Glyn had been the Column's nominal commander, though his role had been overshadowed by Chelmsford's presence and he had succumbed to a fit of depression following the annihilation of five companies of his battalion at Isandlwana. A feeling of gloom and despondency settled over the garrison. The men had no tents and no clothes other than those they were wearing, having lost everything else at Isandlwana. Even when tents were sent down the line, Glyn refused to allow them to be pitched outside the walls of the fort, and conditions remained cramped. Sentries had to improvise greatcoats from empty mealie-bags, cutting holes in the bottom and sides for head and arms. Dead bodies of Zulus, which by now were decomposing, were turning up with disconcerting regularity. Each night brought some new alarm as unusual sights and sounds played on the men's frayed nerves. On one occasion the alarm was sounded in the middle of the night by a civilian doctor attached to the Column, '...a good fellow' who, however, '...had had a bad go of fever and his nerves had all gone to pieces though he still did his duty'. When the troops had stood-to and taken their places around the barricades, someone asked the doctor why he had given the alarm. He replied, 'Good God! don't you hear them, sir? Why the frogs, sir. The Zulus are waking them as they advance!' On a wet night in summer in Zululand, the noise made by the frogs could be heard halfway to Pietermaritzburg.

The rain, which had held off for a few days before the battle, returned with a vengeance shortly afterwards. With no tents or coats, the men could do nothing but endure it, lying in the slush and mud, and sleeping fitfully under the long spears of rain. An exception was made in the case of 'B' Company whose men were allowed to sleep in the attic of the storehouse. The thatch had been removed, but a tarpaulin had been thrown over the rafters and this kept off the worst of the wet. The water did, however, tend to collect when the tarpaulin sagged between the rafters, and from time to time it would be given a push to sluice off the surplus. Henry Harford of the NNC described his experience one night when, in company with Doctor Reynolds, he tried to find a dry place to bed down:

'Suddenly we hit upon the idea of lying down under the eaves of B Company's roof, so coiled ourselves up in our soaking wet blankets, thanking our stars that at all events there would be no river running under us, when presently swish came about half a ton of water clean on top of us — B Company were emptying their tarpaulin! It was useless moving, as we could not better ourselves, and wet as we were, thanks to the temperature of atmosphere and the heat of our bodies, were comfortably warm as long as we stayed still.'

Such conditions were obviously far from ideal for men recovering from wounds received in the action, and on the 26th most of the wounded were shipped up to Helpmekaar, where it was anticipated there would be better facilities for them. In fact, things were little better for them there, though they had the attention of a dedicated and conscientious Surgeon of the Army Medical Department, D. Blair Brown, who commented:

'The wounded from Rorke's Drift, on arrival at Helpmekaar, were accommodated in the end of a corrugated zinc shed. This was one of several, filled with commissariat stores, chiefly bags of maize. Many of them had been exposed to the heavy rains then prevailing before being stored, and were decomposing and giving off the most offensive smell. Long square boxes containing biscuits were arranged along the side of the building, and empty sacks laid over them. This was all the bedsteads and bedding obtainable for more than a fortnight, during which time stores were making their way from the base of operations.'

Brown left detailed case notes on several of the injured, and they are worth quoting at some length because they strip away the façade of glory which has become rather too glibly attached to the story of the battle, and suggest something of the brutal reality beneath. Brown found that Corporal Mayer of the NNC was still suffering from the effects of the stab wound he had received at Sihayo's homestead:

'As there was no bleeding, I simply ordered the limb to be kept as quiet as possible. Next day, however, haemorrhage — which was found by two civil surgeons who attended to be impossible to control — took place. When I arrived he had fainted, and his pulse could only just be felt. No further bleeding took place for two days, when it burst forth again. Assisted by Surgeon McGann and others, the patient being put under chloroform, I enlarged the wound to look for the bleeding vessels. Having made the incisions, I found a large cavity filled with coagulated blood extending up the limb amongst the muscles ... after the clot was cleaned out, numerous points of bleeding were seen, none of which could be seized for torsion or ligature.'

After further investigation Brown managed to stem the flow and '...the wound healed rapidly'. On 15 February he left Helpmekaar for base hospital. He returned to duty and joined 'Buller's Horse', with which famous body he went through all reconnaissances and battles, including Ulundi.' Corporal Lyons, however, was a more difficult case. When Lyons reached Helpmekaar he was still suffering terribly from the gunshot wound that he had received while defending the back barricade;

an entrance wound was visible on the left side of his neck, but despite the efforts of 'several surgeons', the bullet could not be found:

'He complained of great pain in the neck on the slightest movement. When in bed, the pillow caused an increase in this. He had lost almost all the use of his arms and hands, especially the right one, which he described as "quite dead". Painful 'twitchings' were experienced in the arms. Whenever he wished to move his head from the bed someone had to support it between their hands before he could do so ... I put him under chloroform and made a prolonged attempt to find the bullet. The course I found it had taken was in a direct line with the spinal cord. I made a free opening in the middle line as far down the course as possible, and again attempted to reach the bullet. I found by digital examination now that the processes of two adjacent vertebrae were smashed. I could also feel the spinal cord itself. Pressure thereon instantly caused the patient to turn pale and the pulse to be almost imperceptible, and necessitated the immediate withdrawal of the chloroform and the adoption of artificial respiration.'

Brown had to abandon his attempt to find the bullet, and Lyons was sent down to Ladysmith where his condition had not improved a month later when he once again came under Brown's charge. 'He was suffering greatly from pain in his arms, and wished to have them both off to relieve him from it'. On examination, Brown found a lump beneath the muscle that had not been present before, and on opening it up discovered '...an ordinary round bullet with a rather long rough projection extending from its smooth surface'. Lyons healed rapidly and was sent home to England; he kept the bullet as a souvenir, wearing it on a watch-chain for the rest of his life.

Fred Hitch proved as tough as ever. Brown found that '...there was a great swelling on the whole shoulder... and ecchymosis. The tract of the wound was sloughing. Poultices and cold water sufficed to allay this, and the case did well.' Corporal Scammell of the NNC was also suffering from a shoulder wound:

'The bullet hit the back of the head at the posterior margin of the left sterno-mastoid at its origin, and took a course towards the middle of the scapular base, where the bullet had lodged subcutaneously, from which position it had been removed when I took charge of him ... the whole of the shoulder was greatly swollen and painful, requiring poultices. This case, after the usual slough came away, got on well.'

Corporal Allen had been lucky; the bullet which wounded him had '...entered near the insertion of the deltoid muscle to the humerus, and made its exit at the upper angle of the scapula, no bone or joint being touched. This wound sloughed and

Above: The musket ball which injured Corporal John Lyons, and which he later wore on his watch-chain. (RRW Museum, Brecon)

then very rapidly healed up.' Acting Assistant-Commissary Dalton's wound, however, aroused Brown's medical curiosity:

'The bullet entered about half an inch above the middle of the clavicle, and then made its escape posteriorly at the lowest border of the trapezius muscle. The course taken was curious, regularly running round the shoulder and down the back, escaping all the important structures ... After the slough came away the usual tenax was applied. The whole of the field medical equipment having been captured by the enemy at Isandhlwana, I had no antiseptic to use. I thought of quinine, which I knew was a wonderful preserver of animal tissues, and used a solution of that, experimenting in this case. It seemed to answer, as the wounds got on well after being injected several times with it...'

After Blair Brown had done his best for them, most of the patients were sent back to Ladysmith. They were well off away from Rorke's Drift, which became more insanitary and pestilent by the day. Captain Walter Parke Jones, RE, Chard's company commander, describes how sickness took a grip of the garrison, including Chard himself:

'One of my men died of diarrhoea yesterday, and that and fever have nearly knocked all my men over. Quite half the company is in hospital really ill, it is most depressing. My civilian sergeant is a shadow of his former self, ditto my groom. My senior sub, Chard, had to be sent to Ladysmith in an ambulance, very weak with fever. I cannot account for it at all as the place used to be very healthy. Of course, being crowded together in a fort with rotten meal and other stores, and difficulty about sanitary arrangements, has something to do with the question.'

Chard was struck down with fever in the middle of February; No doubt, as with most of the defenders, the traumatic events of the battle had exhausted him. According to an anonymous friend, the battle preyed on Chard's mind:

'He used to say that he fought Rorke's Drift many times over, as the events of that night were so firmly impressed on his memory that for several nights after he dreamt that the affair was happening again and that he was once more in command...'

On 17 February he was taken down to Pietermaritzburg in a wagon, escorted part of the way by a frontier farmer named Thomas Munro Carbutt, who had raised a particularly piratical volunteer unit, Carbutt's Rangers. Chard stayed with the Rangers' medical officer, Dr George Hyde, at his farm Aller Park. According to a local account, Chard was nursed back to health by Hyde's wife using a traditional remedy — wrapping him in a fresh goat's hide, to draw the fever! Dunne, too, was taken ill shortly afterwards:

'Fever and dysentery broke out which the Medical Officer had no means of combatting, for all the medicines had been destroyed in the Hospital when it was burnt by the Zulus. Things improved after a time, but not before many men had been laid low. I, too, sickened with typhoid fever and was sent off, early in March, in an ambulance to Helpmekaar, where a field hospital had been established. When we arrived it was raining heavily; a tent was pitched for me on the wet ground, some blankets were thrown inside, on which I flung myself too ill to do anything more, and there I was left to my own devices.'

Fortunately an officer of the Natal Mounted Police came to Dunne's rescue, and nursed him for three weeks until the fever subsided and he was well enough to be sent to Ladysmith.

There had been significant changes in the post at Rorke's Drift. Following the arrival of half of No. 5 Company, RE, the garrison had set about building a secure permanent fort. The ruins of the hospital were pulled down except for one wall which was incorporated into the defence, and a high, loop-holed stone wall was built around the store. Stone was taken from the cattle-kraals and from the boulder-strewn terraces nearby. Although the position remained cramped and insanitary, it was largely safe from Zulu attack. This fort seems to have been known as Fort Bromhead, although it is possible that this name referred only to the temporary fort of mealie-bags thrown together before the attack.

In fact, the Zulus did not press their advantage. For the best part of a month after Isandlwana, the inhabitants of Natal lay quaking in their beds in nightly expectation of a Zulu raid, and all along the border civilian farmers either rushed into hastily improvised laagers or fled to the safety of the Transvaal. Yet King Cetshwayo had never had any intention of invading Natal and, indeed, he hoped to win political advantage by holding his hand when the odds were so obviously in his favour. But he missed his chance to secure peace on favourable terms precisely for that reason, since his restraint merely allowed Chelmsford to regroup and reorganize. While the British government was embarrassed by Isandlwana, it was not prepared to bring the war to a halt until British prestige had been restored, and reinforcements were hurried to South Africa by the ship-load. It is unlikely, however, that Cetshwayo, even if he had wanted to, would have been able to launch an offensive immediately. Isandlwana and Rorke's Drift combined had been a terrible shock to the Zulus, and it took the *impi* more than a month to tend its wounds and recover. It was not until March that the king was able to call his men together to face a renewed British offensive.

Neither the king nor the nation were much impressed by the outcome at Rorke's Drift. Dabulamanzi's reputation suffered as a consequence and, as Mehlokazulu kaSihayo explained, most Zulus thought him, '...not a good general; he is too impulsive'. Despite wild rumours in the Natal Press that Dabulamanzi had been executed for disobeying the king's commands, he merely returned to his homestead outside Eshowe until public derision subsided. The uThulwana, too, had made themselves the laughing-stock of a nation who could not understand why they had attacked Rorke's Drift in the first place, nor why they had been beaten by only a handful of men:

'The Mbozankomo [uThulwana] regiment was finished up at Jim's — shocking cowards they were too. Our people laughed at them, some said "You! You are no men! You are just women, seeing that you ran away for no reason at all, like the wind!" Others jeered and said, "You marched off. You went to dig little bits with your assegais out of house of Jim, that had never done you any harm!"'

This was a particularly harsh judgement on men who had endured so much suffering, and it must have been deeply galling to the once proud warriors of the uThulwana. But their defeat had merely shown that they had had their day, and it was time to let the younger generation have their turn at the glory. Much of the honour for the victory at Isandlwana went to their rivals, the iNgobamakhosi.

When no Zulu attack materialized, the garrison at Rorke's Drift began to regain confidence and sent patrols out along the Mzinyathi to look for the bodies of fugitives killed on the 22nd, or to harry Zulus living on the far bank. One of these patrols recovered the Queen's Colour of the 1/24th, which Lieutenants Melvill and Coghill had tried to save but died in the attempt. For 'B' Company, the everyday duties of garrison life must have come as something of a relief. Hook was appointed batman to Major Wilsone Black of the 2/24th. A dynamic Scotsman, Black was the mainspring for the garrison's gradual return to offensive operations;

Above: *Major Gonville Bromhead; a sensitive portrait which captures something of the man's retiring personality. (Ron Sheeley collection)*

Top right: *The remains of Rorke's store, photographed c.1000. This is a similar view to an earlier photograph, but the building is more dilapidated; it has lost the glass from the window (left) and the attic door has collapsed. ('SB' Bourquin)*

Right: *The interior of Fort Bromhead, with Rorke's store on the right. The outline of the cattle-kraal can be seen on the ground to the left. The fort seems very large from this sketch, although these engravings were often extremely accurate. (Author's collection)*

Hook thought him, '...a nice gentleman ... I like him very much'. Black, whose shrill Scottish accent was commented on by several observers, could be heard, '...above the fort calling "H-o-o-k!" many times a day. So the men had their little joke, and whenever Hook was called for they shouted for Hook and then yelled out, "I think he's hooked it sir!", which always caused great merriment." '

In the aftermath of Isandlwana, the defence of Rorke's Drift took on a particularly heroic aspect. Since the Zulus had not pushed forward into Natal, it began to look increasingly as if the defence had saved Natal from the horrors of a Zulu invasion. This achievement seemed all the more positive when contrasted with the gloomy events of Isandlwana. It might perhaps be stretching the point to suggest that Chelmsford deliberately promoted Rorke's Drift as a means of obscuring the depth of his defeat on 22 January, but there can be little doubt that it did serve to divert awkward questions about the failings of his own generalship, and to re-assure the public, both in England and Natal, that the British red-coat was more than a match for the Zulus. This was the beginning of a process which has gradually shifted the focus of popular historical consciousness away from Isandlwana and on to Rorke's Drift. The tendency has been to present Isandlwana as the backdrop to the more dramatic events at Rorke's Drift, whereas in fact Rorke's Drift was merely a tactical side-show of no great strategic consequence, a bungled mopping-up operation in the aftermath of the far more important events across the river.

Chelmsford was certainly keen to draw attention to the defence, and as early as 1 February sent a note to Glyn which expressed the '...hope you have sent off Lt. Chard's report of the defence of Rorke's Drift post — I am anxious to send that little gleam of sunshine home as soon as possible'. Neither Chard nor Bromhead struck their seniors as being of the stuff of heroes, however. Major Francis Clery, Glyn's Staff Officer, was the man charged with prising a report out of Bromhead. Clery could be waspish in his judgement of others, and the picture he paints of Bromhead is scarcely a sympathetic one, but it does suggest the extent to which Bromhead's already reticent personality shied away from the attention he had aroused. Indeed, although the concept of post-traumatic shock was alien to Victorian society, which preferred not to dwell on the psychological effects of battle, such an horrific experience must have left wounds on the psyche as well as the body, and there are suggestions that this was the case:

'Well, Chard and Bromhead to begin with: both are almost typical in their separate corps of what would be termed the very dull class. Bromhead is a great favourite in his regiment and a capital fellow at everything except soldiering. So little was he held to be qualified in this way from

Above: 'All's well!' A corner of Fort Bromhead known as 'Bromhead's post', built on the angle he defended during the battle.(Author's collection)

unconquerable indolence that he had to be reported confidentially as hopeless. This is confidential, as I was told it by his commanding officer. I was about a month with him at Rorke's Drift after Isandlwana, and the height of his enjoyment seemed to be to sit all day on a stone on the ground smoking a most uninviting-looking pipe. The only thing that seemed equal to moving him in any way was any allusion to the defence of Rorke's Drift. This used to have a sort of electrical effect on him, for he would jump up and off he would go, and not a word could be got out of him. I used to find him hiding away in corners with a

Above: The interior of Fort Melvill, down by the Drift; note the two-wheeled water-cart, left. It may even have been the one that was inside the perimeter during the fight! (Author's collection)

Right: Drummer Keefe, a Rorke's Drift defender, photographed on his wedding day in the 1880s. (RRW Museum, Brecon)

friend helping him to complete this account, and the only thing that afterwards helped to lessen the compassion I felt for all this, was my own labour when perusing this composition — to understand what it was all about. So you can fancy there was not one who knew him who envied him his distinction, for his modesty about himself was, and is, excessive.

'Chard there is very little to say about except that he too is a "very good fellow" — but very uninteresting. The fact is that until the accounts came out from England nobody had thought of the Rorke's Drift affair except as one in which the private soldiers of the 24th behaved so well. For as a matter of fact they all stayed there to defend the place because there was nowhere else to go, and in defending it they fought most determinedly.'

Indeed, no report, official or otherwise, has survived from Bromhead. Chard's report, however, was both thorough and concise, and has formed the basis of any understanding of the battle for more than a century. Walter Parke Jones, Chard's company commander, found his subaltern similarly frustrating:

'Chard makes me angry, with such a start as he got, he stuck to the company doing nothing. In his place I should have gone up and asked Lord Chelmsford for an appointment, he must have got one, and if not he could have gone home soon after Rorke's Drift, at the height of his popularity at home. I advised him, but he placidly smokes his pipe and does nothing. Few men get such opportunities.'

Clery's judgement on the battle is particularly telling. In the aftermath of Isandlwana, the army in the field fully understood that Rorke's Drift was a brutal and desperate struggle in which the defenders had had no option but to fight. As Walter Dunne had said, it was a case of, 'Do or Die'. This does not detract in any way from the raw courage of the men concerned, who had faced up to a dreadful ordeal and come through alive. Nevertheless, many in the army did not feel that the enthusiasm with which the story was greeted in the Press in Britain was entirely appropriate. The Victorian public had, in any case, a decidedly ambivalent attitude towards its Army. On the

whole, it despised the men in the ranks, yet it thrilled to its adventures overseas and romanticized both its victories and defeats. Kipling perfectly encapsulated this ambiguity:

'It's Tommy this, an' Tommy that, an' Chuck him out, the brute!

But it's "Saviour of 'is country" when the guns begin to shoot.'

While the more sedate of the weekly illustrated papers, *The Illustrated London News* and *The Graphic*, published comparatively accurate renditions of the scene, the more popular papers such as *The Penny Illustrated* depicted stalwart red-coats holding back savage hordes, establishing an image of the battle in the public consciousness which has endured ever since.

It is difficult to tell, now, how the defenders themselves reacted to this nineteenth-century media hype. Certainly Victorian society had far less qualms about the celebration of military exploits than is the case today; the concept of glory

remained a valid one until the currency was devalued in the blood-letting on the Western Front during the First World War. Of course individual personality shaped many of the participants' reactions; Chard seems to have come to terms with his role as a public figure quite easily. Others were no doubt simply modest, a virtue which was particularly prized in those days. Nevertheless, those with experience of combat are often only too aware that the reality did not match the public perception, and, given the opportunities available to them to make their thoughts known, the defenders of Rorke's Drift remained surprisingly reticent. Chard left two accounts, his official report and a longer letter written at Queen Victoria's request in January 1880. Bromhead left no account, nor did Dalton. Dunne's account was written much later in life. Several of the private soldiers wrote letters to their families at the time, and they are largely concerned with the horrors fresh in their minds — 'I am thankful at having

Above: 'A Vote of Thanks'; Mr Punch congratulates Chard and Bromhead on the defence of the post in a cartoon published on 22 March 1879. (Colonel Ian Bennett)

Above: The hero of Rorke's Drift; John Chard, looking very dashing in his full-dress uniform. (Keith Reeves collection)
Above right: Chard photographed shortly after the war — still wearing a beard — in the RE officers' blue patrol jacket. (Natal Museum)

been saved from the cruel slaughter and bloodshed that we had all gone through for the last four days,' wrote Sergeant George Smith to his wife — but only a handful wrote full accounts. Fred Hitch prefaced one of his accounts with, 'As I have been asked many times to give my illustration of Rorke's Drift, I cannot say it was a pleasure for me to do so and to think back to that terrible night of the 22nd January 1879.' The grandson of Sergeant Gallagher told the author during the Centenary Commemoration in 1979 that he remembered Fred Hitch visiting his father from time to time, and that, as a small boy, he was always shooed away, because they did not consider their reminiscences fit for him to hear.

The men of the garrison were showered with awards. Some of these were of an immediate and practical nature, and clearly much appreciated, as George Smith describes:

'...the people of Pietermaritzburg are so well pleased at the manner in which my company kept the stores from being taken by the enemy that they cannot do enough for us. They have subscribed £150 for us to buy the troops a lot of clothing, and pens, ink, and paper, matches, pipes, and a lot of everything, and sent them to us to be given to the troops at Rorke's Drift. They also sent word that they consider we have been the means of saving the whole of the colony from being taken by the Zulus, and I don't think they are far wrong...'

Chard, Bromhead, Dunne and Reynolds all received promotions valid from the day after the battle. This was just the beginning, however. On 2 May *The London Gazette* announced the award of the first Victoria Crosses, the supreme award for valour, to the garrison. They were given to Chard and Bromhead, and six members of 'B' Company: Corporal Allen, Privates Hitch, Hook, Robert Jones, William Jones and John Williams. The choice of these particular individuals is interesting. Chard and Bromhead, as the officers in command, were obvious candidates. Of the rest, four were defenders of the hospital, reflecting the view, summed up by Clery, that, '...the private soldiers of the 24th behaved so well'. Nevertheless, Chard was apparently not consulted in the selection of these awards, and it was clearly felt that others had been equally deserving. Indeed, a certain amount of behind-the-scenes wrangling followed, and it is difficult to avoid the conclusion that the final selection of awards owed as much to the desire of the authorities to recognize the contribution of the various units present as it did to individual merit. Following the announcement of the initial awards, questions were asked in the House of Commons regarding the apparent neglect of Surgeon Reynolds's service. Colonel Stanley, Secretary of State for War, replied that it was '...premature to consider what rewards or honours should be given in regard to the present campaign,' and pointed out that Reynolds had already been promoted to the rank of Surgeon Major. Nevertheless the award of the Victoria Cross for him was announced on 17 June. When a cartoon appeared in the satirical magazine *Punch* as early as March, an anonymous officer, who clearly knew something of the circumstances of the action, wrote:

'In your cartoon of March 22, you, as a worthy head of the British Army, thank Lieutenants Chard and Bromhead for their heroic defence of Rorke's Drift. In the background are seen some men of the 24th Regiment, and scattered about are some Commissariat Supplies. Cannot you find some corner of a memorial to the only officer who was killed that night while gallantly doing his duty, Assistant Commissary Byrne? Should you ignore the only officer "severely wounded" to whom all are indebted for his advice and skill in turning his supplies of flour and biscuits into parapets, Assistant Commissary Dalton? or the young officer who gained the admiration of all by erecting the last defence under heavy fire, Assistant Commissary Dunne?'

The Commissary General, Sir Edward Strickland, orchestrated a campaign for Dunne and Dalton's services to be recognized, and obtained letters from Chard to support their claim. When the appeal finally reached the Duke of Cambridge, the Commander-in-Chief commented, 'We are giving the VC very freely, I think, but probably Mr Dalton has as good a claim as the others who have got the Cross for Rorke's Drift Defence. I do not think there is a case for Mr Dunne.' Dalton's award was gazetted on 18 November 1879. A few weeks later *The London Gazette* announced that Corporal Schiess had also been granted the award. Apparently considerable pressure had been brought to bear by the colonial authorities in South Africa to recognize the efforts of the local troops.

In all, therefore, the defenders of Rorke's Drift were given a total of eleven VCs, which remains a record for any single action. It is in poignant contrast to the Isandlwana débâcle, where only one man, Private Samuel Wassall of the 80th Regiment, serving with the Mounted Infantry, was given the award for saving the life of a colleague at Fugitives' Drift. At least two other men were considered for heroism during the flight, but their cases were rejected. The posthumous awards for Lieutenants Melvill and Coghill were not given until 1906. Clearly Isandlwana was better off forgotten.

Five men were awarded the Silver Medal for Distinguished Conduct: Colour-Sergeant Frank Bourne, Second-Corporal Francis Attwood of the Army Service Corps, Private William Roy of the 1/24th, Second-Corporal Michael McMahon of the Army Hospital Corps, and Wheeler John Cantwell, of N/5 Battery, Royal Artillery. No citations were published for the award of the DCM, but significantly, all these men were singled out for mention in Chard's official report, and, once again, they reflect a cross-section of the units represented in the defence. McMahon's award, incidentally, was later withdrawn because he deserted from the army.

By the time the last awards were announced, the Anglo-Zulu War had long been over. The garrison at Rorke's Drift remained cooped-up in Fort Bromhead until May by which time a new fort had been built down by the river. This had been started in early March under Lieutenant R. da C Porter of No. 5 Company, RE, and had been completed with the help of some of the 2/24th and Major Bengough's battalion of the NNC. It was built on a steep rise directly overlooking the ponts, and was an impressive structure with high stone walls, an outer ditch, and towers at two corners. It was named Fort Melvill in honour of Lieutenant Melvill, who had been killed attempting to save the 1/24th's Queen's Colour at Isandlwana. The first troops of the 2/24th occupied part of it in April, and by May it had been completed. The stores housed in Witt's old church were then moved down, and by the middle of May what remained of the old post at Rorke's Drift had been abandoned.

The fortunes of war had already swung significantly against the Zulus. King Cetshwayo's failure to follow up his victory at Isandlwana had given Chelmsford time to regroup, and by March it was clear that a new offensive was about to begin. Chelmsford's original Right Flank Column, under Colonel Pearson, had been stranded under siege at the old Mission at Eshowe since January, and Chelmsford had formed a relief force to go to its aid. The preparations had been all too apparent to King Cetshwayo, who had mustered his *impi* once more, and directed it against the largest British column still active in Zululand, Colonel Wood's Left Flank Column. The *impi* drew near to Wood's camp at Khambula on the 27th, and caught and badly mauled a mounted force at Hlobane mountain. But when the Zulus attacked Khambula

Above: A famous photograph of the members of 'B' Company, probably taken at Pinetown. The Company is much reduced and, though it is tempting to try to identify the defenders, it is impossible to do so with confidence; Colour-Sergeant Bourne is on the extreme left, however, and Bromhead is on the left of the front row, looking left. Second to the right of him is Sergeant Gallagher. The man behind Gallagher to the right may be John Williams. Those members of the Company who had been wounded during the battle had been invalided home before this picture was taken. (Local History Museum)

itself the following day they were heavily defeated after several hours of desperate fighting. A few days later, at the opposite end of the country, Chelmsford defeated the local Zulu forces investing Eshowe at the battle of Gingindlovu on 2 April. Having inflicted two serious defeats on the Zulus within a week, Chelmsford pulled back to the Natal border and began to prepare his second invasion. This time, the tide of war would pass Rorke's Drift by. Chelmsford's new plan was a greatly simplified version of the first: he intended to make a major thrust from the sector along the upper Mzinyathi/Ncome Rivers, supported by a march in tandem with Wood's Column. A new column would advance up the coastal sector, being supplied by sea. Chelmsford himself would accompany the main thrust which once again was aimed at Ulundi. He had no desire to expose the troops fresh out from England to the horrors of the battlefield at Isandlwana — where the dead still lay unburied — and so decided not to cross into Zululand at Rorke's Drift, choosing instead the village of Dundee, a little farther north, as his new advanced supply depot, and intending to cross the Ncome at Landmans Drift. From there his

Column would skirt round Isandlwana, and then join the route planned for the old Centre Column.

The launch of the new invasion was heralded by a major expedition to Isandlwana. Public pressure had been mounting to bury the remains of the dead, and in any case Chelmsford, whose transport crisis remained desperate, needed to retrieve any surviving wagons for use in the new offensive. The troops required for this operation — chiefly the newly arrived Cavalry Brigade, 17th Lancers and 1st (King's) Dragoon Guards, with elements from the local Volunteer units, 2/24th, Artillery and NNC, were marched up to Fort Melvill, and early on the morning of 21 May they crossed the Mzinyathi at Rorke's Drift and moved up to Isandlwana. The bodies of those killed in the battle still lay mouldering in the long grass, and the visit was a moving experience. In the afternoon the expedition returned to Rorke's Drift bringing away such wagons as were serviceable.

Within a few days the troops had returned to the assembly points for the new invasion columns. The 24th had hoped for a chance to avenge itself for their losses at Rorke's Drift, but to their disappointment they were detailed to guard the

Right: Wheeler John Cantwell, N/5 Battery, RA, who was awarded the DCM for his part in the defence, photographed in his full-dress uniform after being presented with the award by Queen Victoria. (Royal Archives, Windsor)

posts on the lines of communication. Two companies of the 2/24th were left to garrison Fort Melvill, with a detachment of Dragoons and some black auxiliaries. The 24th were under the command of Wilsone Black whose batman was still Henry Hook. 'B' Company, still under Bromhead, now a Major, was moved to posts at Conference Hill and Koppie Alleen, and was still there when the war ended.

Chard, when he had recovered from his illness sufficiently to return to his duties, was attached to Colonel Wood's Column. He did not overly impress either Wood or Wood's right-hand man, Lieutenant-Colonel Redvers Buller, with his efficiency; as they later told Lord Ponsonby, the

Queen's Private Secretary, when they were invited to Balmoral after the War:

'The defence was brilliant and stubborn. But the puzzle to them was — who was the man who organized it — for it showed a genius and quickness neither of which were apparently qualifications of Chard. A dull, heavy man, scarcely ever able to do his regular work. One day Wood sent him to clear some ground. And when he arrived later he found nothing done and Chard asleep. Another day he was sent to find a ford and make it passable. Fearing his man and that a halt might be inconvenient to the Army, Wood rode forward; found Chard quite helpless. He didn't seem to take in clearly what a ford was — and had done nothing. Wood ordered his men to do it. Yet Chard's dispatch was a good one. They hoped his portrait would not appear in Mrs Butler's picture — he was so ugly he would spoil the work of art.'

The latter judgement seems a little harsh; there is nothing in Chard's portrait photographs to suggest he was particularly ugly, but then Evelyn Wood was rather vain so perhaps looks bothered him. In any event, Chard got his face into Lady Butler's painting.

He also saw out the Anglo-Zulu War, and was with Lord Chelmsford's Column when it finally reached Ulundi on 4 July. After the failure of a flurry of last-minute peace negotiations, Chelmsford drew up his forces in a large hollow square on the rolling plain opposite the king's homestead, and for three-quarters of an hour withstood the Zulu attacks. But these were not as determined as they had been; Isandlwana and Khambula had knocked the heart out of them. The senior regiments, including the uThulwana, were seen to advance from Ulundi itself, but the artillery landed several shells among them before they reached rifle-range, and they hung back. No doubt Rorke's Drift had taught them a lesson about the futility of attacking British concentrations. Number 5 Company, Royal Engineers, was in the centre of

the square, and was brought up to support one of the outer faces when one Zulu rush threatened to close to hand-to-hand. Sadly, Chard seems to have left no impression of his feelings that day. When the Zulus faltered Chelmsford unleashed the 17th Lancers who chased them from the field. Ulundi was looted and set ablaze, and that same day Chelmsford retired across the White Mfolozi River, and shortly afterwards resigned his command.

He had, in any case, already been superseded. The Home Government, unhappy at the continuing expense of the War, and Chelmsford's increasingly difficult relationship with Natal's civil administration, had sent out Sir Garnet Wolseley to replace him. Wolseley was a rising star in the Army, the epitome of the reformist element in the younger generation, who had proved himself in colonial warfare on the West Coast of Africa. To his disgust, however, he arrived at the front too late to supervise the final battle, and it was left to him to complete the mopping-up operations and pacify the country. Wolseley had brought out some of the VC awards with him, and on 16 July he presented the medals to both Chard and Surgeon Reynolds in the camp at St. Pauls. At the beginning of August he passed through Rorke's Drift, and on the 3rd presented the VC to Henry Hook, '...within seven

Below: *The presentation of the VC to Private John Williams at Gibraltar in 1880. (Ian Castle)*

or eight hundred yards of the hospital'. Hook was therefore the only one of the defenders to be presented with his award within sight of the battlefield itself. At Utrecht Wolseley decorated Bromhead and Robert Jones in separate ceremonies. Yet Wolseley himself did not share the public adulation of the heroes of Rorke's Drift:

'...it is monstrous making heroes of those who saved or attempted to save their lives by bolting or those who shut up in the buildings at Rorke's Drift could not bolt and fought like rats for their lives which they could not otherwise save.'

No doubt Wolseley's disappointment at being cheated of the glory of the conclusion of the Zulu campaign had affected his opinion of Chelmsford's officers. Nevertheless he too found Chard, '...a hopelessly dull and stupid fellow, and Bromhead not much better'.

Of the remaining VC winners, Dalton was presented with his award by General Hugh Clifford at Fort Napier, Pietermaritzburg, on 16 January 1880. Schiess received the award from Wolseley at Pietermaritzburg on 3 February 1880. Fred Hitch and William Allen had been invalided home because of their injuries, and Hitch was presented with his award by Queen Victoria at the Royal Hospital at Netley on 12 August. Allen also received his from the Queen, in a ceremony at Windsor Castle on 9 December 1879. On the same occasion William Roy was presented with his DCM. William Jones had also been invalided home, suffering from chronic rheumatism, in September 1879. He was decorated by the Queen at Windsor on 13 January 1879.

As the invading army gradually broke up, and the troops were marched off, destined now for the dull routine of colonial garrison duty, or to be sent to some other hot-spot across the empire, 'B' Company, 2/24th, had something of a triumphal return. When the 2nd Battalion marched through Pietermaritzburg, they were hailed as, '...the battalion that saved Natal', and the men of 'B' Company spotted an old friend in the crowd. *The Natal Witness* of 16 October 1879 explains:

'The spectators in Church Street could not make out why one Company of the noble 24th suddenly raised a deafening cheer on coming to the Club House.

'The fact was that B Company, the gallant defenders of Rorke's Drift, under Major Bromhead, VC, had recognized amongst the spectators Assistant Commissary Dalton, one of the leaders of that night.'

Apparently one of the Company spotted Dalton and cried out, 'Why, there's Mr Dalton cheering us! We ought to be cheering him! He was the best man there!,' and he was hauled out of the crowd and made to march with them down the street, to the accompaniment of thunderous cheers. In Durban the Mayor presented the survivors of 'B'

Company, but none of the other defenders apparently, which hardly seems fair, with an inscribed scroll of honour, 'Out of gratitude for their courage, loyalty and duty, in the face of the darkest cloud of invasion that had ever lowered over the wild frontier of the British Dominion in Africa.'

On 21 October the 2nd 24th went into camp in Pinetown, outside Durban, where they were stranded for several months because of delays in obtaining transport. Then, in mid January 1880, they embarked at Durban and sailed to their next posting at Gibraltar. There, on 1 March, the last of the VCs, John Williams, was presented with his award by Major-General Anderson before the assembled garrison on the Almeda Parade Ground.

John Chard returned home to a hero's welcome in England. He arrived at Spithead in the transport HMS *Eagle* on 2 October, and the Duke of Cambridge came aboard to greet him with an invitation to dine with the Queen. An audience took place at Balmoral on the morning of 14 October. Lieutenant-Colonel A.F. Pickard, a member of the Household, describes the occasion:

'He explained the defence of Rorke's Drift to the Queen, Prince Leopold and the Grand Duke of Hesse and Princess Beatrice in the Queen's private room and did it all very clearly and modestly.

'After dinner, he did ditto to us in the Billiard room on the table, where Store House and Hospital were books and boxes, and mealie-bags and biscuit tins were billiard balls.

'The Queen liked his quiet unassuming manner and the modest way in which he told his story.'

Public recognition was showered upon the garrison. Chard was given a presentation sword by the citizens of Plymouth, and Bromhead a revolver by the tenants of Thurlby Hall, his family seat in Lincolnshire. The other ranks were each given a souvenir Bible by a group calling themselves The Ladies' Rorke's Drift Testimonial Fund.

Queen Victoria was genuinely impressed by the affair and asked for photographs of those who had distinguished themselves; some of these are reproduced in this book. She also wanted a permanent record of the action and commissioned the successful military artist, Elizabeth Thompson, the wife of Major William Butler, to paint a picture of Rorke's Drift. Lady Butler visited the 1st Battalion, 24th which had returned to Portsmouth at the beginning of October, and found that the officers were only too helpful:

'Nothing that the officers of that regiment and the staff could possibly do to help me was neglected. They even had a representation of the fight acted by the men who took part in it, dressed in the uniforms they wore on that awful night. Of course, the result was that I reproduced the event as nearly to the life as possible, but from the soldiers' point of view — I may say the privates'

Above: *The presentation of the VC to James Dalton at Fort Napier, Pietermaritzburg. (Natal Museum)*

Right: James Langley Dalton's VC, with his Long Service medal, right, and South Africa medal left. The South Africa medal is an unofficial replacement, the original having been lost. (RCT Museum)

ACTING ASSISTANT COMMISSARY
JAMES LANGLEY DALTON, V.C.

MR. DALTON WON THE VICTORIA CROSS AT
RORKE'S DRIFT. 22ND JAN. 1879
WHERE HE ORGANIZED THE DEFENCES AND
EXHIBITED OUTSTANDING GALLANTRY IN THE SIEGE.

point of view — not mine, as the principal witnesses were from the ranks.'

This comment needs amplification. Of course, few of the men at Portsmouth could actually have been at Rorke's Drift, because the 2nd Battalion, 'B' Company included, was at that time still on its way down through Natal en route for Gibraltar. But it is possible that individuals, such as Sergeant Wilson and Private Roy, who had both been patients in the hospital during the fight, were on hand to tell their story. Lady Butler was also, apparently, able to interview those members of 'B' Company that had been invalided home, Hitch among them. Chard also sat for his portrait; it is often said that Bromhead did the same, though it is difficult to see how he could have been in England at the time. The painting posed a number of difficult technical problems, particularly with regard to the lighting, since the scene was set at dusk, only illuminated by the flames of the burning hospital. Although in her battle scenes it was her rule never to show figures actually engaged in violence, on this occasion Lady Butler went so far as to depict a Zulu on the far side of the barricade snatching at the rifle of one of the defenders, using as a model some one from a London show.

Lady Butler's was not the only painting of the action completed with the aid of the participants. The French battle-painter, Alphonse de Neuville, who specialized in scenes of the Franco-Prussian War, was apparently introduced to the subject by the commander of the 2nd Battalion, Lieutenant-Colonel Henry Degacher, who had known him in earlier life. Degacher, who had been with

Top left: *Queen Victoria decorating heroes of the Zulu War; among them are Private Roy, second from the left, and Corporal Allen, centre. (Author's collection)*

Left: *Sir Garnet Wolseley decorates Chard with the VC at St. Pauls in Zululand. (Author's collection)*

Above: *The Duke of Cambridge greets Chard at Portsmouth on his return aboard the transport Eagle (Author's collection).*

Right: *When the 1/24th and John Chard returned to Portsmouth on 2 October 1879, crowds cheered them through the streets as the 'Heroes of Rorke's Drift' — despite the fact that only a handful of the 1/24th had been present at the defence. (Rai England collection)*

Revolver presented to the late Major Gonville Bromhead VC by Friends at Thurlby in memory of Rorkes Drift 22nd January 1879. The following is a copy of the address which accompanied the revolver.

"We the undersigned living in Thurlby, being justly proud of the part which you took in the heroic defence of Rorkes Drift, beg your acceptance of the accompanying revolver as a token of our esteem and admiration of your gallant conduct which has brought honour to the name of England and especially to Thurlby your native place. We would at the same time, take this opportunity of offering to you our congratulations on you obtaining the rank of Captain and Brevet Major; and of your receiving the Victoria Cross.
We trust that you may be spared to a long life of usefulness in the service of our country and that we may see you amongst us again at Thurlby. We hope that you may never find yourself face to face with such numbers as you successfully met at Rorkes Drift, but should this occur, we trust that our revolver may not fail you in the hour of need and we are certain that it could not be held by a worthier hand."

Acc No R 93 58

Chelmsford's party on the morning of the 23rd, sent de Neuville two excellent water-colours which he had made on the spot, one featuring a wagon built into the barricade, and the other a panoramic scene of the post. Harry Lugg of the Natal Mounted Police also sent him a sketch. From these de Neuville worked up a detailed reconstruction of the fight.

Both paintings are, of course, extremely attractive works of art, and fascinating as representations of the historical event. But it is interesting to see how the artists tackled the subject, since this has helped to shape the public perception of Rorke's Drift ever since. Both pictures follow the broad conventions of late nineteenth-century battle paintings by including a number of tableaux featuring incidents from the battle. In Lady Butler's picture, Fred Hitch, his

arm strapped beneath his waist-belt, carries an armful of ammunition to the line, while Louis Byrne is struck dead in the act of passing a drink to the wounded Corporal Scammell. In the background, Chaplain Smith hands out ammunition, while Corporal Schiess leaps over the barricade to get at the Zulus beyond. In de Neuville's painting, Surgeon Reynolds, his dog 'Dick' at his side, tends the wounded Dalton, and again, Corporal Scammell — here depicted incorrectly in the uniform of the 24th — hands his cartridges to Chard. Bromhead points dramatically towards the barricades, while Smith is once again handing out ammunition. Both paintings are set in the yard, and in both the sick are seen being evacuated from the hospital, although from a chronological point of view, this is inaccurate. Both paintings capture something of the feel of the fight,

thereby assume the righteousness of the British cause. The subject might have been approached very differently; de Neuville painted some excellent, fluid studies of men moving forward, struggling in heroic assaults, and a composition could equally have been found which addressed the role of both participants. Such paintings were rare in the iconography of Victorian military campaigns, but not unknown; the Sudan Wars, for example, produced several paintings that gave equal emphasis to the African enemy. The shortcomings of this approach, when taken to its logical conclusion, becomes apparent in C.E. Fripp's famous painting, 'The Last Stand of the 24th at Isandhlwana'. This similarly concentrates on a group of the 24th who are making a stand against the overwhelming masses of the Zulus, who are seen slaughtering soldiers in the background; Fripp went so far as to add a stalwart sergeant and a young drummer-boy, figures so conventional as to be clichéd, in the centre of his picture. Fripp was a war-artist who covered the later stages of the Zulu War, and his eye for accurate detail probably outstripped any of his rivals. Yet, by emphasizing the 'thin red line's' attempts to hold the frontiers of Empire, Fripp was employing the same imagery as the Rorke's Drift paintings but in an even more inappropriate context: at Isandlwana, after all, it was the British, who were the aggressors, and the Zulus who were defending their homeland. Such an interpretation is not at all apparent in Fripp's painting. The case may be less clear cut at Rorke's Drift, but the same point applies.

The Reverend Witt was one of those who questioned the way the War was interpreted by the public. He wrote:

'Who wins your warmest sympathy — the Captain, who, knowing that he is lost, stops a moment to spike the cannon and die; or the Zulu who, in his excitement, leaves his fellow soldiers behind, and alone makes the attack on the hospital at Rorke's Drift, resting his gun on the very barricade, and firing at those inside? Is your admiration greater for the ninety-five who entered the commissariat stores at Oscarsburg and defended it against 5,000 Zulus than for those 5,000 who fought outside the whole night, trying to overpower the whites, and who withdrew, leaving 1,000 dead, hundreds of whom were lying even on the very verandah of the house? Indeed, your admiration ought to be as great for the one as for the other. Where did you find greater courage or contempt of death than theirs?'

This was a fair question, but Witt found himself out of touch with the spirit of the times, and his humanitarian attitude — he also publicly criticized the treatment meted out by Natal colonists to black Africans — earned him the contempt of the local Press.

Witt returned to reclaim his property sometime

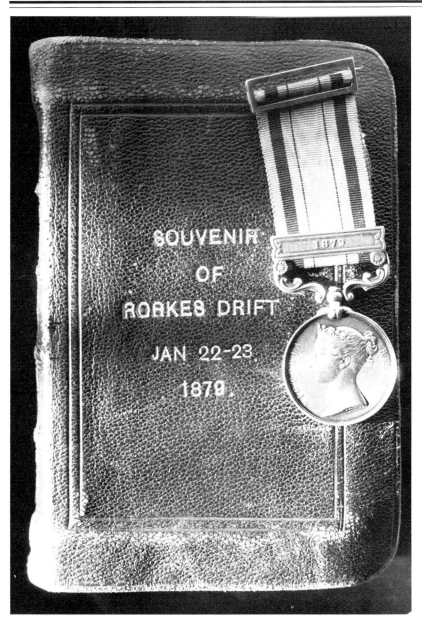

Above: The Rorke's Drift Bible and South Africa 1879 medal belonging to Sergeant Milne. (Family collection)

but de Neuville's is the more natural of the two; Lady Butler's is rather static, and her reliance on posed figures is just a little too obvious.

It was, of course, only natural to stress the role of the defenders, but the Zulus hardly feature in either painting, being reduced to shadowy figures beyond the parapet. Lady Butler chose a viewpoint directly above the barricade, so that the Zulus are squeezed out to the left of the composition; in the de Neuville, the men along the barricade physically blot out the Zulus, apart from a couple of dead and dying figures that have fallen into the yard. The British remain steadfast and static; there is no sense of the ebb and flow of battle; by excluding a Zulu viewpoint, the effect is to stress the isolation of the garrison and their steadfast stand against the anonymous and savage mass of darkest Africa. Both paintings are essentially eulogistic, and

BRAVO, CHELMSFORD !

after the end of the War. His house had been destroyed completely, and the stone walls of the fort built after the battle still surrounded his church. Over the next couple of years Witt gradually re-established the Mission at Rorke's Drift. The storehouse and fort walls were demolished and the stone used to build first a new house, on the site of the hospital, and then a proper church. In November 1881 a British traveller, Mr R.W. Leyland, found Witt living near the site, and work in progress on the house. A trader named

Craft had taken over Fort Melvill down by the Drift, which was in, '...a very dilapidated condition', and had built a solid stone dwelling next to it. Leyland found that cartridge cases and other evidence of the battle could still be found around the Mission, but by the time Bertram Mitford made his pilgrimage to the battlefields in 1882, he was disappointed to find:

'Few or no traces of the old fortification were to be seen, but a large house was in the course of construction, the residence of Mr Otto Witt, the

Swedish missionary, whose name, it may be remembered, was before the public at the beginning of the war. Much carpentering and joining was going on in the verandah; outhouses stood around, hard by was the chapel belonging to the Mission, but of the defences not a trace. Save for the little cemetery, where are lying the few who fell of that handful of defenders, it would be difficult to realize that one stood on the site of the most brilliant feat of arms of our day. To the cemetery I passed; a modest burial ground enclosed by a sod wall, the names of its silent denizens graven on an obelisk in the midst.'

The Swedish Mission, not unnaturally, had no desire to remember the terrible night of bloodshed that had taken place on its soil, and which went so much against its own philosophy. No attempt was made to preserve any vestige of the old post. Witt's new house was built on the site of the hospital building, and much resembles it; however, an archaeological survey carried out in 1988-9 discovered that it was not built on exactly the same

Right: '*B*' *Company's daily order book, covering the period after the battle at Rorke's Drift. (RRW Museum, Brecon)*

Right: *A decorated pin-cushion made by the sick and wounded after Rorke's Drift, using bits of uniform cloth. (RRW Museum, Brecon)*

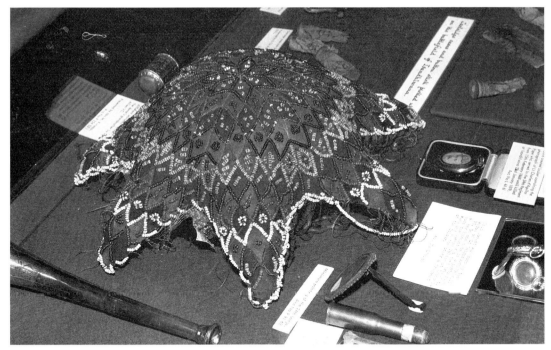

foundations. Similarly, the lines of stone set into the grass, which have so long been a feature of the site and which supposedly mark the outline of the barricades and the plan of the storehouse were also found to be not entirely correct; the church was built almost exactly over the site of the storehouse. During the course of this excavation, a large number of relics was discovered dating to more than a century of civilian occupation of the site, but a number of relics of the battle were also found. These included smashed crockery and fused glass, believed to date from the burning of the hospital, cartridge cases and spent bullets.

When the British Army withdrew from Zululand, the Home Government refused to countenance the expense of annexing the country, and Frere's discredited policy of Confederation was abandoned. Instead, Sir Garnet Wolseley imposed a peace settlement which was designed to break down the political and economic institutions of the old Zulu kingdom. King Cetshwayo himself was captured and sent into exile, and the country was

Left: *The surrender of Prince Dabulamanzi on 12 July 1879. The Prince's fondness for European clothes is well captured here. (Author's collection)*

Below: *An interesting and unusual photograph of Rorke's Drift after the war, showing the party led by Major Stabb (with butterfly net) that erected the monument to the Prince Imperial. The wall in the right foreground may be the remains of the rough cattle-kraal. (Keith Reeves collection)*

Right: *Another photograph taken on the same occasion, with kwaSingqindi hill in the background. (Killie Campbell Africana Library)*

divided between thirteen chiefs whom the British considered safe to leave in charge. The country soon gravitated towards pro- and anti-royalist factions, and by 1882 a civil war had broken out. The situation became so unstable that in January 1883 Cetshwayo was allowed to return to part of his own territory in the hope that this might restore order. But this had precisely the opposite effect to the one desired, and merely provoked an attack by the anti-royalists. In July 1883 Zibhebhu kaMapitha, the same man who had turned back from the foray into Natal at Fugitives' Drift, led a surprise attack against the king at his reconstructed homestead at Ulundi. The king's followers were caught unawares and massacred. Among them were a number of the uThulwana, some of whom had probably fought at Rorke's Drift. The king managed to escape but died a few months later, a broken man. The civil war spluttered on for another four years, and British outposts were once again established in Zululand. One of these was at Fort Northampton, an impressive stone and earthwork bastion built above the Zululand bank at Rorke's Drift, just a few hundred yards from the pont. Photographs of this fort show that a military ferry was still in operation at the site, on the same spot where Chard once guarded the ponts. It was not until 1888, however, that red-coats once more took the field against the Zulus. The royalist faction, led by Cetshwayo's son Dinuzulu, whom many regarded as the rightful king of the Zulus — a position the British refused to acknowledge — rose in rebellion, but was easily suppressed. There

was no fighting in the vicinity of Rorke's Drift.

Prince Dabulamanzi was one of the casualties of this troubled time. During the remainder of the Anglo-Zulu War, he had achieved considerable notoriety among the British troops as one of the most daring and dashing of the Zulu commanders, and was credited with having played a prominent part in most of the major battles, '...quite irrespective', as Mitford observed, 'of such trivialities as time and place'. In fact, he had fought at the battle of Gingindlovu, since the Eshowe district fell within his personal territory. Indeed, when Chelmsford relieved Eshowe, his last act before returning to the Thukela was to mount a foray to destroy eZulwini, the prince's personal homestead nearby. The homestead was set ablaze, and Dabulamanzi traded shots with the British from a nearby eminence. He did not take part in the battle of Ulundi, but he did not surrender to the British until 12 July, more than a week after the final battle. In the post-war settlement he was placed under the charge of John Dunn, but agitated for the return of King Cetshwayo. After Cetshwayo's death he transferred his allegiance to Dinuzulu, but on 22 September 1886 he was murdered by the Boers in the northern part of the country. The Transvaal Republic had become deeply involved in the Zulu civil war, and had been given a slice of land in north-eastern Zululand by Dinuzulu as a reward for helping him defeat his enemies. The extent of the Boer claims led to bitter disputes, however, and Dabulamanzi had been arrested on a charge of cattle-stealing which had

Left: The Mission church, built on the site of the storehouse, photographed with its congregation in the 1890s. (Natal Museums Service)

Left: The Reverend Otto Witt, his family, and some of his converts, photographed at the restored Mission in the 1880s. (Bryan Maggs)

arisen from these disputes, and which he hotly denied. Dabulamanzi escaped with his son into British territory, but the Boers pursued them and tried to arrest them again. In the struggle Dabulamanzi was shot by a Boer named Paul van der Berg, who was known to the Zulus as Peula. Dabulamanzi's son, uMzingeli, described his death:

'Peula and my father then struggled together, my father seizing hold of Peula's bandolier. After a bit they separated, my father having possession of the bandolier and Peula of my father's knobkerrie. I was prevented from assisting my father by the other Boer who threatened to shoot me. Peula said, "Give me back my bandolier." My father replied "Return me my knobkerrie." My father threw the

bandolier to Peula who then seized the gun from Wilhelm and said he would shoot my father if he wouldn't go to Vryheid. My father replied, "You wouldn't shoot me on Government ground." Peula said he would, and after some more words he shot my father who was standing within two or three yards of him, through the body, the bullet entering his stomach below the left side and coming out above his right hip. My father ran away and as he was doing so, Peula shot him again twice, the first shot struck him above the left hip, the second passed through his right elbow and left wrist. Peula then fired two shots at me as I was riding away on the horse which bucked me off and I sprained my knee. My father, after receiving the second shot, fell close to me; he had only run about 200 yards.'

The Boers rode off leaving some local Zulus to tend Dabulamanzi's wounds, but he died the next morning. His body was taken back to the site of eZulwini and buried. It was a sad and rather squalid end to the man who had led his country's troops in what had already become the most famous battle in his nation's history.

Of the British participants, Chard continued to enjoy his role as 'The Hero of Rorke's Drift', and enjoyed the Queen's favour, for several years. He served in a number of overseas postings, including Cyprus and Singapore, but did not see active service again. He rose to the rank of colonel, but in 1896 he was afflicted with cancer of the tongue. Despite several operations, the condition did not improve, and he retired to Hatch Beauchamp in Somerset, where his brother was the vicar of St. John the Baptist Church. Queen Victoria inquired

about his progress and sent him a Diamond Jubilee Medal. His condition worsened, and he died on 1 November 1897, aged forty-nine. He was buried four days later, and the Queen sent a wreath with an inscription in her own hand as, 'A mark of Admiration and regard for a brave soldier from his sovereign.'

One of Chard's visitors in his last months was the Reverend George Smith. Smith had also accompanied Chelmsford's advance on the Zulu capital, and had been present at Ulundi. His incumbency of the Mission at Estcourt expired in 1880, and on 1 January of that year he was appointed Chaplain of the Forces of the Army Chaplains' Department, a post awarded in recognition of his services at Rorke's Drift. He returned to England and was Chaplain at Aldershot until 1881, when he was sent to Cork. He went to Egypt with Wolseley's Egyptian Expeditionary Force, and was present at Tel-el-Kebir. He was awarded the Queen's Medal for Egypt and the Khedive's Star. When the Mahdist revolt broke out, he was present at the Battle of Ginniss. In 1887 he returned to Britain where he enjoyed a number of posts, and for a brief spell in 1903-4 returned to South Africa where he was based at Harrismith in the Orange Free State. In 1905 he retired to Sumner's Hotel, Fulwood, at Preston, Lancashire, where he had spent several years as a Chaplain. He died on 27 November 1918, at the age of seventy-three.

Gonville Bromhead did not long survive the Zulu War. He was promoted to the rank of Major in 1883 and served with the 2nd Battalion in the

Burma campaign of 1886-8. On 9 February 1891 when the Battalion was in India, he succumbed to typhoid fever and was buried in the New Cantonment Cemetery at Allahabad. Lord Roberts, the Commander-in-Chief, telegraphed his condolences to the regiment:

'Please let all ranks of the South Wales Borderers know how much the Chief sympathises with them in the loss of Major Bromhead, V.C., who behaved with such conspicuous gallantry at Rorke's Drift, and so well supported the reputation of his distinguished regiment.'

Walter Dunne enjoyed a varied and adventurous career. After his recovery from the fever which struck him at Rorke's Drift, he returned to the field and was present at Ulundi. Placed in charge of the supply depot at St. Pauls, he witnessed King Cetshwayo being brought in as a prisoner. 'From what I had heard I expected to see an obese, ill-looking savage,' he wrote:

'...but on the contrary, he was a fine looking, intelligent man with good features. He descended slowly from the ambulance, and walked with natural dignity to the tent provided for him, raising his head to cast a steady glance on those who were in front of him; a glance which seemed to show that as a king he felt his altered position, but bore up against it. His demeanour was manly and dignified, and not unworthy of a captive king...

'Thus we had ocular proof of the downfall of Cetewayo, and the end of the unhappy war which cost so many valuable lives.'

From Zululand Dunne was sent north to help in the final campaign against the persistently recalcitrant King Sekhukhune of the Pedi and was present at the storming of Sekhukhune's stronghold in November 1879. In 1880 he was sent to join the garrison at Potchefstroom in the Transvaal. The Transvaal had never been reconciled to British rule, and when the republic's Boers rose in revolt, the Potchefstroom garrison was besieged for four months. Once again Dunne distinguished himself at the barricades. The garrison was forced to surrender, but marched out with full military honours. Dunne returned home to England, but was soon dispatched to Egypt where he took part in the Battle of Tel-el-Kebir. After another brief spell at home, he joined the Suakim expedition in the Sudan. He rose to the rank of Colonel, and retired to Rome where he died in 1908.

James Dalton was given a permanent commission as a Commissariat Officer in recognition of his services at Rorke's Drift, but in December 1879 he was put on half-pay and returned to England. He went back to South Africa a few years later, and bought a share in a mining concern at Barbeton in the eastern Transvaal. He

spent Christmas 1886 with an old friend who ran a hotel in Port Elizabeth, in the eastern Cape, but fell ill and died quite suddenly on 7 January 1887.

James Reynolds, on the other hand, lived a long and active life. His career prospered, and he reached the rank of lieutenant-colonel, without seeing further active service, and retired from the Army in January 1896. In November 1929 he was one of three senior VC holders who attended a VC dinner given by the Prince of Wales in the Royal Gallery at the House of Lords; one of the others was John Williams. Reynolds died in London in 1932 at the grand age of eighty-two.

The subsequent histories of 'B' Company's VC winners were varied, and there is a strain of blight which runs through one or two, suggesting that they never really overcame the trauma of that night in January 1879. Their stories may be taken as typifying the experience of the rest of the garrison, some of whose lives are less easy to trace. William Allen's injured arm never fully healed, but he continued to serve with the South Wales Borderers' 4th Volunteer Battalion as a sergeant-instructor of musketry, based at Monmouth. He succumbed to an epidemic of influenza in March 1890, aged forty-six. Fred Hitch's wounds rendered him unfit for further military service and he was discharged

from the Army in August 1879, still in his early twenties. He joined the Corps of Commissionaires, and later became a cab driver. In 1901 his VC was stolen from his coat, and he was presented with a replacement by Lord Roberts in 1908. He died of pneumonia in January 1913 aged fifty-six. Henry Hook sailed with the 2nd Battalion to Gibraltar, but bought himself out of the Army in 1880. He went to London where he found a job at the British Museum which he held until his retirement. He became involved with various Rifle Volunteer Clubs until he joined the 1st Volunteer Battalion of the Royal Fusiliers, with whom he became a sergeant-instructor of musketry. After the turn of the century his health declined and he returned to Gloucester to escape the smog of London. The move was not entirely successful, however, and he died of pulmonary consumption on 12 March 1905, aged fifty-four. He was buried at Churcham, outside the city, in a funeral attended by a crowd of several thousands, including representatives from 23 regiments. Fred Hitch attended the ceremony, and one of his sons, a corporal in the South Wales Borderers, was one of the pall-bearers. John Williams, whose real name was John Fielding, stayed with the Battalion until 1883 when he retired into the Army Reserve. He worked at

Above: *The impressive defences of Fort Northampton, on the Zulu side of Rorke's Drift, 1884, with the distinctive outline of Shiyane in the distance. Note the wall of mealie-bags! (Bryan Maggs)*

Top right: *An interesting photograph of the Mission, c.1884; a detachment of military drummers is playing in the cemetery.(Natal Museums Service)*

Right: *Officers' quarters, Fort Northampton, 1884. (Bryan Maggs)*

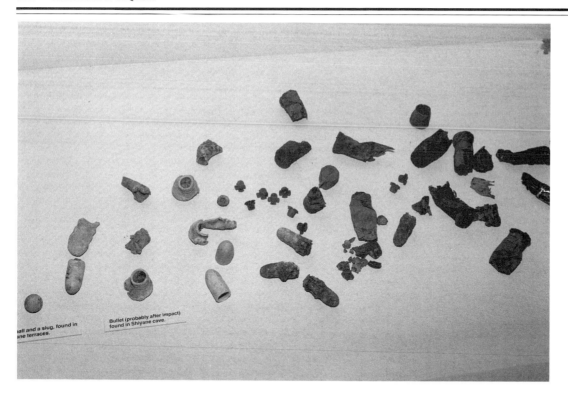

Left: Relics discovered during cable-laying near the hospital building, September 1991; Victorian pottery, broken glass, animal bones and, centre, a flattened Martini-Henry bullet. (Author's photograph)

Brecon Barracks until his retirement in 1920. One of his sons was killed in the First World War fighting with the South Wales Borderers. Fielding died of heart failure in 1932. It is said that his hair had turned quite white at an early age because of his experiences at Rorke's Drift. Robert Jones left the Army in 1881 and went to work as a groundsman for a retired officer in the village of Peterchurch, near Hereford. He was apparently troubled with severe headaches resulting from a wound — not, apparently, sustained at Rorke's Drift — and on 6 September 1898 he went into the garden with a shot-gun, put the muzzle into his mouth and blew off the top of his head. He was forty-one years old. It is never wise to make glib assumptions about what drives a man to such

Right: The foundations of the original hospital, discovered beneath the floor of Witt's house by archaeologists, 1988-9. (Natal Museums Service)

Below: A sample dig to locate — successfully — the foundations of the old storehouse, 1988-9. (Natal Museums Service)

despair, but one wonders just how much the past had haunted him. William Jones was discharged as unfit because of rheumatism in 1880, and he went to live in Manchester where he occasionally made ends meet by appearing on a local stage to recite an account of Rorke's Drift. In 1887-8 he toured with Buffalo Bill's Wild West Show. He did not prosper, however, and in later life he was apparently plagued by nightmares which sometimes caused him to run out of the house in the middle of the night. In 1912 he was found wandering the streets of Manchester in a state of confusion, and was taken to the Workhouse until his wife could collect him. He died in April 1913, aged seventy-three.

Schiess's end was the most tragic of all. After the Zulu War he worked for a while in the telegraph office at Durban, but by 1884 he was out of work and soon became destitute. He was offered a free passage to England in the transport *Serapis*, but his health had been broken, and he died at sea on 14 December 1884 at the age of twenty-eight. He was buried at sea off the coast of West Africa. He has no grave to remember him by, nor has any portrait of him ever been authenticated.

Frank Bourne is thought to have been the last survivor of the garrison. His career was a distinguished one, and he rose through the ranks to become a lieutenant-colonel. In 1934 he attended the Northern Command Tattoo, with four other veterans of Rorke's Drift, then-Corporal Alfred Saxty and Privates William Cooper, John Jobbins and Caleb Woods. In December 1935 he recorded an account of the battle for the BBC in a series entitled 'I Was There'; although a transcript of this

talk appeared in *The Listener*, the recording was
destroyed in the 1960s because it was considered to
be no longer of interest. Whenever he was asked
about Rorke's Drift, he would say that he,
'...considered myself lucky to have been there'; he
commemorated the anniversary of the battle with a
family meal. He died in May 1945 at the age of
ninety-one, having seen the fall of not only the
Zulu kingdom, but the decline of Hitler's
Germany.

The last Zulu survivors have long since departed
the scene, for the men of the uThulwana had been
about seventy at the turn of the century. By 1950
the Battle of Rorke's Drift had passed out of living
experience, and into the realm of legend. At the
site itself, the Mission went quietly about its
business, and the station was gradually extended
with the addition of extra buildings. Very few
visitors went out of their way to find Rorke's Drift,
and the battle seemed destined to slide into
obscurity, a footnote in an increasingly
unfashionable era of the past. Then, in 1963, the
Welsh actor Stanley Baker, co-produced a film
about the battle called simply, *Zulu*.

The cinema had, indeed, taken a look at Rorke's
Drift once before. As early as 1918 a company
called African Film Productions had made a silent
epic about the Anglo-Zulu War, F. Horace Rose's
'Great National and Patriotic Drama of the Zulu
War of 1879', *Symbol of Sacrifice*. This seems to
have been an extraordinary amalgam of a typical
silent melodrama — young British hero falls in love
with the daughter of a Boer farmer on the Zulu
border — and an historical tableau, which
recreated a number of set-piece incidents from the
War. These included such stirring moments as the
last stand of the Natal Carbineers at Isandlwana,
Melvill and Coghill's dash with the Colours, the
death of the Prince Imperial, and the burning of
the royal homestead at Ulundi. Inevitably, the
defence of Rorke's Drift played a prominent part,
and it is no coincidence that the film's stated
intention was, '...to remind the present generation,
war-torn and weary as it is, that heroism and
devotion are no monopoly of the World's Great
War whose agony has been unfolding before our
eyes'. Already Rorke's Drift had become a potent
source of imagery, although it must be said that
Symbol of Sacrifice, for all its epic qualities, seems to
have made no very great impact on the history of
world cinema.

Zulu had a rather more ambivalent attitude
towards its subject matter. It was made during the
last great period of the cinematic epic, and relied
for much of its appeal on spectacle, yet it reflected
the war-weary cynicism of the 1960s. The story
was simply a retelling of Rorke's Drift, with Baker
playing Chard as a dour professional engineer, out
of place in the old school tie world of the officer
class, represented by Gonville Bromhead.

Above: *John Chard, photographed in later life. (Keith Reeves collection)*

Bromhead was played by a young actor named
Michael Caine, turning in a fine performance not
at all in keeping with his usual screen character.
Zulu perfectly encapsulated the myth of Rorke's
Drift, moving the action away from the rather plain
scenery of Shiyane and its surroundings, and
transposing it to the breath-taking Natal National
Park, where it was framed by a spectacular
mountain amphitheatre; the archetypal exotic
Africa. It is a film extremely rich in visual appeal;
the bright scarlet of the soldiers' tunics, the white
of their helmets and glare of their helmet-plates are
offset against the brilliant blue sky and the green of
the hillsides; the conspicuousness the soldiers of
1879 sought to avoid makes marvellous cinema. It
also provides a series of stock characters who are

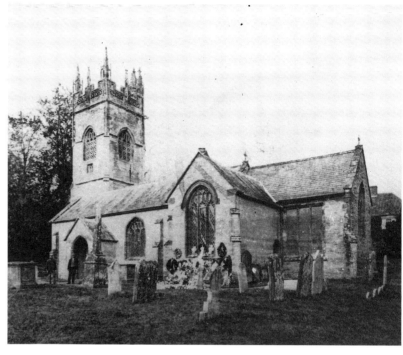

Chard's funeral at Hatch Beauchamp, Somerset, November 1897, showing the wreath (top left) sent by Queen Victoria. (Keith Reeves collection)

every bit as artificial as the stalwart sergeant and the drummer-boy in Fripp's Isandhlwana painting. Hook is depicted as a rascally other-ranker, who shows his true mettle when the chips are down, while Colour-Sergeant Bourne, a superb portrayal by Nigel Green, is the ultimate British NCO, dependable, reliable, a father-figure to the young and unsure. By giving the Zulu attacks much more order than was the case, the brutality of the battle is replaced by an epic grandeur. The Zulus are depicted as an extension of an alien and forbidding landscape — they appear over the crest of hills, or rise out of the long grass — which threatens to swallow up the tiny garrison. Each appearance cranks up the tension still further, and is released in a series of progressively spectacular charges and bouts of mêlée. There is no Zulu perspective in the film; indeed, the very choice of the title serves to draw on the air of mystery and savagery which has become attached to the Zulus in the British mind since the war itself. In this respect, Zulu captures an image of the battle which would have been instantly familiar to the battle-artists of the nineteenth century. Nevertheless, it boasts some superb moments which perhaps suggest something of a greater truth about the battle than can be found in a mere attention to surface detail. The fight in the hospital is suitably desperate and claustrophobic, and the final image of the battle, where a carpet of dead and dying Zulus sprawls

Left: Henry Hook, photographed as a Sergeant-Instructor of Musketry in the 1st Volunteer Battalion, Royal Fusiliers. (Keith Reeves collection)

Right: *Frock-coat belonging to Gonville Bromhead; the medal ribbons include his VC and Zulu War campaign medal. (Newark Museum, Nottingham)*

right up to the feet of the defenders, is surely one of the most striking in any historical war film. Indeed, it is precisely because its imagery is so potent that *Zulu* was a hugely successful film. It is wonderfully enjoyable, and it brought the story to an international audience. Although its message is less clear-cut, it is probably true to say that it was primarily responsible for the image Rorke's Drift enjoys in the public consciousness, as a heroic stand against the overwhelming forces of

Left: *A group of South Wales Borderers' VC winners photographed at the turn of the century; Robert Jones is on the far left, back row, with Henry Hook centre, and Robert Jones, right. David Bell — who won the VC in the Andaman Islands in 1867 — is sitting far left, then Edward Browne, who was decorated for gallantry with the Mounted Infantry at Hlobane Mountain in Zululand, Fred Hitch and John Williams. (Author's collection)*

Below left: *Memorial to Henry Hook, Brecon Cathedral. (Author's photograph)*

Below right: *Memorial to Gonville Bromhead, Brecon Cathedral. (Author's photograph)*

barbarism. When, only two years after *Zulu's* release, the American author Donald R. Morris published his extraordinary, popular history of the Zulu nation, *The Washing of the Spears*, a best-seller which is still in print at the time of writing, almost thirty years later, the legendary status of Rorke's Drift was assured.

It took some time for this popular appeal to filter through to the site itself, which has remained steadfastly off the beaten track. Helpmekaar is no less desolate now than it was in 1879 —in 1992 it consisted of a police station, a dilapidated store and two or three fine old stone buildings, gone to ruin — and until David and Nicky Rattray opened the Fugitives' Drift Lodge a few miles down the road in 1990, the nearest hotel was miles away, at Dundee. Rorke's Drift was at the end of the tourist road, and only the most dedicated enthusiast risked his suspension on the long and bumpy dirt road. Gradually, however, a greater awareness within South Africa and changing attitudes in the world outside have led to a steady increase in tourism, and Rorke's Drift has found itself figuratively and literally on the map once more. A steady stream of visitors are prepared to follow in Bertram Mitford's footsteps and wander, '...through the Zulu country', and the appeal of its dramatic past is not to be denied. In January 1992 the Natal Museums' Service opened the first museum on the battlefield in the house Otto Witt built over the ruins of the hospital, and it much resembles it both internally and outside. It is a moving experience to look at the exhibits which reconstruct incidents on the very ground where they took place.

Above: *Several of the defenders of Rorke's Drift continued to serve in a very different age of warfare; Evan Jones, who was a Private in 'B' Company, photographed as a lance-sergeant in the Royal Welsh Fusiliers, c.1918. Jones died in 1931 at the age of 72. (RRW Museum, Brecon)*

Right: *The remains of the ramparts and trenches of Fort Melvill, with Shiyane in the background, 1990. (Author's photograph)*

Left: An over-view of the Rorke's Drift site in 1991, photographed from above the Shiyane terrace. The site is still a working Mission, although there is now a battlefield museum there; at the centre of this photograph is the site of the original buildings. (Author's photograph)

Above: Glittering prizes: Walter Dunne's medals. Left to right, the CB (awarded in 1897 for distinguished service), the South Africa medal with bar 1877-8-9, the Egypt medal, with bars for Tel-el-Kebir and Suakim 1885, and the Khedive's Star. (RCT Museum/Colonel Ian Bennett)

APPENDIXES

ROLL OF RORKE'S DRIFT DEFENDERS

Officer Commanding
Lieutenant J.R.M.Chard, 5th (Field) Company, Royal Engineers
Staff
Sergeant G.W. Mabin
'N' Battery, 5th Brigade, Royal Artillery
Bombardier T. Lewis
Wheeler J. Cantwell
Gunners A.Evans and A. Howard
5th Field Company, Royal Engineers
Driver E. Robson
2nd Battalion, 3rd (East Kent) Regiment 'The Buffs'
Sergeant F. Millne
1st Battalion, 24th Regiment
Sergeant E. Wilson
Privates W. Beckett, P. Desmond, W. Horrigan, J. Jenkins, E. Nicholas, T. Payton, W. Roy, H. Turner, J. Waters
2nd Battalion, 24th Regiment
Lieutenant G. Bromhead
Colour-Sergeant F. Bourne
Sergeants H. Gallagher, R. Maxfield, G. Smith, J. Windridge
Lance-Sergeants J. Taylor, T. Williams
Corporals W.W. Allen, G. French, J. Key, J. Lyons (1112), A. Saxty
Lance-Corporals W. Bessell, W. Halley
Drummers P. Galgey, P. Hayes, J. Keefe, J. Meehan
Privates R. Adams, J. Ashton, T. Barry, W. Bennett, J. Bly, J.Bromwich, T. Buckley, T. Burke, J. Bushe, W.H. Camp, T. Chester, J. Chick, T. Clayton, R. Cole, T. Cole, T. Collins, J. Connolly, A. Connors, T. Connors, W. Cooper, G. Davis, W.H. Davis, T. Daw, G. Deacon, M. Deane, J. Dick, W. Dicks, T. Driscoll, J. Dunbar, G. Edwards, J. Fagan, E. Gee, J. Hagan, J. Harris, G. Hayden, F. Hitch, A.H. Hook, J. Jobbins, E. Jones, J. Jones (970), J. Jones (1179), R. Jones, W. Jones, P. Judge, P. Kears, M. Kiley, D. Lewis, H. Lines, D. Lloyd, T. Lockhart, J. Lodge, T.M. Lynch, J. Lyons (1441), J. Manley, J. Marshall, H. Martin, C. Mason, M. Minehan, T. Moffatt, A. Morris, F. Morris, T. Morrison, J. Murphy, W. Neville, R. Norris, W. Osbourne, S. Parry, W. Partridge, S. Pitts, T. Robinson, J. Ruck, E. Savage, J. Scanlon, A. Sears, G. Shearman, J. Shergold, J. Smith, T. Stevens, W. Tasker, F. Taylor, T. Taylor, J. Thomas, J. Thompson, M. Tobin, P. Tobin, W.J. Todd, R. Tongue, J. Wall, A. Whetton, W. Wilcox, J. Williams (1395), J. Williams (934), J. Williams (1398), C. Wood
90th (Perthshire Volunteers) Light Infantry
Corporal J. Graham
Commissariat and Transport Department
Assistant Commissary W.A. Dunne
Acting Assistant Commissary J.L. Dalton
Acting Storekeeper L.A. Byrne
Army Service Corps
Second Corporal F. Attwood
Army Medical Department
Surgeon Reynolds
Mr Pearce
Army Hospital Corps
Corporal R. Miller
Second Corporal M. McMahon
Private T. Luddington
Chaplain
The Revd G. Smith
Natal Mounted Police
Troopers R. Green, S. Hunter, H. Lugg
Natal Native Contingent
Lieutenant J. Adendorff
Corporals M. Dougherty, J.H. Mayer, C.Scammell, C.F. Schiess, J.Wilson; one unknown private
Civilian Mr Daniells

Note. A number of authenticated rolls of the Rorke's Drift garrison exists, and there are some discrepancies between them. Their relative merits are carefully assessed in Norman Holme's *The Silver Wreath* (1979), and I have followed his conclusions with regard to the men of the 2/24th. It should be noted that only some 95 of the men of the 2/24th were with 'B' Company, the remainder being mostly patients in the hospital.

BRITISH CASUALTIES AT RORKE'S DRIFT

Killed:
Acting Storekeeper L.A. Byrne, Sergeant R. Maxfield,
Privates R. Adams, J. Chick, T. Cole, J. Fagan, G. Hayden, W. Horrigan, J. Jenkins, E. Nicholas, J. Scanlon, J. Williams,
Trooper S. Hunter, Corporal Anderson, NNC, unknown private, NNC

Mortally wounded / died of wounds:
Lance-Sergeant T. Williams, Private W. Beckett
Wounded:
Acting Assistant Commissary J.L. Dalton,
Corporals W.W. Allen, J. Lyons, Corporals (NNC)
C. Scammell, C.F. Schiess, Drummer J. Keefe,
Privates J. Bushe, P. Desmond, F. Hitch, A.H.
Hook, R. Jones, J. Smith, W. Tasker, J. Waters,
Trooper R. Green
NOTE: Corporal Anderson was apparently killed by
British fire.

AWARDS

Victoria Cross:
Lieutenant J.R.M. Chard
Surgeon J.H. Reynolds
Acting Assistant Commissary J.L. Dalton
Lieutenant G. Bromhead
Corporal (1240) W.W. Allen
Private (1362) F. Hitch
Private (1373) A.H. Hook
Private (716) R. Jones
Private (593) W. Jones
Private (1395) John Williams
Corporal F.C. Schiess, NNC

Distinguished Conduct Medal:
Colour-Sergeant (2459) F. Bourne
Private (1542) W. Roy
Wheeler (2076) J. Cantwell, RA
Second Corporal (24692) Francis Attwood, ASC
Second Corporal M. McMahon, AHC (Award
withdrawn)

CAST AND CREDITS OF THE MOTION PICTURE *ZULU*

Cast:

Lieutenant John Chard	Stanley Baker
Rev. Otto Witt	Jack Hawkins
Margareta Witt	Ulla Jacobsson
Private Henry Hook	James Booth
Lieutenant Gonville Bromhead	Michael Caine
Colour-Sergeant Bourne	Nigel Green
Private Owen	Ivor Emmanuel
Sergeant Maxfield	Paul Daneman
Corporal Allen	Glynn Edwards
Private Thomas	Neil McCarthy
Private Hitch	David Kernan
Private Cole	Gary Bond
Private 612 Williams	Peter Gill
Lance-Corporal	Tom Gerrard
Surgeon Reynolds	Patrick Magee
Private 593 Jones	Richard Davies
Gunner Howarth	Dafydd Havard
Private 716 Jones	Denys Graham
Corporal Schiess	Dickie Owen
Hughes	Larry Taylor
Sergeant Windridge	Joe Powell
Stephenson	John Sullivan
Sick Man	Harvey Hall
Adendorff	Gert van den Bergh
Commissary Dalton	Dennis Folbigge
Company Cook	Kerry Jordan
Bugler	Ronald Hill
Cetewayo	Chief Buthelezi
Jacob	Daniel Tshabalala
Red Garters	Ephraim Mbhele
Dance Leader	Simon Sabela
Narrator	Richard Burton

Credits:

Director	Cy Endfield
Produced by	Stanley Baker and Cy Endfield
Associate Producer	Basil Keys
Production Manager	John D. Merriman
Art Director	Ernest Archer
Editor	John Jympson
2nd Unit Director	Bob Porter
Director of Photography	Stephen Dade, BSC
Screenplay by	John Prebble and Cy Endfield
From an original story by	John Prebble
Original music composed and conducted by	John Barry
Make-up created by	Charles Parker
Wardrobe Supervisor	Arthur Newman

1964. Certificate 'U' in UK. Length 12,494 feet.
Running time 138 minutes. Registered No. BR/E
29156. Filmed in Technicolor® and Technirama®.
A Paramount picture. A Diamond Films Ltd.
Production. Presented by Joseph E. Levine.

BIBLIOGRAPHY

There are surprisingly few eye-witness accounts of Rorke's Drift. John Chard wrote two detailed accounts: his official report, contained in the War Office file WO 32/7737 in the Public Record Office, and published with others in *The Historical Records of the 24th Regiment*, by Glennie, Paton and Penn Symons (1892), and a longer letter written at Queen Victoria's request in 1880. This was published — together with accounts by Colour-Sergeant Bourne, Sergeant George Smith, Corporal John Lyons, Privates Hitch, Henry Hook, John Waters, and John Jobbins — in Norman Holme's *The Silver Wreath* (London, 1979). This work also includes invaluable notes on the military records and subsequent careers of the members of 'B' Company. Another account by Hitch, together with other important and vivid descriptions of the campaign by participants — including Lieutenant Weallans' letter — can be found in Frank Emery's *The Red Soldier* (London, 1979). Hook told his story several times in later life, with minor variations in detail; they appeared variously in *The Strand* magazine half-yearly volume January-June 1891, *The Royal Magazine* of February 1905, *Macmillan's Magazine* for October 1898 and *The Daily Graphic* of March 1905. The same volume of *The Strand* also includes short accounts by Robert Jones and William Jones. William Roy's account appeared in a letter in a Dundee newspaper, apparently in 1879, but I have not so far been able to trace the source of the cutting in my possession.

A number of anecdotes have been gleaned from obituaries published on the death of participants, notably in the case of George Edwards (Orchard) and Henry Martin. Spalding's report can be found in War Office file WO 32/7738 in the Public Record Office. Walter Dunne's story appeared in the *Army Service Corps Journal* in 1891, and formed the basis of Colonel Ian Bennett's *Eyewitness in Zululand* (1990). The Reverend Smith's account is included in both *The Historical Records of the 24th* and Canon Lummis's *Padre George Smith of Rorke's Drift* (1978). Smith was also apparently the author of an article 'The Defence of Rorke's Drift By An Eyewitness' which appeared in the *Natal Mercury* on 7 April 1879. A copy of Surgeon Reynolds's report was published as an Appendix to the Army Medical Department report of 1878. Otto Witt's account was published in *The Graphic* of 22 March 1879. Harry Lugg's description of the battle, first published in *The Bristol Observer*, is reprinted, together with further anecdotes, in H.C. Lugg's *A Natal Family Looks Back* (1970).

Zulu views of the fight can be found in 'A Zulu Boy's Recollections of the Zulu War', edited by C. de B Webb, in *Natalia*, December 1978. By far the best analysis of the Zulu movements during the battle is John Laband's *Kingdom in Crisis: The Zulu Response to the British Invasion of 1879* (1992). The same author's chapter 'The Zulu At Rorke's Drift' in *Kingdom and Colony At War* (with Paul Thompson, 1990) also contains a detailed list of official and other reports referring to the battle. Also in that book, Paul Thompson's 'The NNC At Rorke's Drift' sorts out much of the confusion regarding Stephenson's company and the Native Horse during the battle.

The aftermath of the battle is described in George Hamilton-Browne's *A Lost Legionary in South Africa* (London, c.1913); Daphne Child (ed.) *The Zulu War Diary of Colonel Henry Harford* (1978); Horace Smith-Dorrien's *Memories of Forty-Eight Years' Service* (London, 1929); John Maxwell's *Reminiscences of the Zulu War* (ed. by L.T. Jones, 1979) and Henry Fynn's 'My Recollections of a Famous Campaign' in *Natal Witness* of 22 January 1913. Blair Brown's comments on medical aspects of the War can be found in *Surgical Experiences In The Zulu And Transvaal Wars*, 1882. For the views of Crealock and Clery, see the Alison letters in Sonia Clarke's *Zululand At War*, 1984. Sir Garnet Wolseley's comments can be found in *The South African Journal of Sir Garnet Wolseley, 1879-80*, edited by Adrian Preston, 1973. John Laband and Paul Thompson's *The Buffalo Border* (with Sheila Henderson, 1982) and *The Zulu War and the Colony of Natal* (eds. G.A. Chadwick and E.G. Hobson, 1979) both include useful material on the settler communities along the upper Mzinyathi.

R.W. Leyland's *A Holiday in South Africa* (1882) and, more particularly, Bertram Mitford's *Through The Zulu Country* (1883, rep. 1992) both contain descriptions of the site in the early years after the battle; Mitford also includes general conversations on the topic with Zulu participants. James Bancroft's *The Zulu War VCs* (1992), as its title suggests, provides brief biographies of some of the principal British participants.

For the literature of the Isandlwana campaign, see the author's *Zulu: The Battles of Isandlwana and Rorke's Drift* (1992), and for an assessment of accounts of the war as a whole, *Brave Men's Blood* (1990).

INDEX

Numbers in italic refer to illustrations